Relentless Progress

Can fairy tales subvert consumerism? Can fantasy and children's literature counter the homogenizing influence of globalization? Can storytellers retain their authenticity in the age of consumerism? These are some of the critical questions raised by Jack Zipes, the celebrated scholar of fairy tales and children's literature. In this book, Zipes argues that, despite a dangerous reconfiguration of children as consumers in the civilizing process, children's literature, fairy tales, and storytelling possess a uniquely powerful (even fantastic) capacity to resist the "relentless progress" of negative trends in culture. He also argues that these tales and stories may lose their power if they are too diluted by commercialism and merchandising.

Stories have been used for centuries as a way to teach children (and adults) how to see the world, as well as their place within it. In *Relentless Progress*, Zipes looks at the surprising ways that stories have influenced people within contemporary culture and vice versa. Among the many topics explored here are the dumbing down of books for children, the marketing of childhood, the changing shape of feminist fairy tales, and why American and British children aren't exposed to more non-western fairy tales. From picture books to graphic novels, from children's films to video games, from the Grimms' fairy tales to the multimedia Harry Potter phenomenon, Zipes demonstrates that while children's stories have changed greatly in recent years, much about these stories has remained the same—despite their contemporary, high-tech repackaging.

Relentless Progress offers remarkable insight into why classic folklore and fairy tales should remain an important part of the lives of children in today's digital culture.

Jack Zipes is Professor of German at the University of Minnesota. An acclaimed translator and scholar of children's literature and culture, his most recent books include *The Collected Sicilian Folk and Fairy Tales of Giuseppe Pitrè*, *Why Fairy Tales Stick*, *Hans Christian Andersen: T̲ l Angiola*, and *The Robber with the Witch's Head*.

Relentless Progress

The Reconfiguration of Children's Literature, Fairy Tales, and Storytelling

Jack Zipes

Routledge
Taylor & Francis Group

NEW YORK AND LONDON

First published 2009
by Routledge
270 Madison Ave, New York, NY 10016

Simultaneously published in the UK
by Routledge
2 Park Square, Milton Park, Abingdon, Oxon OX14 4RN

Routledge is an imprint of the Taylor & Francis Group, an informa business

© 2009 Taylor & Francis

Typeset in Berkeley by
RefineCatch Limited, Bungay, Suffolk
Printed and bound in the United States of America on acid-free paper by
Walsworth Publishing Company, Marceline, MO

Library of Congress Cataloging in Publication Data
Zipes, Jack David.
Relentless progress : the reconfiguration of children's literature, fairy tales, and storytelling /
Jack Zipes.
p. cm.
Includes bibliographical references and index.
1. Children's literature—History and criticism.   2. Children's literature—Social aspects.
3. Children—Books and reading.   I. Title.
PN1009.A1Z56 2008
809'.89282—dc22
2008021844

ISBN10: 0–415–99063–7 (hbk)
ISBN10: 0–415–99064–5 (pbk)
ISBN10: 0–203–92756–7 (ebk)

ISBN13: 978–0–415–99063–9 (hbk)
ISBN13: 978–0–415–99064–6 (pbk)
ISBN13: 978–0–203–92756–4 (ebk)

For Carolina,
Who has taught me l'arte del vivere con lentezza e con speranza

Contents

Preface

"Progress," once the most extreme manifestation of radical optimism and a promise of universally shared and lasting happiness, has moved all the way to the opposite, dystopian and fatalistic pole of anticipation. It now stands for the threat of relentless and inescapable change that augurs not peace and respite but continuous crisis and strain, forbidding any moment of rest; a sort of game of musical chairs in which a second's inattention results in irreversible defeat and exclusion with no appeal allowed. Instead of great expectations and sweet dreams, "progress" evokes an insomnia full of nightmares of "being left behind," of missing the train or falling out of the window of a fast accelerating vehicle.

Zygmunt Bauman, *Liquid Life* (2005)

In *Liquid Life* and many of his other publications at the beginning of the twenty-first century, the astute social critic, Zygmunt Bauman, has endeavored valiantly to make sense out of the immense socio-economic changes of the last twenty or thirty years that go by the name of globalization. Like numerous other concerned thinkers, he fears that global market conditions have totally altered the way we human beings relate to one another, and that they have practically destroyed the possibility for developing community identity and civic responsibility. Human bonds and interactions are predicated on the laws of consumerism and waste so that there is very little left of firm and durable value in the civilizing process for people to use as models to develop the trajectories of their lives. Whatever hope for humanity to survive the onslaught of globalization can only be maintained by preserving and redeeming the hopes of the past, not simply in preserving the past. The hopes of the past were closely tied to discontentment with arbitrary rule and efforts to transform society into a more just and enlightened society. More and more, these hopes have disintegrated in our rapid and relentless progress toward perfection in a world out of our control and run amuck.

Bauman does not have a recipe for redeeming the hopes of the past and offsetting the relentless pace of globalization that both unites and separates us at the same time. But he does recommend cures such as empowering people to rebuild the deserted public spaces so that they can converse and exchange ideas about private and communal interests, rights, and responsibilities. In addition, he argues almost vehemently that intellectuals have disgraced themselves and broken a compact that they once had with the common people to uplift and guide them into history. In the present situation, instead of seeking to play a deterrent role in the way history is being perversely played out, intellectuals seek to benefit from the privileges provided by globalization.

> The descendants of the intellectuals of yore, the knowledge elite, having shared in the "secession of the contented", now move in a world sharply different from, and certainly not overlapping with, the many and different worlds in which the lives and the prospects (or their absence) of the "people" are ensconced and locked.[i]

Citing such critical thinkers as Theodor Adorno, Hannah Arendt, Pierre Bourdieu, and Jean Baudrillard, Bauman calls for radical thinking that does not explain or reinterpret the world but is an act of defiance against the events of the world and the ways in which these events are explicated, rationalized, or justified.

> "Radical thought" is *not* born of philosophical doubt or of frustrated utopia. It moves all the way towards questioning the world, *including* its utopian critique and the philosophy arising out of the void separating the two. The practitioners of radical thought in Baudrillard's rendition "dream of a world in which everybody laughs spontaneously when some one says 'this is true', 'this is real'."[ii]

I would like to think that the essays in my book move in the direction of the radical thought called for by Bauman. At one point I wanted to call the essays "interventions," for all of them were originally held as talks at universities or conferences, and I purposely wrote them to intervene in the debates about particular topics that concerned me and the audiences to which I was speaking. To intervene, for me, does not mean to negotiate a position, but to negate radically what is happening in my profession, to critique the present state of affairs in a socio-political context, to examine my own perspective self-critically, and to offer alternative ways of thinking about culture that will keep alive the hopes of the past that have not been fulfilled. Cultural interventions as radical thought call for a full stop, a pause, time to reflect, and time to determine whether we can invent and create viable options that enable us to gain control over our lives.

We already have control over the lives of our children. We always have had control. When we bring children into the world, we immediately define their positions and possibilities. Not only are our children biologically determined, hard-wired, as some might say, but culturally determined according to social class, gender, and ethnicity. The French sociologist Pierre Bourdieu talks about the habitus, the predispositions, that we all acquire from our parents and social status ultimately to become what we would like to become but always within conditions and frames, not of our own making. Our free will and volition have limits, and our individuality consists in our pursuit to extend or go beyond these limits.

While redefining ourselves in a configuration that we call the socio-economic system of our nation, we have reconfigured ourselves and are reconfigured to assume certain vital functions that maintain the system. The transformations and transitions that we make are generally smooth, but in times of crisis and worldwide uncontrollable events that have in part been engendered by the immense changes wrought by global capitalism, also known as globalization during the past thirty years, the transformations and transitions have been bumpy. The future is unpredictable because of the unstable times, and we are still in the process of seeking to stabilize or slow down the progress that we thought we had been making in all domains of society. It is truly time for critical reflection.

My essays are endeavors at critical reflection and are closely tied to the work that I have been doing at the University of Minnesota as a professor of German and comparative literature, as the founder and director of a storytelling/creative drama program, Neighborhood Bridges, for elementary schoolchildren in the Twin Cities, and as a writer and lecturer. The first four essays in the book, "The Reconfiguration of Children and Children's Literature in the Culture Industry," "Misreading Children and the Fate of the Book," "Why Fantasy Matters Too Much," and "The Multicultural Contradictions of International Children's Literature: Three Complaints and Three Wishes," focus on the immense changes in the field of children's literature. Beginning with the argument that children have become reconfigured into nodal points as consumers prompted to purchase primarily goods that are advertised to raise their status in society, I also address the corporate changes in the book publishing industry, the book as commodity, the significance of new literacies, mistaken notions about the meaning of fantasy, and the impossibility of developing a multicultural children's literature when American publishers translate very few foreign books, and American teachers are not trained to read other languages and understand other cultures. The next two essays, "What Makes a

Repulsive Frog So Appealing: Applying Memetics to Folk and Fairy Tales" and "And Nobody Lived Happily Ever After: The Feminist Fairy Tale after Forty Years of Fighting for Survival," concentrate on significant transformations in the field of folklore and fairy-tale studies. "What Makes a Repulsive Frog So Appealing" is a long, elaborate, controversial "treatise" on why it is important to consider using theories from the social sciences such as memetics, evolutionary psychology, and cultural anthropology to grasp why tales from the oral tradition are transformed and stick with us as memes. I have already dealt with this topic in my previous book, *Why Fairy Tales Stick: The Evolution and Relevance of a Genre*, and the present essay elaborates my position in more detail and, I hope, with more clarity. In "And Nobody Lived Happily Ever After," I try to gauge what has happened to the radical beginnings of the feminist fairy tales that I first studied in my book, *Don't Bet on the Prince* in 1986. The tone and style of the original optimistic and critical fairy tales written by women writers seem to have been altered and become more acerbic, and I explore some of the more recent feminist writings in light of the backlash against feminism. The final essay in the book, "Storytelling as Spectacle in the Globalized World," brings together many of the strands of critical thinking that I have developed throughout the book. It is based on my forty-year experience as an active storyteller with children and adults, and I meditate on how the role of the storyteller has been transformed as globalization has threatened, if not devastated, communal life, and how storytellers have been tempted to commodify themselves rather than resisting forces of a society of spectacle.

Though at times my remarks may seem too provocative and skeptical with regard to globalization, I believe we live in exciting times when new cultural and economic technologies can bring about "true" globalization rather than divide us and cause conflict. By true globalization, I mean more substantial connections between people in our own country and with people from other cultures, more sensitivity to issues of poverty, race, and gender that separate us, more dedication to using modes of communication to create greater understanding between diverse groups of people, more straightforward and candid talk by political and religious leaders instead of lies and hypocrisy, and more sincere care for the young and aged by all of us involved in trying to restore some human compassion into the relentless motor of present-day capitalism. We have experienced eight wasted-chance years in America from 1992 to 2000 and eight bitter ruthless years from 2000 to 2008, sixteen years in all, when progress in humanity was relentlessly and arrogantly dashed aside. This is why critique must intervene, resist, and defy the barbaric side of relentless progress.

Acknowledgments

For the past ten years I have been greatly influenced by the works of Pierre Bourdieu, Guy De Bord, Zygmunt Bauman, Richard Dawkins, Daniel Dennett, Dan Sperber, and Giorgio Agamben, and their imprint can be felt, I believe, in all the essays. As I mention in the preface, all the essays were originally talks that have undergone constant revision, and I want to thank my friends and colleagues who have offered me encouragement, support, and important advice. They are, in alphabetical order, Alma Flor Ada, Cristina Bacchilega, Karen Balliett, Claire Bazin, Marie-Claude Chenour-Perrin, Theda Detlor, Klaus Doderer, Don Haase, Betsy Hearne, Bev Hock, Wolfgang Mieder, Pat Ryan, Myra Smith, Hans-Jörg Uther, and Mike Wilson.

At Routledge, Matt Byrnie initiated and guided this project with great care. Stan Spring provided me with all the necessary support that I needed with thoughtful consideration. As usual, Siân Findlay did a superb job in overseeing the entire production with grace and efficiency, and I am extremely grateful for Alice Stoakley's meticulous copyediting and sound advice.

Most of all, I want to thank my wife, Carol Dines, to whom I dedicate this book. She has borne my "grumpy" years with trust, patience, and wisdom—and a twinkle in her eye.

Prologue

Singing the Song of Globalized Futurism

While I was putting the final touches to my book in Rome, I attended a fascinating exhibition at the Palazzo delle Esposizioni that had the title "Il Mito della Velocità" (The Myth of Velocity). Most of the early enthusiasm for velocity in Italy at the beginning of the twentieth century was cultivated by the futurists. On February 29, 1909, the poet Filippo Tommaso Marinetti published "The Futurist Manifesto" in the French newspaper, *Le Figaro*. It included the following points:

1. We want to sing the love of danger, the habit of energy and rashness.
2. The essential elements of our poetry will be courage, audacity, and revolt.
3. Literature has up to now magnified pensive immobility, ecstasy, and slumber. We want to exalt movements of aggression, feverish sleeplessness, the double march, the perilous leap, the slap, and the blow with the fist.
4. We declare that the splendor of the world has been enriched by a new beauty: the beauty of speed. A racing automobile with its bonnet adorned with great tubes like serpents with explosive breath . . . a roaring motor car which seems to run on machine-gun fire is more beautiful than the Victory of Samothrace.
5. We want to sing the man at the wheel, the ideal axis of which crosses the earth, itself hurled along its orbit.
6. The poet must spend himself with warmth, glamour, and prodigality to increase the enthusiastic fervor of the primordial elements.
7. Beauty exists only in struggle. There is no masterpiece that has not an aggressive character. Poetry must be a violent assault on the forces of the unknown, to force them to bow before man.

8. We are on the extreme promontory of the centuries! What is the use of looking behind at the moment when we must open the mysterious shutters of the impossible? Time and Space died yesterday. We are already living in the absolute, since we have already created eternal, omnipresent speed.

9. We want to glorify war—the only cure for the world—militarism, patriotism, the destructive gesture of the anarchists, the beautiful ideas which kill, and contempt for woman.

10. We want to demolish museums and libraries, fight morality, feminism, and all opportunist and utilitarian cowardice.

11. We will sing of the great crowds agitated by work, pleasure, and revolt; the multi-colored and polyphonic surf of revolutions in modern capitals; the nocturnal vibration of the arsenals and the workshops between their violent moons; the gluttonous railway stations devouring smoking serpents; factories suspended from the clouds by the thread of their smoke; bridges with the leap of gymnasts flung across the diabolic cutlery of sunny rivers; adventurous steamers sniffing the horizon; great-breasted locomotives, puffing on the rails like enormous steel horses with long tubes for bridle, and the gliding fight of aeroplanes whose propeller sounds like the flapping of a flag and the applause of enthusiastic crowds.

It seems to me that 100 years later, the dreams and wishes of the futurists have been fulfilled in uncanny ways. Some contemporary, stalwart warriors of futurism are happily singing the song of globalization and relentless progress. But most of us are simply entangled in the songs and visions of the futurists that have reconfigured us in the spectacle of our reality. Marinetti's celebration of velocity has become our dilemma.

Jack Zipes
June 7, 2008

The Reconfiguration of Children and Children's Literature in the Culture Industry

1

The question must be asked in the sharpest terms. Are we ready in this global age of the free market to continue to protect children from the competitive pressures of the market? Since the United States provides a major engine for global capitalism and world trade, we might be tempted to let the market set its own boundaries, overlooking the harms done to children as we once overlooked the harms done to slaves. I wonder also whether the particular, romantic, Western vision of the sentimental child may not have outgrown its usefulness, to become so cliché ridden that it can no longer cover the needs of children. Can we do this by at once valuing the needs of children (and children do have special needs) while recognizing the exigencies of the many evolving economies and cultures in which child labor, and even child prostitution, are necessary?

Paula Fass, *Children of New World: Society, Culture, and Globalization*[1]

It is simply impossible to discuss children and children's literature today without situating them within the complex of the cultural field of production in which young people are introduced to a variety of commodities connected to a book, story, or poem that they may be reading. When a child encounters a book, often mediated by a teacher, librarian, parent, or friend, the relationship with the book is no longer the young reader and the text, but young consumer and a myriad of products associated with the text that the child will be encouraged to buy and to buy more of the same: video tapes, CDs, DVDs, games, dolls, toys, t-shirts, watches, cups, clothing, food, and so on. Three international examples are the Disney Corporation's *Beauty and the Beast* (1991) with its numerous sequels, Luc Besson's *Arthur and the Invisible* (2007), and Tony Di Terlizzi and Holly Black's

The Spiderwick Chronicles (2008), not to mention J. K. Rowling's Harry Potter novels.[2] These books are accompanied by numerous artifacts such as films, DVDs, and branded articles and promoted by effective advertising and informational networks throughout the world. They also spawn sequels in print and in other forms and can be found in numerous places on the Internet. Moreover, writers and publishers produce imitations also known as copycats, to capitalize on the success of blockbusters. Needless to say, there will be numerous offshoots of any new book that captures the imagination and pocketbooks of adults and children. The best-selling books for young readers between three and eighteen are now produced and marketed globally in a manner that has altered the reading and reception of children's literature, and, consequently, this kind of production also has an impact on the way critics analyze children's literature and culture today. Nobody can avoid the consequences of the massive reconfiguration of children and children's literature.

In fact, numerous critics in the 1990s and the first decade of the twenty-first century in North America and Great Britain are very aware of the shifts in the culture industry, particularly in the mass media, and have been debating what all the changes mean for childhood and the culture of young people. The debates form the basis of such essay collections as *The Children's Culture Reader* (1999), edited by Henry Jenkins, *Kids' Media Culture* (1999), edited by Marsha Kinder, and *Adolescents and Literacies in a Digital World* (2002), edited by Donna Alverman, among other important books by individual authors.[3] One of the crucial questions being asked is whether the young are being victimized by the commercial interests of those corporations and publishers that produce cultural artifacts for children. Are they being made more violent, sexual, and sick by the images of brutality, sex, and horror on the big and little screens of television, the Internet, and the cinema? Are the new digital technologies transforming literacies and the way children read so that they are no longer reflective and capable of sustained reading? How does advertising affect the brains of children from infancy throughout their teens? What are they actually imbibing? What are they learning if they are learning? What do they do with what they experience? Are children creative and sophisticated consumers of the new products marketed specifically for them, or are they subtly (and not so subtly) influenced and manipulated to buy particular objects and to keep buying?

Activist groups ranging from the religious right to the radical left have been formed to protect children from pornography and works of moral turpitude that are shown on television and the Web and in movie theaters and published as books.[4] Scholars and activists have taken different positions on all these questions, and I propose to examine some of the more relevant works that bear light on the transformation of children and children's literature in a cultural field of production that embraces commodities to be consumed primarily by young people from five to eighteen in the United States. What I have to say, however, is not limited to American culture but pertains to an uneven global development that stamps the reconfiguration of children and children's literature.

But before I discuss these works, I should like to define what I mean by children's literature as a field of production within the culture industry and how children and their reading matter have been configured in the industry in a new way. In my opinion, the crucial question with regard to children's culture is not whether the literature, films, television programs, toys, clothing, computer games, and such like are harmful to children. This has always been a false or misleading question that diverts attention from a more significant issue—how children are now configured within the culture industry of the civilizing process to consume products indiscriminately and at high speeds to assume functions within a socio-economic system that furthers exploitation of individuals of all ages and the communities in which they live. And here I maintain that the recent reconfiguration has radically transformed reading habits and the manner in which literature and other cultural artifacts are distributed and consumed by young people. The reconfiguration has, in fact, brought about a radical change of childhood. As Paula Fass, one of the most important historians of children's history, has remarked,

> As we look around us today, we can observe the growing emphasis in the United States on adult sentences for young children from which the juvenile court was supposed to protect them; a new insistence on schooling as a form of competitive skills preparation rather than individual moral development and playful creativity; the hyper-sexualization of children in advertising; the inundation in the news of portrayals of young children as bloodthirsty murderers. All these do not bode particularly well for the continuation of our twentieth-century views of vulnerable childhood as a period of playfulness and of respite from the market whose payoff is a better future for the human race.[5]

It may be too early yet to assess the effects of this reconfiguration that is connected to the operations of the commodity market. However, I believe that we are positioning children to experience and to read the world in a manner that alienates them from families and communities and causes immense problems in identity formation, and these problems are the ones that need our immediate concern. As Daniel Thomas Cook has argued,

> The problematic of children's consumption cannot fruitfully be engaged with as an either/or proposition; rather, it must be recognized that commercially imposed meaning *and* personal identity creation blend together at the level of practice early in the life course and that this confluence supports consumer capitalism and its current globalizing tendency.[6]

The Cultural Field of Children's Literature

More than ever before the meaning of an individual reading of a literary text by a child depends on the socio-cultural situation of the child, whose very act of reading a book, story, poem and all the multi-modal materials in books and on screens, is produced to further adult aims and the power of the market. These aims include the pedagogical purpose of teaching and improving the reading skills of a child, the moral and ideological didactic purpose of the author and adult who provides the reading for the child, the commercial designs of publishers and corporations that seek to animate the reader to read more of the same, and the cultural reproduction of a labor force to maintain the ongoing developments of a particular society. As soon as a child is born today, he or she will gradually be regarded as a discursively configured child, that is, as a cognitive reader, who is virtually produced under material conditions that are organized around the interests of an adult world influenced by the global growth of the culture industry. Clearly, children produce their own private meanings as well and use books and screens for self-development and pleasure, but they are predisposed by genetics, social status, and environmental influences to experience and to read the world within socio-cultural contexts. In America, the cultural field of production has increasingly become influenced by market conditions to such an extent that the child's capacity to read without interference from the media and advertising has become next to impossible. In her significant study *Born to Buy* (2004), Juliet Schor remarks:

> Marketing is also fundamentally altering the experience of childhood. Corporations have infiltrated the core activities and institutions of childhood, with virtually no resistance from government or parents. Advertising is widespread in schools. Electronic media are replacing conventional play. We have become a nation that places a lower priority on teaching its children how to thrive socially, intellectually, even spiritually, than it does on training them to consume. The long-term consequences of this development are ominous.[7]

In Robert McChesney's highly important study, *Rich Media, Poor Democracy: Communication Politics in Dubious Times* (1999), he discusses the increased concentration of power in growing international conglomerates such as Disney, Time Warner, Universal, Gannett, and others, and he comes to the conclusion that the ramifications of this concentration and conglomeration are negative because the products of the culture industry are linked more and more to the needs of a handful of powerful corporations that influence all political and educational institutions in North America and Great Britain, if not in the world. Moreover, there has been a hyper-commercialization of the media fare that is calculated to bring about the greatest possible profit from cultural products.

> Book publishing, even more than music, has seen the greatest change as a result of concentration and conglomeration. Only a generation ago, U.S. book publishing was, for better or for worse, a moderately concentrated industry. Since the early 1980s there has been a shakeout in the number of firms, and now most of the remaining publishers are part of the corporate media conglomerates. This has changed their operating logic considerably. In addition to shaping what manuscripts are considered market-worthy and what authors "bankable," there is increased pressure to publish and record writers and artists whose work complements products produced in other branches of these far-flung empires. . . . Although more titles than ever are being published—often due to the work of marginalized and struggling "independent" publishers—the big commercial publishers are emulating the Hollywood model of seeking out super-profitable blockbuster bestsellers and eschewing titles that might sell moderately well but have little chance of attaining blockbuster status. Moreover, concentration within the industry has been accompanied by a sharp decrease in the attention given to book quality.[8]

For children's and young adult literature, the increase in production and the decrease in quality have been highly visible, but it is not so much this phenomenon that is of concern. Rather it is the way reading and viewing are framed by the rapidly changing culture industry that configures children and teenagers into its calculations as consumers and as saturated nodal points of mass information which makes it difficult for the young to establish particular identities and a sense of autonomy. While it would be foolish and misleading to regard the young as under the total control of the corporate capitalist world and hence "victimized"[9] and manipulated in a process that produces homogenized recipients of media fare, it is, nevertheless, important to grasp the institutionalized mediations through which knowledge and cultural products are manufactured. Children are not passive victims, but they are also not free creative individuals. They learn to know the world through object relations that determine their cognitive interests. It is in their interests, their parents know, that they, the young, learn strategy techniques of survival and that they learn to *read* the cultural codes and symbols successfully to find their roles and functions within the socio-economic order. The basis of our socio-economic order is predicated on hegemonic relations of power that reward those young individuals who master linguistic and scientific skills and foster the interests of a global capitalist system in an age where constantly changing information stamps the means of production. Learning to read all kinds of texts and images is thus essential to any youngster who wants to succeed in this system, and whether it is fiction or non-fiction, the child reads and views all signs to position him or herself within the world and to discover opportunities to fulfill his or her desires and needs. At the same time the child reads and views signs, he or she is being configured by the material conditions of a particular social class, ethnic group, region, and genetic background within a particular field of children's literature production.

What does being "configured" mean in the field of children's literature production? What is the field, and how has this field changed? In his insightful essay, "The Field of Cultural Production, or: The Economic World Reversed," Pierre Bourdieu remarks that

> the literary or artistic field is a *field of forces*, but it is also a *field of struggles* tending to transform or conserve this field of forces. The network of objective relations between positions subtends and orients the strategies which the occupants of the different positions implement in their struggles to defend or improve their positions (i.e. their position-takings), strategies which depend for their force and form on the position each agent occupies in the power relations [*rapports de force*].[10]

Ever since literature and literacy began to play a major role in the civilizing process in the fifteenth and sixteenth centuries, the field of children's literature began to assume importance as a training ground for future administrators of society. As Harvey Graff and R. A. Houston have pointed out,[11] literacy is a technology or set of techniques for communication and for decoding and reproducing written or printed materials. To master this technology—and it is important to remember that we are not born to read, that is, we are not genetically hard-wired to read— and to become literate meant and means to distinguish oneself as capable of deciphering codes and using them to advance our understanding of phenomena and putting our knowledge to use for the benefit of a particular society if not humanity. Progress depends on literacy. To become literate meant and means to obtain mastery of technologies of communication and a certain degree of power and status within a given society. To be literate also implies distinction, a distinguished position, in opposition to others who are allegedly inferior, illiterate, or dysfunctional. These "others", the lower classes, are forces who allegedly negate, question, or challenge literacy and must be trained to conform to the standards of the literate. To figure into and play a role within the civilizing process of most modern societies has necessitated a certain mastery of reading and writing, and the early configuration of children demanded literacy if parents wanted to establish places of distinction for themselves and their children. This is one of the reasons why children's literature of all kinds from textbooks to fiction became at first privileged items of the upper classes and why literacy was at first kept from women, the lower classes, and slaves. As literacy became more accessible and widespread, children's literature became vital for socialization and the cultivation of all social groups, and thus struggles to influence the mores and behavior of children were played out in part through literature and literacy campaigns. Today, within the field of children's literature production, distribution, and consumption, the contending forces are constituted by the writer, the literary agent, the publisher, the family, the school, the mass media, bookstores, the Internet, and lastly by the child.

The writer/illustrator produces a book to articulate his or her needs and views and to share them and promote them on the market designated broadly for the young from three to eighteen. The literary agent monitors the product, decides which category of the market might be best suitable to sell the product, and negotiates the terms for publication that generally include property rights for spin-offs. While the agent is supposed to act for the author, he or she is most concerned for the agency and for the status of the literary agent within publishing. In the publishing house itself, key decisions about the publication of a book for children will be determined by the editorial staff and the marketing division, often at odds with one another. Once a decision is made to publish a book, the publishing firm will seek to maximize profits through advertising and the possible creation of spin-offs such as toys, clothing, videos, films, or audio cassettes. Marketing and distribution are the key to success, and it is important to position the book in the proper network, institutions, and stores. Though children buy books, they prefer to buy toys, tapes, DVDs, CDs, games, food, and clothing more than literature. Therefore, the key purchasers of children's literature, especially for the very young, will be adults, if they buy books at all. Schools and libraries are the most dependable purchasers, though they often do not buy what children "want" and desire and they do not explore why children are "influenced" to read (Ninja Turtles, Power Rangers, X-Men, Pokémon, etc.). By far, the most important market for children's books today is constituted by a variety of new outlets. As Judith Rosen has explained,

> In 1983, Random House transformed its children's division into a "merchandise group," incorporating editorial, sales and marketing and offering traditional books as well as other products (books on tape, videos, the Happy House line) to reflect a new emphasis on merchandise. Others, including Simon & Schuster, Harcourt and DK, soon followed suit by adding merchandise lines. At the same time, a consumer revolution was taking place. Mass merchandisers, such as Wal-Mart, Target and Kmart, were not only responsible for changing "the way American shops" for clothes and home furnishings, but they also began adding books to their product mix and opening new stores at an accelerated place. Suddenly bigger was better, whether it was Barnes & Noble or Borders superstore or a massive warehouse outlet for home building or office supplies."[12]

Film companies and television may also promote a book by adapting it for the big or little screen. Some books are written to appear simultaneously with a film as in the case of *Toy Story* or after a particular toy or doll has become famous as in the case of Barbie and such books as *The Barbie ABC Book* and *The Barbie Activity Book*. The Internet has also become a means to publish, advertise, and sell books and stories for young readers as well as a place where children can voice their views about books they are reading. As readers, children are part of the force field of children's literature as consumers of a culture constructed for them by adults and transformed to a degree by the young either in conformity with or rebellion against market conditions. Despite the fact that there are various contending groups seeking to win the attention of the young through literature, the reconfiguration of children within the force field of production places children and teenagers at the same nodal point, even if some are marginalized. It is over and through their bodies that information is rapidly processed to increase the productivity of labor and capital and profit taking.

One could possibly use another term to designate the function of children in the field of literature production such as players, learners, negotiators, or developers, but this is not the way they are configured today. The most frequent definition of "configure" is to set something up for operation in a specific way. For instance, we configure computers with software programs that make the machine function in a particular way, or the machine itself is configured to respond in a certain manner. The parts or components of a machine are arranged or configured to form a pattern so that they will operate efficiently and smoothly. In the case of children in the field of literature production, dissemination, and consumption, children were at one point configured to learn and amuse themselves. The book or story was published primarily to provide an individual reading experience within a socio-economic context that emphasized the cultural and educational value of the text. Up through the middle of the twentieth century, certain books lent distinction and status to the reader. From the early development of children's literature or literature in general, books were recognized to contain cultural capital. As time has passed, books have gradually lost value and become more like common commodities, indistinguishable from other products. The lines between book, film, video game, booklet for a doll, advertisement, and image on a computer screen have been blurred. Books are becoming more and more multimodal. It does not matter what young readers do with all the material that they consume, just as long as they are predisposed to buy and keep consuming an assortment of images and icons that do not vary much in meaning and substance. From a production viewpoint that is common in book publishing, toy manufacture, clothing, and advertising, children's needs and desires are taken very seriously but only to make them more operable and operational within the market system established by the conglomerates that are much more advanced than most educational institutions in the world, for they have learned how to infiltrate and influence the network of reading and learning that children do from infancy through the teenage years and beyond. Highly trained researchers have explored practically every aspect of how children consume cultural artifacts, including how the brain functions in response to advertising. In discussing brain imaging and scanning with Robert Reiher, a media psychologist, Juliet Schor reported that

> he is very concerned about how advertising can manipulate viewers' attention mechanism and "downshift" the brain, that is, activate the emotional midbrain and the instinctive reactive centers. Such downshifting makes it virtually impossible for critical thinking and effective reasoning to occur while watching an ad. In combination with age-inappropriate content, Reiher believes that downshifting can have negative impact on brain development in children."[13]

One major purpose of marketing and advertising is to endow children with a false sense of power and autonomy based on the material interests of the socioeconomic system along with a real sense of how to manipulate new technologies of literacy. Corporations love to talk about how savvy and sophisticated children have become as though they always know their own minds. As a result children buy to feel empowered by all kinds of commodities including books and other reading materials in the age of information. They have become more productive users of books as commodities which, in their fetishized form, stimulate children to accumulate more objects and to play with them as they wish. Publishers are not concerned about the educational and social effects of their books, just as long as children as a target audience learn to buy more and more of their books in whatever form they assume and just as long as their corporate products are linked to the texts.

In the United States up until the 1950s, books and reading matter for the young were generally part of a shared experience either in the family, school, or library that prepared children to learn about the world and provided pleasure during leisure time. It should also be noted that reading and the acquisition of books depended on social class and race, and that the books had gender- and race-specific content and purposes. Very rarely were books and reading material linked to toys and cultural artifacts in a seemingly natural and seamless web. It was only at the beginning of the twentieth century that publishers and manufacturers took advantage of new means of advertising. For instance, in the case of *The Wonderful*

Wizard of Oz (1900), L. Frank Baum and W. W. Denslow created artifacts to profit from their creations. They set a trend that can be traced in the dolls manufactured from Johnny Gruelle's Raggedy Andy and Raggedy Annie books in the 1920s as well as all the bears and other products that emanated from the Winnie the Pooh books. By the 1930s Walt Disney and his brother Roy were quick to manufacture products based on their films and formed Mickey Mouse clubs that used Disney books and other artifacts so that children would bond through the Disney brand. In 1937 the production of *Snow White and the Seven Dwarfs* added luster to the Disney Corporation, which continues to market hundreds of products in more sophisticated digital ways in the present century. Despite early signs that children might be mined for their consumer potential in the first half of the twentieth century, most publishing houses, however, did not directly appeal to children as their primary purchasers. Parents, librarians, and teachers were their major target audiences as they had been in the nineteenth century, for the adults read and monitored most of the reading that was done within the socially constructed spheres of childhood activity. This does not mean that the young were always reading what the adults wanted them to read. Indeed, they have always been reading manifold signs in the world around them from birth, but adults had not always been aware of the productive ways children read or studied the myriad ways in which children read or do not read. That is, most children do not read many books or stories, unless they come from affluent families, because they cannot afford them or are not exposed to them. As Shelby Anne Wolf and Shirley Brice Heath have pointed out,

> until the 1980s, in the relatively small amount of research on children reading outside the context of school lessons, "reading" referred almost exclusively to making meaning from written texts for the purpose of pleasure. Yet closer looks at children interacting with print outside school settings revealed that their reading texts were prompts: commercial logos from brand-name products, television advertising, and T-shirts stood as guides for actions. These studies called attention to the ways in which children became familiar with print in their everyday lives, and how the extent of print in commerce, trade, and religious life enabled them to acquire an early familiarity with the shapes, alignments, and even the meanings of script systems. Studies of children's response to literature after the 1980s also urged educators to look well beyond occasions of interaction around the book itself to the economic, social, and cultural contexts of reading. By the end of the twentieth century, scholars had come increasingly to recognize children's capacity to reconstruct their worlds (if allowed to do so) with words and rules from both life and literature.[14]

Of course, it is nearly impossible to do a complete study of how children were reading their worlds before the advent of what Manuel Castells calls "the network society" in the 1980s, just as it is impossible to develop a comprehensive study of how today's children relate to literature and books and how they read. There are just too many factors to be taken into consideration such as: gender, ethnic group, linguistic codes and capabilities, social class, age, region, school, teacher, family, and religion. Yet, we can make certain discreet generalizations of how societies have produced or constructed children as readers, and continue to do so. We can talk about how they were and are configured in the culture industry of the civilizing process as readers. We can study the transformation or shifts in the configuration of children as active and productive consumers of literature.

If the immediate post-war period after 1945 was some kind of worldwide watershed or marker for historians—and it certainly was because we became more aware of just how barbarian we were in an age of modern enlightenment, and we have continued many barbaric practices in the Cold War, Middle East Wars, Korean War, Vietnam War, and Iraq War. I would suggest that 1989 and the period immediately preceding the fall of statist communism now loom as perhaps much more significant because of the great technological revolution that has taken place. Manuel Castells has made this clear in his highly significant three-volume study of the information age:

> the information technology revolution has been instrumental in allowing the implementa-
> tion of a fundamental process of restructuring of the capitalist system from the 1980s
> onwards. In the process, this technological revolution was itself shaped, in its development
> and manifestations by the logic and interests of advanced capitalism, without being
> reducible to the expression of such interests.[15]

He maintains that the restructuring led to a series of reforms both at the level of institutions and in the management of firms that were aimed at four main goals:

> deepening the capitalist logic of profit-seeking in capital–labor relationships; enhancing the
> productivity of labor and capital; globalizing production, circulation, and markets, seizing
> the opportunity of the most advantageous conditions for profit-making everywhere; and
> marshaling the state's support for productivity gains and competitiveness of national econ-
> omies, often to the detriment of social protection and public interest regulations.[16]

What has all of this restructuring meant for the young, not just in the United States, but throughout the world? What will it mean? One major shift, as I have already maintained, is a reconfiguration of children and children's literature because children are being predisposed to read and view the world in entirely new ways due to changes in technology, the processing of information through children, advertising, and the emphasis on rapid capitalization of investments and profit taking. This is a global shift that entails a global reconfiguration. But since I am most familiar with the situation in America, my focus will be mainly on the effect of the shift in that country.

A child born at the beginning of the twenty-first century in America, no matter what class, color, or gender, has already been bombarded with messages and texts through design, electronics, and print by icons, signs, and sounds that come from adults, clothing, television screens, the radio, the movie screen, toys, games, and books. Among the logos will be McDonalds, Wendys, Kentucky Fried Chicken, Arbys, Nike, and Coke Cola, and associated with the logos will be actual places and characters or toys that appear in those places. For instance, McDonalds has often had special gifts for children emanating from the Disney corporation or designs on their cups to lure children into their parlors. As we know American children watch an average of at least three hours of television and videos a day, and children have become accustomed to viewing many shows that do not make a distinction between the products they are advertising and the actual stories that are projected onto the screens. Therefore, a character or symbol can come to stand for a food product, a book, a film, or a place. It is insignificant if the child between one and five can make distinctions. What is important is that the child feels the urge to procure, to possess, or to become attached to the image that he or she registers. Even educational television with the Sesame Street characters, the Muppets, and Barney have been predicated on the child's desire to identify with these figures or to own them. In addition, it is also important that the child constantly sees babies as in the Michelin adds or Pamper commercials or youngsters delightfully selling all kinds of clothes and sports items, making deals as little Wall Street brokers, or identifying with the products by eating them, playing with them, admiring them, wearing them, driving in them, and so on. Reading and viewing the world becomes associated with the incorporation of product and the use of the product. The bodily consumption of all kinds of wares is projected positively as a pleasurable experience through icons and letters. By the time a child is five or six years old and is ready for formal training in reading and introduction to books, he or she already has developed predispositions and techniques of reading and familiarity with sign systems and codes that conditions the child to read in bites and to be familiar with conventional narratives where children appear to be empowered as autonomous consumers. This empowerment is crucial, for all stories developed by television and movies are bound up with stimulating material desires of children. Children are literally being empowered to buy and to compete for products. They are being empowered to advertise themselves as commodities and compete for status and distinction. The child, who has always played some role within the socio-economic system as worker, disseminator, consumer of products, has been reconfigured into a hyper-commercialized world of signs that is unlike the environment experienced by other generations of young people.

Whereas a child might have read a book as a separate or individual work of art without associating it with a commercial product of clothing, food, or toy during the period before the 1980s, it is virtually impossible for a child to pick up a book inside or outside the family or school and not associate it with other products or a sequel of the book that he or she is reading. The network of production of children's literature today is such that it is geared to configure the child on all levels, psychological and material, as a functional consumer that will perpetuate the system by profiting from it and playing the game or games that this network of information installs and develops at a lightning pace. This does not mean that the conglomerates that have been formed during the 1980s and 1990s have discovered a way to stimulate children to read as Pavlovian dogs. But it does mean that market researchers have conducted exhaustive and refined studies to try to guarantee that, when a book is bought to be read, the young reader will read it not to discover new things about himself or herself—although this may occur—but will want to become associated with a symbolical system of goods that lends the boy or girl status. To make a crass argument, one does not read a Harry Potter book to learn something about oneself or the world but to say that I have read it and am associated with it.

We have always read in part to say we have read. But never before has the urge to read and the reading of a book or gazing at images been associated in such a consummate way with consumerism. There are indeed many pieces of delectable literature that we simply eat and spew from our systems like candy bars that provide instantaneous pleasure but are not nutritional or long lasting. The problem with children's literature today is that it is configured to be long lasting because the same kind of book, story, or image is being reproduced constantly on the same day so that it has a lasting effect. Each book reinforces the desire to buy books that "promise" the same happy narrative which features an empowered child as hero, male and female, in different colors, shapes, and sizes. This is due to the restructuring of capitalism and the rise of the network system that fosters reinforcement of generic symbols, icons, codes, and conventions. The repetition and redundancy of the same programs, advertising, toys, and books is so overwhelming that the subject as agent is easily bewildered yet knows that he or she needs power. Thus information leading to the acquisition of power becomes an important goal in the reading of literature and other texts designed for the young. This is perhaps the most disturbing effect of the reconfiguration of children's literature and children. Whereas one could argue that books and stories led young readers to a point of withdrawal where they could establish and assess identities in their imagination, they no longer can guarantee safe conduct to neutral and independent zones for the imagination, which has also been loaded through a saturation of designed signs. Reading a book is to provide immediate gratification, a quick fix of power and a guarantee that the world is ordered in a conventional plot. Free association in the process of identity formation has been severely limited by the reconfiguration of children's literature and children. Despite the fact that the glut of children's literature in the past thirty years has grown and contains numerous books of quality and diversity, the socio-cultural process of reading inhibits particular identity formation and contributes to a paradox that not only pertains to the young, but also to adults: the more information we imbibe in the capitalist restructuring process, the less we know about ourselves and the more we are becoming reified to operate functionally in the network system to empower ourselves without questioning what this system is doing.

All this does not mean that we are becoming automatons, that it is impossible for us to make judicious decisions, or that we cannot attain great pleasure and learn through cultural activities such as reading a book or watching a film. But it does mean that the way we are linked or not linked to the network system controlled by contending groups within the state and the global corporate world prepares children to operate functionally according to capitalist interests and values. It means that predispositions and tendencies are cultivated in children by design and by chance to desire, need, and consume cultural materials manufactured to maintain those desires, needs, and habits of consumption.

Critical Reflections on Commercialism, Consumption, and Reconfiguration

At this point I want to cite some concrete examples of how children and literature have become reconfigured, and I want to suggest that the reading and the teaching of reading under present conditions in the culture industry must become contentious and subversive acts if children's creativity and productivity are to be cultivated and channeled in a way that they do not regard themselves and other people to whom they relate in the private and public spheres as commodities. As it is, children are basically empowered through the reading of the codes of their everyday activities to sell themselves on the market according to values established by the market. The prostitution of children does not take place only on the streets but within the network system in very legal ways. As Daniel Thomas Cook states,

It is, indeed, nearly impossible to avoid encountering the goods, icons and media characters produced for children's use and consumption when one walks down the street, enters a school or supermarket, flips through a magazine, scans television channels or pays even scant attention to one's own children. We see inscriptions of consumer media culture painted on the walls of nurseries, sewn on school backpacks, emblazoned on the faceplates of mobile phones and encoded in the array of branded breakfast cereals strategically slotted at children's eye level in grocery store aisles.[17]

Given the enormous amount of children's literature and associated products in North America—well over a million new books are published every year, not to mention millions of other commodities directed at children—and their different uses and receptions by young consumers, I want to focus my attention on a short essay by Karen Klugman, "A Bad Hair Day for G. I. Joe," (1999), Stephen Kline's *Out of the Garden: Toys and Children's Culture in the Age of TV Marketing* (1993), Ellen Seiter's *Sold Separately: Parents & Children in Consumer Culture* (1995), and Anne Haas Dyson's *Writing Superheroes: Contemporary Childhood, Popular Culture, and Classroom Literacy* (1997). In conclusion, I shall make a few remarks about the essays in a special issue of the *Journal of Consumer Culture* dedicated to children's consumer culture, and the essay, "Kids and Commerce," by Viviana Zelizer in *Childhood*, for they raise extremely important questions about the reconfiguration of children and children's literature in the network system of the culture industry. I should also like to preface my remarks by stressing again that the quality of children's literature is not at issue here nor the quality of children's potential as readers and producers of their own meanings, rather it is the manner in which children and children's literature are configured within the network system of global capitalism that concerns me most.

Klugman's 1999 autobiographical essay about shopping for toys and raising two girls and a boy is instructive because her engagement or rather confrontation with the culture industry is still common to that experienced by many mothers to one degree or another—and not only in North America. Contrary to what one might believe, she maintains that differences between the genders continue to be created, manufactured, and marketed at birth through color coding, toys, and dolls. Despite the advances made by the feminist movement, the toy industry, television, Hollywood, and advertising have remained almost immune to pressures by activist groups that seek to change the negative images conveyed by all sorts of cultural objects that influence social roles and relationships. She claims that

the way dolls are packaged and advertised further stereotypes [of] gender roles. Many packages of girls' dolls feature photographs of girls holding, grooming, or otherwise caring for a doll or sometimes just gazing at the doll in the plastic wrapping. These images of girls, like the layering of accessories from doll to owner, create a link between fantasy play and real life that you will not find in the marketing of boys' dolls.[18]

Not that the dolls, figurines, and games for boys are much better than those for girls, for they stress action in war, combat for the sake of learning how to fight and compete, and learning technical skills for the mastery of an opponent. The major difference is that they encourage young boys to determine their own destinies, whereas the girls' playthings are predicated on beauty, luck, or miraculous intercession to bring about their happiness. Without drawing direct parallels with literature or books, Klugman discusses dolls and toys that are already intertwined with narratives that children know by the time they are of school age, whether they can read texts or not. Though these narratives may shift depending on the product, and though new characters and plots are created annually if not monthly by publishers and toy companies, the gender roles have only been slightly modified to open up alternatives for both girls and boys. Klugman makes the point that

> as science continues to discover biological explanations for behaviors previously regarded as environmentally determined—for example, a gene that controls obesity and a physiological difference in the hypothalamus of gay males—perhaps toys that encourage Stone Age tendencies of women to prepare food and men to hunt and gather will prove to be justified by our genes. But in our modern world of fast-food drive-thru and hormone-injected cattle, the toy market has responded to revolutionary changes in our occupational options by adding pink microwaves to the girls' Small Appliance section of Toys 'Я' Us and by giving boys herds of grotesque creatures to shoot at.[19]

Klugman discusses how she sought to prevent the "invasion" of such gender stereotyped toys and games from entering her house, but she, like most mothers and fathers in America, had to relent because of her children's desires and/or needs to consume what their friends were purchasing and what they saw on television or in the public sphere. Her concerns about consumerism and the impact that it has had on children are at the heart of Stephen Kline's more thorough and provocative study *Out of the Garden: Toys and Children's Culture in the Age of TV Marketing* (1993). Kline focuses on the rise of the toy industry and television because toys are the prototypical possessions of children that they use, control, and gain pleasure from during the first three years of their lives and because by the time an average child graduates from high school in the United States he or she

> will have spent over 20,000 hours watching television and only 11,000 in the classroom. A child will be exposed each year to 18,000–21,000 commercial messages. Heavy-viewing preschoolers may spend up to one third of their waking days in front of the tube. They will forget many of the facts that they learn in this TV-watching but will retain vague impressions

from the thousands of stories they see. Because of this incidental cultural learning, they will also accumulate an encyclopedic knowledge of the preferred patterns of speech behaviour and social interaction in our popular culture.[20]

His study is highly significant because he demonstrates through careful research how children's socialization and their changing culture in North America from the nineteenth century to the present has gradually been shaped by commercial interests. Indeed, he claims that advertising firms, television and movie companies, and, of course, publishers take children, analyze their needs, wants, and desires, and respond to them more carefully than educators and psychologists because their business depends so heavily on them. Moreover, they have expertly learned to induce desires, needs, and wants based on their research and are most adept in producing enticing subliminal messages. The creation of particular character types to be emulated through toys, television shows, and film have become essential to the profit-making purposes of commercial companies during the rise of the technological age, and therefore, conventionalized codes were gradually construed to prompt viewers to decode stories, signs, and images in particular ways that influence their behavior as consumers.

> This social decoding process is precisely what the character marketers saw as the appeal of character toys; the careful construction of fantasy-world back-stories and attractive imaginary characters was the basis of their craft. They themselves became ethnographers of children's daydreams in order to create mini-worlds that resonated with the social knowledge and preferences of their target markets—all so their product lines would stand out.[21]

Although it may be an exaggeration to claim that it does not matter what shows children watch or what toys they play with, for the message is the same, Kline does reveal very similar patterns in the narrative structures of programs and commercials such as He-Man, Care Bears, G. I. Joe, My Little Pony, Barbie, and others. "Most of the new children's television animations," he claims,

> have been created explicitly for selling a new line of licensed goods. It is simply not sufficient for a programme to be popular with kids. The programme must instil in them the promise of an imaginary world that can be entered not just by watching television but also by owning and playing with a specific toy line. Children must want to have the characters and props, to own and to play with them to re-create their imaginary universes within their own play spaces.[22]

Kline discusses how the free play of children has been filled with commercialized figures that set the parameters for their games. Their imaginations and

interactions are prescripted by templates "through which children are being introduced into the attitudes and social relations of consumerism."[23] Though there are
no conclusive studies that reveal the immense harm done to children by having
their imaginations limited and steered by consumer culture, Kline maintains that
children today are basically learning to mimic what they see and read in a preda-
tory environment that exploits children's skills, talents, and energies. One of the
problems is that adults do not see the dangers of a consumer society because they
are fully immersed in the marketplace. For Kline, the only solution to the present
problem is for adults to recognize what the real problem is, namely that children
are being socialized to read signs of a socially constructed world and to compete for
a place in that world as if it were the only and best world that people could possibly
create.

Whereas Kline is skeptical about the possibility of changing the network
society of consumerism, Ellen Seiter and Anne Haas Dyson are more optimistic.
Seiter's starting point in *Sold Separately: Parents and Children in Consumer Culture*
is that we must accept the fact that the consumer society is here to stay:

> all members of modern developed societies depend heavily on commodity consumption,
> not just for survival but for participation—inclusion—in social networks. Clothing, furni-
> ture, records, toys—all the things that we buy involve decisions and the exercise of our own
> judgment and "taste." Obviously we do not control what is available for us to choose from in
> the first place. But consuming offers a certain scope for creativity. The deliberate, chosen
> meanings in most people's lives come more often from what they consume than what they
> produce, and these meanings are not individual but social and deserving of much more
> attention from academics interested in culture.[24]

Her perspective emanates from the tradition of the Birmingham School, which
has been influential in the area of cultural studies in America and has been stimu-
lated by the works of John Fiske, who has sought to demonstrate how people play
with popular culture in a subversive and emancipatory way. Similarly, Seiter,
whom I believe is much more sophisticated in her analyses than Fiske, argues that
children are not passive watchers of television and consumers of snacks, toys, and
clothes. Moreover, she maintains that the culture industry for children is not one-
dimensional. In fact, she claims that it has always been somewhat contradictory.
While promoting products and stimulating the urge to consume no matter what
the product is, television and advertising, according to Seiter, are also utopian and
educational and provide hope and meaningful experiences for children. Seiter
herself appears to be on a curious contradictory crusade: "I believe it is necessary to
defend U.S. consumer culture against many of the elitist moral judgments against
it; at the same time, I think it is absolutely necessary to criticize the gross economic

inequities that are expressed in, negotiated through, and created by advertising and marketing."[25]

Throughout her book she offers examples of how children take the commercial products such as My Little Pony and Ghostbusters that have been made into toys, videos, films, books, t-shirts, figurines, and other artifacts, play with them, and transform them into their own wish-fulfillment dreams.

> Children's interest in consumer culture involves much more than greed, hedonism, or passivity: it involves the desire for community and for a utopian freedom from adult authority, seriousness, and goal directedness. As a mass culture, toys and television give children a medium of communication—this is why I have described it as a lingua franca. Consumer culture does, however, limit children's utopian impulses. When engaged with consumer culture, children promote some identifications—those of a same-sex peer group while demoting others. Peer groups offer a limited basis for social alliances when considered apart from other aspects of social identity—race, ethnicity, gender, class, region.[26]

In the end, Seiter tends to minimize the alleged "negative" effects that commercial television and toys might have on young people by placing these products within a subversive tradition in children's literature and childhood culture without fully discussing this literature or culture. No doubt there are subversive currents in all cultures, but they cannot be easily divided into adult and child, for the lines between the two have always been fluid. Nor should one readily accept her thesis that the appeal of toys and television shows for children depends on the propensity to invert adult values. It is very questionable whether the literature she cites, fairy tales and nursery rhymes, are subversive.

Though Seiter's work is refreshingly provocative, there is also a populist tendency in it that celebrates what I would call calculated and contrived subversion, a kind of artificial negativity that has no other meaning for children than to get them to consume. What might have been considered subversive or provocative in the past has been domesticated through the market and changing tastes and values. That children and adults as producers of meaning make more out of the signs, images, and icons they appropriate from books, toys, and television shows is obvious, but the parameters of the market system and network society provide little room for genuine opposition, and the result of the games played out by children as adults tends to turn into degenerate utopias much in the same manner in which the Disney theme parks have been realized.[27]

A critique of the culture industry and the devastating effects it has on the disposition of children and their configuration within the socialization process is not always elitist, especially when it recognizes the necessity to engage commercial and popular culture, to take it seriously, not to celebrate its utopian and subversive potential, and to grasp why it is being consumed and used by young people. In Anne Haas Dyson's book, *Writing Superheroes*, she seeks

> to contribute to discussions of contemporary culture by portraying ways in which young people, like their older counterparts are active interpreters of the media, who "reconstruct its meanings according to more immediate [social] interests." Indeed, sometimes children themselves are superheroes who overcome the ideological constraints of media offerings, not to save imagined others, but to live more equitably and/or more harmoniously with real others. Moreover, I aim to argue that educators may both foster and influence these interpretive processes if school curricula are "permeable"—not impervious—to children's playful appropriations and critical examinations of diverse cultural material. Teachers, and more broadly, communities do have a responsibility to make judgments about, and provide the young access to, valuable cultural products—but they also have a responsibility to attend to those cultural materials children themselves find accessible and meaningful. To fail to do so is to risk reinforcing societal divisions of gender and socioeconomic class.[28]

There are two key features of Dyson's study that are important: 1. commercial culture is ideologically slanted and geared to perpetuate stereotypes that do not lead to critical literacy; 2. the role of educators and parents is not to ignore or necessarily condemn the commercial media, central to contemporary childhood in America, but to work with this material critically and imaginatively so that children fully grasp the significance of the cultural products they are fed and can appropriate them in a more socially meaningful way. If such educational work does not become part of the socio-cultural practices in schools, Dyson stresses, there is little chance to counter the negative aspects of the culture industry and to provide alternatives to current socio-political thinking.

Dyson's book is largely devoted to a two-year project conceived by a young teacher named Kristin in an East San Francisco Bay school. Contrary to the traditional method of teaching writing and reading, Kristin created a practice called "Author's Theater," in which children could choose their classmates to act out stories that they created largely out of their association with commercial culture. Over the course of two years the theater became a kind of public forum in which the texts that they created spoke back to the media, spoke to their own needs, and spoke to the classmates and conditions in the class. Kristin taught the same class of approximately twenty-eight children for two years from second through third grade, and Dyson collected an immense amount of data through classroom and playground observation, tapes, and interviews. The heroes on which the children chose to base their stories came from the movies, television, comic books, and video games: *Aladdin, Batman Returns, Beauty and the Beast, Jaws, Jurassic Park, Star Wars, Teenage Mutant Ninja Turtles, Superman, Barney, Martin, Power Rangers, Star Trek, X-Men, Mortal Kombat II*. Throughout her book, she comments theoretically on the interactions and changes that she observes. Although she makes many illuminating observations, I found that her description of the process as struggle was most significant. In other words, what struck me most was how the children had to struggle over the portrayal of the characters and how to use words and images to articulate their *personal* needs and wishes. At the same time they had to negate commercial influences and degenerate utopic images and were not always able to overcome racial and gender stereotypes. The conflicting tension of the project reveals all the more the importance of developing such experimental projects like Author's Theater. As Dyson comments,

> ideological tensions, revealed during free writing and Author's Theater, helped children problematize and, in fact, conceive of their choices of roles and plots as matters of authorial choice. Because sensitivity to textual decisions was linked to sensitivity to community response (e.g., along the lines of gender or race), learning to write became linked to socio-ideological awareness and community participation—and bridge building. In this way, composing and, more particularly, the social and ideological dynamics that undergirded it, helped children learn about their interconnectedness as "fellow planeteers," to quote a child I once knew, even as that interconnectedness informed their learning to write.[29]

It is the interconnectedness and the reconfiguration of children within the global network society that it is crucial to grasp if we want to understand the role of children's literature today, what children's literature actually is, and how children learn to read and react to the materials that surround them.

Factors of Children's Consumer Culture

The configuration and reconfiguration of children in socio-economic networks varies throughout the world. But there are several relatively "stable" or reliable factors that are triggering the great transformation of children and children's literature in the relentless process of globalization that determines their interconnectedness. To conclude this chapter, I shall try briefly to summarize what factors are necessary to consider when discussing the reconfiguration of children and children's literature. Certainly, when one studies children and children's literature, we cannot separate them from the broader fields of culture as is normally done at universities, especially in departments of English or cultural studies. Children are not separate from the civilizing process and socio-economic activity; they are nodal points for understanding the nature of progress and civilization of which they are part. Their reconfiguration and the reconfiguration of children's literature must change the way we view the anxieties and problems that we, adults, have when we wonder why children are becoming rootless in a fluid life. And now let me suggest some "stable" factors that, I believe, should play a role when we think about reconfiguration.

1. Children have become more active participants in the socio-economic fields of their respective countries. As Viviana Zelizer has remarked,

> Recent research provides new ideas and information about children's place in economic production, consumption and distribution. It also helps identify three somewhat different sets of economic relations in which children regularly engage: with members (including adult members) of their own households, with children outside their households and with agents of other organizations such as outside households, schools, store, firms, churches and voluntary associations. Contrary to cherished images of children as economic innocents, we discover children actively engaged in production, consumption and distribution. We also discover that their economic activity varies significantly from one category of social relations to another.[30]

When Zelizer refers to children as active participants in economic activity, she includes young people between the ages of five and sixteen, but I should like to expand this grouping to include the young from the ages of three to eighteen. The involvement of very small children in economic activity begins with trips to super-markets and other stores and with watching and reading commercials on TV and advertisements in restaurants. By the time a child becomes a teenager in twenty-first century America, he or she is a formidable expert of market conditions.

2. Not only are children more active in economic processes, they have also become more or less agents of cultural capital. In his book, *The Commodification of Childhood: The Children's Clothing Industry and the Rise of the Child Consumer*, Daniel Thomas Cook argues that

> markets shape persons in and through the consumer culture of childhood. Markets make persons in their capacity as power structures to "hail" or call into being particular subjects and subjectivities, akin to Louis Althusser's understanding. The ideological process that I describe, however, consists of commercially focused institutions addressing and indeed encouraging active, agentive beings rather than state apparatuses creating subjects helplessly subjected to them.[31]

Early in their lives, children are spurred to consume and to consume to profit and have become key players on all markets. Not only are they shaped by market forces during their infancy, but they are later *trusted* to shape market forces. They use capital to distinguish themselves and create their self-worth in different commodi-fied forms.

3. The new technologies invented and developed during the last thirty years have radically changed the way children read and engage with their worlds and

negotiate their way through the world. No longer viewed as precious or sacred or considered vital for the development of a particular tradition, children sense that they are "free" to desire and present and even advertise themselves on the market the way they want. This is the sense of empowerment that they feel as they mature and use the television, cell phones, portable media players, computers, CD and DVD players, and all types of digital gadgets to exercise their power. As Beryl Langer has observed,

> the global children's culture industry can only be sustained if children can "be relied on to keep buying" when their rooms are filled to overflowing with toys and games. Hence, the emergence of "commoditoys", characterized by a capacity to stimulate rather than satisfy longing and a short but intense "shelf life" as objects of desire. Their essential feature is that satiation is endlessly postponed. Each act of consumption is a beginning rather than an end, the first or next step in an endless series for which each particular toy is an advertisement: first, because its package is also a catalogue; and, second, because it is part of a tantalizing universe without which the one just purchased is somehow incomplete. The presence of "marked and marketed spaces" for children in chain stores, shopping malls, fast food restaurants and superstores maximizes children's exposure to the universe of "commoditoy" possibility. What Ritzer (1999)[32] identifies as "the new means of consumption" thus play a major role in reproducing the cycle of perpetual desire in which consumer capitalist childhood is embedded.[33]

Langer believes that there may be unintended consequences of the unsatiated desires produced by the market insofar as they might lead to a resistance to globalization because it does not satisfy their desires.

4. Though the social production and manipulation of desires is fundamental to the successful operation of the capitalist market and consumerism, the formation of dispositions to make children receptive to the appeal of certain goods is key to understanding why children ultimately had to be reconfigured in the civilizing process to become as active as they are as consumers. In "Bringing Children (and Parents) into the Sociology of Consumption" (2004) Lydia Martens, Dale Southerton, and Sue Scott make use of Pierre Bourdieu's concepts of consumption and *habitus* to explain why children (and adults) consume the way they do. They remark that Bourdieu sees

> consumption as a process of reproducing dispositions that constitute differential tastes and emanate from the *pursuit of the conduct* of a life that is subjectively acceptable in the context of objectively given circumstances. These objective circumstances related to class-based constraints associated with an individual's material wealth (economic), types of knowledge (cultural) and access to networks (social), all acting as resources (accumulated to form capital) that are deployed when judging taste in the pursuit of social practice.[34]

In other words, the way everyone (children and adults) consumes is bound to a socially class-defined comportment that will influence his or her tastes and choices in the consumption of knowledge and material goods and in his or her use of skills and articles. Our comportment depends on our habitus which is a set of acquired dispositions determined at first by the social class, ethnicity, nationality, and religion of the family into which one is born. A child will internalize the dispositions at the same time that he or she is structuring the dispositions (gestures; tastes of dress, music, literature; speech and accents; etc.) to form his or her identity under the conditions of a particular civilizing process. A child reproduces them while acquiring other dispositions that will distinguish him or her in a hierarchical society that associates and recognizes a habitus in almost every social and non-social occupation. A habitus is dynamic. That is, though one is marked through life by one's early habitus, primarily influenced by parents and relatives and one's immediate environment, it is possible to cultivate and assume another habitus as one develops and assumes an adult role in society. A child's habitus is a crucial indicator for how he or she will relate to consumption, production, and dissemination of material and cultural goods. As Martens, Southerton, and Scott note,

> If the internalization of habitus relates to the learning of cultural values, how to consume and what is competent social conduct, and if habitus is structured according to the objective constraints of capital, then it is in the external social conditions (such as the influences of school and social networks) and the transfer of capital (especially cultural) between parents and children that the role of consumption in social reproduction will be revealed.[35]

Whether a child resists or participates in the transfer of capital, it is only through the capitalist market and the civilizing process of globalization that he or she can form a habitus and determine his or her private and social identity. While a child is bound to reproduce his or her parents' orientations in the domain of consumption, the changed objective conditions of capitalist production and consumption lead children to experiment and act in ways that lead to a thinking and comportment that also may differentiate them from their parents.

5. Children do not read books, use books, or invest in books the way their parents do, and certainly not the way their grandparents did. Nor are books the same "sacred" commodities they once were when they endowed a person with a certain amount of distinction and cultural capital. Children are not as literate as their parents were in the domain of literature, but their parents are also not as literate in the new technologies that are pivotal for their children's acquiring a distinct and distinguished habitus under present cultural and economic conditions. If children are being reconfigured to act primarily as savvy consumers and

supporters of globalized capitalism, alphabetic literature, as we have understood it, is incidental to their major interests. In *Literacy in the New Media Age*, Gunther Kress talks about a revolution in the landscape of communication.

> The former constellation of *medium of book* and *mode of writing* is giving way, and in many domains has already given way, to the new constellation of *medium of screen* and *mode of image*. The logic of image now dominates the sites and the conditions of appearance of all "displayed" communication, that is, of all graphic communication that takes place via spatial display and through the sense of sight. That now includes writing, which is becoming display-oriented. When in the past image appeared on the page it did so subject to the logic of writing, the relation of image to writing which we still know as "illustration". When writing now appears on the screen, it does so subject to the logic of the image.[36]

Kress associates all forms of literacy with social power and maintains that the logic of reading and writing formerly served a more static and conventional society of authority if not authoritarianism. In the "fluid" twenty-first century, though alphabetic literature and reading are still important, the new dominance of design and display in multi-modes of communication is in keeping with the reconfiguration of children within the network of the civilizing process. The slow, deliberate, and reflective process that complex reading entails is being replaced by the quick images, instant recognition, and non-reflective viewing of the screen, big and little. The new multimodal literature for children offers vast opportunities for consumers, but it also does not want the consumers to think too much about what they are reading/viewing.

6. It would be a mistake to assume that the new technologies that entail developing new literacies are necessarily detrimental to the young. Technologies and inventions such as the television, computer, cell phone, computer game, portable media player, and so on are not by themselves dangerous or insidious. What is significant is how they are put to use by corporations that produce and sell them and how they are used by the consumers. Corporations are not concerned about how they are used just as long as they are desired and bought. For instance, in 2008 new cell phones are being produced for 5-year-olds, and cell-phone novels have become fashionable in Japan. The corporations that have produced the cell phones are pleased to train the children in early usage and also pleased that young people are finding imaginative uses for the cell phone. They also want to make their phones more effective, stimulating, and useful. But social value is generally insignificant in their view; their bottom line is the production of desire for profit.

7. The tendency of the reconfigured book for reconfigured children today— and I shall discuss all this in more detail in the next chapter—is to produce a desire for the same type of multimodal text that is to be consumed to reproduce the

market conditions that will keep them as loyal consumers. Loyalty to a family, religion, and nation is being replaced by loyalty to the market. Acclamation and display in a society of spectacle are the manners of comportment demanded by politicians and corporations that promote an interconnectedness alien to the needs of most children.

Misreading
Children
and the Fate
of the Book   2

We are in a muddle about literacy. We worry endlessly that children in Britain are not becoming readers. Report after report comes out, revealing that hundreds of thousands of our children do not read well enough, that we are slipping further and further behind in child literacy levels when compared with other countries.

Michael Morpurgo, "On Teaching Children to Read"[1]

As long as we continue to allow our children's future to be squandered on obscenities like the militarization of outer space (among countless other examples of governmental waste, fraud, and mismanagement), we have no right to lament that those children will not spend enough time reading, or that their reading won't be done in the familiar bound books of our past.

Ralph Lombreglia, "Humanity's Humanity in the Digital Twenty-First"[2]

It is one of the worst kept secrets in the world that, within the past fifty years or so, we have reconfigured our children to act and to behave as commodities and agents of consumerism, and we continue to invent ways to incorporate them flawlessly into socio-economic systems that compromise their integrity and make them complicit in criminal behavior such as mutual economic exploitation and the political maintenance of class division. By teaching children how not to read, to inhibit their expert reading, or to read vacuous books and diverse screens with words and images advertising some sort of seemingly magical commodity, we have succeeded in transforming children into functional literates, nonliterates, and alliterates, who lack any sense of civic responsibility and are predisposed to become consumers in a society gone amuck. Perhaps we should call this process the "endumbment of children," that is, the dumbing down of children so that they will be more docile, flexible, and operational as plug-in adults. And perhaps you may think that I am exaggerating our present dilemma regarding trivial books and mechanical reading programs, but I am not alone. In fact, there is strong concern throughout America, if not throughout the world,[3] about an alleged crisis of literacy that has national consequences, and it is a concern that has been expressed particularly by government ministries and offices that love to produce facts without reflecting self-critically about them.

In 2004, the National Endowment for the Arts (NEA) published the booklet, *Reading at Risk: A Survey of Literary Reading in America*, which included the following statistics:

- Only 47 percent of adults read a work of literature (defined as a novel, short story, play, or poem) within the past year.
- That figure represented a 7-point decline in the percentage of literary readers over a 10-year period.
- Literary reading declined in both genders, across all education levels, and in virtually all age groups.
- The declines were steepest in young adults, accelerating at a greater rate than in the general population.
- Americans were not only reading literature at a reduced rate—they were reading fewer books generally.[4]

This publication caused great alarm among educators, politicians, and the general public, and there was a good deal of finger pointing from all sides. Blame for producing a nation of illiterates and alliterates was placed on television, the Internet, the public school system, the government, and a wide variety of social and commercial institutions. Federal and state governments responded with even more mandated reading policies for schools and more testing in accordance with President Bush's infamous 2001 legislation, No Child Left Behind, to enforce accountability in the teaching of reading. In some cases, however, critics derided the results of the NEA booklet and criticized the report for being skewed, inaccurate, and misleading. Not to be daunted, however, the NEA published a second booklet, *To Read or Not to Read: A Question of National Consequence* in 2007, which not only reinforced the first survey with even more thorough research and even more statistics, but it was also more disturbing than *Reading at Risk*. In his preface, Dana Gioia, Chairman of the NEA, commented:

> The story the data tell is simple, consistent, and alarming. Although there has been measurable progress in recent years in reading ability at the elementary school level, all progress

appears to halt as children enter their teenage years. There is a general decline in reading among teenage and adult Americans. . . . As Americans, especially younger Americans, read less, they read less well. Because they read less well, they have lower levels of academic achievement. (The shameful fact that nearly one-third of American teenagers drop out of school is deeply connected to declining literacy and reading comprehension.) With lower levels of reading and writing ability, people do less well in the job market. Poor reading skills correlate heavily with lack of employment, lower wages, and fewer opportunities for advancement. Significantly worse reading skills are found among prisoners than in the general adult population. And deficient readers are less likely to become active in civic and cultural life, most notably in volunteerism and voting.[5]

Though there has been a slight drop in the rate of book production in America, it still remains relatively high compared to most other countries, and there are over 65,000 different publishing houses and presses in the USA. But most people (including the young) are reading fewer and fewer books. Even when they read, they are often watching a screen or listening to music or the radio. In addition, average household spending on books has dropped 14 percent from 1985 to the present, and 58 percent of middle and high school students use other media while reading, so-called multi-tasking, and they watch two to three hours of television every day. Books are becoming more and more rare in households, and many homes do not even have them. It would seem, from the report, that there is a correlation to be drawn from the lack of books in households, the downward trend in the reading of the books that are being produced, and the quality of civic life. Or, in other words, if more people read books, the NEA booklet argues, there would be greater participation in all forms of culture including sports, and people would be more civically responsible. In short, the NEA appears to be proposing that either culture and civic responsibility in American society have been degenerating because people are spending their leisure time in the wrong places and do not read enough books, or that book reading is a panacea to a country that appears to disparage reading and is indifferent to the consequences of a non-reading public.

While this proposition may be true to a certain extent—and it is important to take the two reports by the NEA very seriously—the focus, in my opinion, is blurred and leads to the misreading of what children read and need—and adults as well. The NEA has unfortunately transformed the book and reading into fetishes that could magically revive American culture. It is part and parcel of the old elitist, genteel veneration of the book as sacrament and book-reading as spiritually uplifting. Preserve the book and reading, namely the novel, short story, poem, and play, and we shall preserve the humanities and arts in America—perhaps prevent the decline of American civilization. Yet, if the book and reading are so crucial to the welfare of American culture, especially for children, it seems to me that there are more important questions to ask, that involve the reconfiguration of children into a socio-economic system that exploits their talents and works against them, not for them, and the commercialization and standardization of the book, than the ones raised by the NEA. While most of the statistics provided by the NEA are valuable, they are essentially quantitative and imply that certain kinds and amounts of book-reading are more enriching and benefit society more than other kinds of reading. But this really misses the point about the significance of reading and books for the young in contemporary American society or in any society. One could even argue that the writers and researchers of the two NEA booklets misread the problems regarding children, books, reading, and culture, and their statistics only serve to perpetuate the problems that continue to plague children and limit the education that they are offered. As Sven Birkerts, author of *The Gutenberg Elegies: The Fate of Reading in an Electronic Age* (1994), has remarked,

> In asking about the fate of the book, most askers really want to talk about the fate of a way of life. But no one ever just comes out and says so. This confirms my general intuition about Americans, even—or especially—American intellectuals. We want to talk about the big things but we just can't let ourselves to admit it.[6]

In light of the major drawbacks of the NEA booklets, which try to talk about the big things but never get to the heart of the matter, I want to focus on the socialization of children, reading practices, children's books, and other cultural artifacts and how young people from about three to eighteen are exposed to them. My concern is not about books, how many are read, and whether children learn to read, but how and why they are taught and prompted to misread, and by consequence, how and why we continue to misread problematic aspects of contemporary culture. By misreading, which is non-reflective reading, geared toward quick absorption of information and signs not elaborated by the brain, I mean that we do not carefully examine all the complex institutional processes that bear upon our reading and our personal and public decisions and commitments and that we do not recognize that the rational and efficient operations in the socio-economic system that affect us and our children's lives lead to exploitative and reified relations among all people. The result is that we tend to treat one another as objects to be used for personal gain and pleasure. Misreading involves ignoring the words, signs, and meanings that foster the rationalization and standardization of daily social life and involves the prevention of profound comprehension and empathetic relations. It is the opposite of reading which the astute professor of child development, Maryanne Wolf, defines as a neuronally and intellectually circuitous act, enriched as much by the unpredictable indirections of a reader's inferences and thoughts as by the direct message to the eye from the text. . . . Biologically and intellectually, reading allows the species to go "beyond the information given" to create endless thoughts most beautiful and wonderful. We must not lose this essential quality in our present moment of historical transition to new ways of acquiring process, and comprehending information.[7]

In her remarkable book, *Proust and the Squid: The Story and Science of the Reading Brain*, Wolf reminds us,

We were never born to read. Human beings invented reading only a few thousand years ago. And with this invention, we rearranged the very organization of our brain, which in turn expanded the ways we were able to think, which altered the intellectual evolution of our species. Reading is one of the single most remarkable inventions in history.[8]

It is this invention and what we are doing to it that the NEA booklets never discuss, nor do they discuss the quality of the books that are being manufactured for young people between the ages of three and eighteen. Moreover, they never ask other crucial questions such as: What is a book for children? How are children exposed to reading materials and taught to use them? What are the diverse sociocultural contexts in which children read? Do other media complement the reading of books? Hasn't the screen replaced the book to produce multimodal reading? Why read what we read, and do we have a choice? What role does social class, race, and gender play in learning how to read?

Books

Simply put, a book for children is a commodity, not the holy grail nor the salvation of civilized society. Of course, it is also a commodity for adults, but I shall largely be talking about books for children and questions of literacy. When John Newberry, the first major publisher of books for children in England, began specifically to produce juvenile works in 1744, he had a clear idea of what a book had to be if it was to be successful in improving the morals of the young and educating them and if it was also to be enjoyable and profitable. As Janet Adam Smith remarks,

Newberry's interest for us here is in his obvious care for the look of his publications, his insistence that a book should be specially designed. He had new woodcuts made for his alphabets, instead of using any that happened to be knocking around; he launched out into some copperplate engravings, and his title-pages were gracefully lettered and laid out. And by covering his books in pretty flowery Dutch papers touched with gilt and charmingly labeled, he made them as attractive as coloured lollipops or gilt-wrapped gingerbread.[9]

For Newberry and most of the book publishers and owners of bookstores during the eighteenth and early nineteenth centuries, the book for children had to be attractive, charming, and magical. No matter what type of book was produced, it was regarded as a thing to be sold that had something of value between its covers and that needed deciphering. It had to appeal to parents and children at the same time, and it had to fulfill its promise advertised on the cover and title page. The importance of design and display was not new in the book publishing industry in Newberry's time, but the appearance of this somewhat new commodity became fundamental for the success of books produced for children. Once bookstores included books for children, these products had to be distinguished from others, and the covers helped signal whether they were bible stories, alphabet books, fairy tales, legends, myths, educational texts, anthologies, poems, songs, picture books, chapbooks, and so on, and whether they were appropriate for girls or boys of specific social classes or for both genders. Forget about children of the working classes, slaves, and minority groups. Of course, since most children could not read books in the eighteenth and nineteenth centuries, book production was largely dedicated to children of the upper classes, primarily boys. Only by the end of the nineteenth century did conditions of literacy in English-speaking countries begin to change, when reading became more widespread with the introduction of com- pulsory education, but it was also more prescribed and conscripted: that is, schools had developed approved disciplines, genres, and canons, and children were compelled to learn—often by rote—what was proper for them to read.

From the beginning, before children were encouraged to read and before there was a market for children's books, that is, from the advent of the printing press in the fifteenth century, books and reading were associated with enlightenment, mor- ality, and healthy recreation, or a meaningful way to pass one's time. As commod- ities, books were always regarded as something special, magical, authoritative, and sacred. They were associated with learning and cultivated people, the upper class, government, and the church. They enabled the right genteel people to assert their authority and determine what culture meant on all levels of society. In short, when books for children and young people began to be manufactured in large quantities and disseminated among the upper classes—and many of them were books of manners—they were considered potent agents of the civilizing process that, according to Rousseau and Locke, were both dangerous and beneficial, even if they were "sacred" and "authoritative." Indeed, in the eighteenth and nineteenth centuries, numerous educators and clergymen warned that wrong reading, espe- cially fantasy works, could arouse the sexual drives of young readers and lead to masturbation and other deviant behavior.

Times have changed a great deal since the eighteenth century. But publishers, or should I say, corporate conglomerates, that manufacture books today in the English-speaking world still make distinctions based on moral and ethical standards that reflect the cultural values and prejudices of a given society. Outright censorship, which played a role throughout the twentieth century, has largely disappeared due to the free market system and globalization, but most of the large publishing houses, in collusion with chain stores and super bookstores, subscribe to "unofficial" censorship through the categorization of appropriate reading and careful selection of books that will be marketable to large readerships. Their policies are intended to manipulate the market for profit, and the children's book can be highly profitable. We cannot speak about *the* BOOK for children and its fate in general terms, because there are literally hundreds of different types and sizes of books with and without substance. But we can note certain tendencies about the manufacturing, dissemination, publicity, and use of books.

The most significant change in the production of books as commodities since the eighteenth century can be discerned by analyzing the ideological shift in the perspective of the producers, sellers, and marketers in the second half of the twentieth century. Whereas the early publishers of children's books were driven more by enlightenment ideals to benefit children by improving their morals, instructing them, and amusing them, and whereas they were tiny publishing houses, often family enterprises that encompassed printing and selling, the major contemporary publishers of books are part of large anonymous public conglomerates, driven largely by a profit motive, and they will indiscriminately publish anything that will increase their own stature, wealth, and power, and anything that will secure their status within the culture industry. In her highly relevant book about bookselling and the culture of consumption, *Reluctant Capitalists: Bookselling and the Culture of Consumption* (2007), Laura Miller notes that the major transformation of the book industry is closely connected to the big question of a way of life, and she argues that communal fun and entertainment have replaced affective ties between community members in large part due to consumerism and the reconfiguration of marketing and shopping, and how all this imparts meaning to our daily activities. In writing about booksellers, she notes,

> the bookstore's foray into the provision of entertaining experiences is of a piece with much of consumer culture. However, to understand why the bookstore has so successfully adopted entertainment retail, one also needs to take into account of how books, specifically, have been incorporated into a culture of entertainment. The widespread use of books as building blocks of entertaining experiences represents the culmination of a process first seen

so clearly in the early amusement park. Kasson[10] claims that Coney Island represented a cultural revolt against genteel expectations that leisure should be connected to moral improvement; instead, the amusement park promoted novelty, excitement, and a release of inhibition. . . . The entertaining bookstore is an indication that the cultural revolt described by Kasson has truly reached deep into the world with transformative results. An important aspect of this transformation has to do with the book's status as a medium of mass communication. The development of the entertaining bookstore reflects the almost complete integration of books into an interlocking entertainment industry. On the one hand, the integration of books into the entertainment industry has been organizational. Beginning in the 1970s, book publishers were acquired by corporations with holdings in film, broadcasting, music, newspapers, and magazines. Today, almost all the major American book publishers are owned by such diversified media conglomerates as Bertelsmann, Time Warner, and Viacom.[11]

Not only are publishing houses parts of large media conglomerates, there is no longer such thing as a stable group of editors, publicists, marketers, or loyalty to a particular house. Though many editors still retain a high regard for serious books and strong relationships with their writers, they are under duress to acquire popular books that will sell well. In a recent article in *Harper's Magazine*, the outspoken, talented writer, Ursula K. Le Guin, who is also concerned about the recent NEA report, has pointed out,

> Moneymaking entities controlled by obscenely rich executives and their anonymous accountants have acquired most previously independent publishing houses with the notion of making quick profit by selling works of art and information. I wouldn't be surprised to learn that such people get sleepy when they read. Within the corporate whales are many luckless Jonahs who were swallowed alive with their old publishing house—editors and such anachronisms—people who read wide awake. Some of them are so alert they can scent out promising new writers. Some of them have their eyes so wide open they can even proofread. But it doesn't do them much good. For years now, most editors have had to waste most of their time on an unlevel playing field, fighting Sales and Accounting. In those departments, beloved by the CEOs, a "good book" means a high gross and a "good writer" is one whose next book can be guaranteed to sell better than the last one.[12]

Though there are a great number of intelligent editors dedicated to the education of children in the publishing industry, their influence on book production is negligible, for the bottom line of every book is indeed its marketability and profitability. Miller has also remarked that within publishing houses the marketing department will often determine what types of books will be produced, and the bookstores, now dominated by chains such as Barnes & Noble, Borders, Dalton, and even Wal-Mart, will sometimes determine which books will be highlighted or distributed.[13] On the Internet, Amazon plays an important role. In short, the market dictates the interests of publishers, writers, and readers, and of course, the market cannot predict everything, but it can quickly take advantage of unanticipated shifts in audience tastes and/or promote those tastes.

For instance, if so-called fantasy books become the rage such as J. K. Rowling's Harry Potter series or Philip Pullman's *His Dark Materials* trilogy, and they are made into films to increase their popularity, then numerous publishers will publish copycat books—and they were doing this even before the Harry Potter craze—in order to find their blockbuster book. If, after a certain amount of promotion, a book does not reap profits and become a bestseller or if it does not become simply profitable, it will be allowed to go out of print, or it will be remaindered. Indiscriminate quantities of books must be manufactured every year for publishers to make money, as if they were playing the lottery, hoping for at least one big winner a year. One obscene example from the American culture industry should serve as an example of how conglomerates operate today.

On August 29, 2005, the following press release was distributed worldwide by PRB newswire:

> Disney Publishing unveiled to the world today its eagerly awaited novel *Fairy Dust and the Quest for the Egg* by Newbery Honor-winning author Gail Carson Levine. This illustrated novel goes on sale in stores in the United States on September 1st and arrives at bookstores in Asia, Europe and Latin America throughout September and October. This book for girls ages 6–10 builds upon the enormous popularity of Tinker Bell and The Walt Disney Company's heritage of creating fairy tale magic for more than 75 years; it releases with a significant one-million book launch in 45 countries, 32 languages and a million-dollar marketing campaign, extraordinary in the world of children's publishing.[14]

Following this declaration without explaining who exactly was eagerly awaiting Gail Carson Levine's novel, the press release informed readers:

> Following Disney Publishing Worldwide's initial launch, The Walt Disney Company will provide unparalleled and synergistic support for Disney Fairies across its business units. The campaign begins with the recent launch of http://www. disneyfairies.com, a global online experience where visitors can explore and learn about Tinker Bell and other Never Land fairies. The entertainment experience will continue with a series of chapter books planned for the spring 2006. In addition, multiple films are currently in development to further extend the storytelling and bring the world of Tinker Bell and her friends to life. Disney Consumer Products will bring Disney Fairies into the homes and lives of girls around with the world with a breadth of products that will inspire, enlighten, and fuel their imaginations—from apparel and toys to home décor and stationery.[15]

Within the following three years, the Disney Company unfortunately was compelled to live up to its promises. The spurious and vapid first novel written by Levine, who basically compromised whatever talents she had, was followed by imitative books by a stable of hack writers, who followed a formula, as did the illustrators, who depicted the trials and tribulations of variations of Tinker Bell like fairies, multicultural, of course. Neither the plots nor the characters were original or dealt with serious social or cultural issues. The entire series was conceived to sell itself and other commodities associated with the original book. Reading one of the books, a child would be basically prompted to read another one of the same books. The pictures of the cute, cuddly fairies were intended to spur girls to buy and cuddle one of the fairy dolls. To read the Disney/Levine conception of fairies and fairy tales, the child would learn nothing about the essence of fairies and their roles in the long tradition of oral and literary fairy tales, not to mention the significance of Tinker Bell in J. M. Barrie's play *Peter Pan*. In fact, the Disney Corporation has appropriated Tinker Bell and has a license on her name because it began producing a series of computerized DVD films in 2008 featuring Tinker Bell and her faux fairy friends. Of course, the series is intended to glorify the fairies in the book series and will continue to perpetuate misleading myths about fairies. The Disney legacy and corporation are all that counts.

One might argue that the example of Disney is not typical of the book publishing industry for children. But that is not true. The impetus to produce books that will replicate themselves, books to produce films that replicate the books, films to produce books to replicate the films, books that will sell books of the same category—this impetus can be found throughout the industry. As far as the publishers are concerned, books are to be manufactured to sell other books, and in the process, the tastes and values of children are to be molded to suit the tastes and values of the culture industry en large, for a book is no longer a single commodity but closely connected if not intertwined with other similar products. If children are to read, they are basically encouraged to consume more and more of the same.

The Spiderwick Chronicles (2003), written and illustrated by Tony Di Terlizzi and Holly Black, and published by Simon & Schuster Books for Young Readers, is another example of how a book is conceived to regenerate itself selfishly into multiple mirror-images in the society of spectacle. In this case, the framework, not unlike that of Disney Fairies, concerns 9-year-old twins and their older sister Mallory, who move to an old decrepit estate in New England and discover that the place is infested with fairies. The children explore the mysterious world of the fairies and have numerous entertaining adventures for five volumes. But there is more, for there are other books beyond the series that explain how you care for and feed the sprites, or how you can find your way around the estate and discern the different types of fairies. There is also *Notebook for Fantastical Observations* (2005), which is allegedly an interactive storybook that basically demands that you purchase the other books in the series in order to be active. As usual, a film and video game based on the series have been produced, and other paraphernalia accompany the books and film.

Generally speaking, sequel literature for children and young adults is often targeted to specific age groups and is gender-oriented and ghost-written, once a single author demonstrates success. This is the case with Cecily von Ziesgar's *Gossip Girl* (2002), published by Alloy Entertainment in New York and followed by eleven other novels and a prequel, *It Had to Be You* (2007). The plots of the novels concern a group of exceedingly rich teenage girls, whose lives are filled with drugs, sex, and shopping and sniping at their parents and at each other. Nastiness and wealth pay well in all the novels, so well, in fact, that they have spawned copycat series such as the "A-List" and "Clique" novels. As Naomi Wolf has pointed out, these series "represent a new kind of young adult fiction, and feature a differ-ent kind of heroine. In these novels, which have dominated the field of popular girls' fiction in recent years, Carol Gilligan's question about whether girls can have a 'different voice'[16] has been answered in a scary way."[17] Gilligan's feminist call for listening to the more empathetic and softer voice that females have to offer and that needs to be recognized has indeed been answered by books empowering girls to be competitive, arrogant, solipsistic, seductive, and wealthy. The protagonists in these novels realize exactly what the advertising industry wants to make out of them— ideal commodified consumers, whose appetites are voracious and can never be satiated. That these books sell in the millions and have been the basis of a television series needs no comment.

The connection to television and the film industry is thus very important. Films and television can often regenerate interest in books published for children in the past, and in some cases they can lead to a renewed interest in popular novels, picture books, classical works, and fairy tales, some with merit and some that deserve to be forgotten. In many cases, a film or series of films can reawaken interest in a mediocre charming book as is the case with *Shrek* by William Steig. Not only have there been three films based on Steig's slim, modest picture book, but the films have also led to the publication of numerous other books such as *Shrek the Halls Lift the Flap Book* (2007, Reader's Digest), *Shrek Cookbook* (2007, DK Publishing), *Shrek* (2007, ultimate sticker books, DK Publishing), *Shrek: The Art of the Quest* (2007, Insight Editions), *Shrek 2* (2004, interactive sound book, Dream-works Pictures), *Shrek the Third: The Movie Storybook* (2007) by Alice Cameron, *Shrek the Third: The Junior Novel* (2007) by Kathleen Weidner, *Shrek the Third Mix and Match Jigsaw Puzzle Book* (2007), *Shrek 2: The Cat Attack!* (2004, storybook with stickers), *Shrek: The Complete Guide* (2007, DK Publishing), *Shrek 2: Who Are*

You Calling Ugly? (2004, with scratch and stink stickers) by Sandvik and Linda Karl, *Shrek the Third 2008 Calendar, Shrek Sweet Treats Cookie Cutter Kit* (2007), and so on. Again, the principle of publishing is: milk the cow when she is full and continue milking until she is empty. If she can't produce any more milk, kill it, skin it, and wear it. In short, the principle is to capitalize on a book as commodity and reproduce it until its market value begins to wane. Then let it become dust.

In the book publishing industry, the contents of a book may be spurious, but any book can be sold to a certain extent as long as it has good advertising and distribution. Children's books can generally pay for themselves, and there is a possibility that they might even pay more if the right conditions are met. One factor, however, must be stressed: the market for books for children is shriveling, and public places for reading books have been eliminated or revamped to adjust to rapid introduction of new technologies into the lives of children. Library budgets have been reduced, and libraries have been revamped to introduce computers and various new technologies of the mass media into their spaces. Independent book-stores have closed. Children prefer to play video games, watch television, view programs on the Internet, and go to the movies. They have portable media players, cameras, cell phones, and computers and communicate through text messages and e-mails. Of course, not all children have these apparatuses, but they are encour-aged to desire and purchase them. A book is probably the last item on their wish list for Christmas and birthday presents. And yet, despite all the changes that have occurred in book production and all the damage done to the book in terms of sales and use, we need not worry about the fate of the book. This special commodity will be with us for many years to come.

The Book in the Context of Reading Practices

The book is more than just a commodity. It has always been and still is what Le Guin calls a "social vector," and she offers an unusual definition of a book:

> In its silence, a book is a challenge; it can't lull you with surging music or deafen you with screeching laugh tracks or fire gunshots in your living room; you have to listen to it in your head. A book won't move your eyes for you the way images on a screen do. It won't move your mind unless you give it your mind, or your heart unless you put your heart in it. It won't do the work for you. To read a story well is to follow it, to act it, to feel it, to become it—everything short of writing it, in fact. Reading is not "interactive" with a set of rules or options, as games are; reading is actual collaboration with the writer's mind.[18]

A book is not only social because it involves collaboration, confrontation, or discussion with the writer, but it can bring a reader together with other readers to discuss the qualities of the printed and illustrated pages. Books as commodities and social vectors were originally meant to be read aloud and discussed in monasteries, places of religious worship, courts, reading societies, families, schools, and many other public places, and they still are read together and aloud in schools, libraries, book clubs, book stores, at public events, and so on. In particular the vast amount of diverse books for children was intended to enable children to develop their talents, their creativity, and their critical thinking so that they might better understand the conditions under which they were living and develop a sense of civic responsibility and affective attachment to other human beings. As social vectors, they also serve as the basis for many products of the mass media including the cinema, television, and Internet. By examining the book as a social vector connected to the bigger question about ways of life, to recall Sven Birkerts, we might be able to understand why the book and reading are still so crucial to the civilizing process and what role they play in the process in different societies. We might understand why governments, corporations, and religious organizations in America have sought to control the way we read, think, relate to each other, and determine the quality of our culture.

In *Reading for Profit: How the Bottom Line Leaves Kids Behind*, a collection of essays by concerned educators, Bess Altwerger notes,

> Reading instruction, and education more generally, seems almost to have transformed overnight with the passage of No Child Left Behind legislation signed by President George Bush in 2001. Suddenly, commercial reading programs are not just offered, but mandated by our school systems. Teachers are "trained" to follow the scripts and directions in the teachers' manuals as if they are unskilled workers. States are refused federal dollars when they stray from officially prescribed components of reading instruction and assessment, and they must resort to hiring federally "approved" consultants, such as Louisa Moats, to right their paths. Even preservice and inservice reading education falls under federal control, with the same chosen few deciding which courses comply with narrowly defined specifications for "scientifically based" reading research and instruction and may therefore be counted toward teacher certification. Children are being left behind by the thousands as their reading scores on commercially published standardized tests don't reach the federally prescribed standard. And sadly, fine schools that have achieved recognition for excellence by their own state are labeled failing and threatened with student transfers and closure for not achieving "adequate yearly progress" on standardized tests.[19]

It is especially in the early crucial years from first to fourth grade that the education system, the publishing industry, government, and entertainment industry are failing our children. Maryanne Wolf writes that recent reports from the National Reading Panel and the "nation's report cards" indicate that 30 to 40 percent of children in the fourth grade do not become fully fluent readers with adequate comprehension. This is a devastating figure, made even worse by the fact that teachers, textbook authors, and indeed the entire school system have different expectations for students from grade 4 on.[20]

What has transpired recently in American education, public and private, has been a long process—and it is a process—of reconfiguration of children, turning them into pawns of the economic system that pervades all social and cultural institutions of American society. As Patrick Shannon has stated in his significant book, *Reading Against Democracy: The Broken Promises of Reading Instruction*,

> The market ideology and its new promise—that reading education will make all students capable of fulfilling the high-skill, high-wage jobs waiting for them in the global economy—distort the balance between the economic and civic rationales to such a point that the civic rationale has all but disappeared. Students are to learn to read in order to perform in the economy, and not to understand themselves, others, and ways texts work for and against them in a democracy. In effect, under market ideology and its laws concerning reading education, we are teaching and students are reading against democracy.[21]

In the process of reconfiguring children (and adults) in the new globalized market economy, what happens then to books, books of all kinds, when misreading is fostered as reading? Are they consumed like all other commodities? Can they have a value as social vectors? Does it really matter whether children and adults are reading fewer and fewer books each year if they are being "trained" to misread by institutions and corporations that want them to misread? What has become of all the educational and cultural reform movements of the 1970s and 1980s that fostered the whole language approach to literacy and multiculturalism? What is the impact of some of the extraordinary books created by talented writers and illustrators to challenge children and to have a dialogue with them? Is it possible for them to buy the books, be aware of them, appreciate them in their leisure, discuss them with friends and parents? Is there any hope, not to return to the genteel appreciation of books for children, but hope to move forward to a real recognition of what books are as social vectors?

Let us not forget: the book is a dead object. By itself it can do nothing. It is inanimate and can only be animated when brought to life. It is brought to life through reading practices. As Allan Luke and Peter Freebody have stated:

> History teaches us that literacy refers to a malleable set of cultural practices that are shaped and reshaped by different, often competing, social and cultural interests. As a result, we do not view how to teach literacy as a scientific decision, but rather as a moral, political, and cultural decision about the kind of literary practices that are needed to enhance peoples'

agency over their life trajectories and to enhance communities' intellectual, cultural, and semiotic resources in print/multi-mediated economies. Literacy education is ultimately about the kind of society and the kinds of citizen/subjects that could and should be constructed.[22]

The number of books produced each year by the 60,000 odd publishers in America amounts to more than approximately 165,000 titles, perhaps a modest estimate. Laura Miller has noted that, "in 2001, there were approximately 167,000 new titles published. When combined with older titles still available, that meant that there were approximately 1.7 million different books in print in the United States."[23] Whatever the figures may be, the existence of these books and whether children read as many as possible are not significant for the development of literacy in any culture. It is how we act upon these books and enact what the contents may or may not provide.

Reading practices and reading have been radically altered in the past twenty-five years, and they are still in the process of radical transformation. Who would have thought that just a year or so ago, Japanese adolescents would be reading cell-phone novels?[24] Text-messaging has become a way of life for millions of young people.[25] Children are exposed to a myriad of reading matter in books, news-papers, magazines, comics, and on television shows and commercials, Internet sites, computer games, movie screens, DVDs, and so on. Much of the reading is done in bytes while listening to music or watching something else at the same time. Protracted and reflective reading practices are difficult to develop in societies that emphasize constant testing, positivist knowledge, quick thinking, efficiency, max-imum productivity at all costs, competition, religious worship as spectacle, and the instrumentalization of other people for political power. This is not to say that everyone is infected by misreading. There are still millions of people, young and old, who have learned and are employing reading practices critically to compre-hend themselves and the world around them and to counter misreading. There are thousands of concerned teachers and parents struggling to come to terms with new literacies and technologies by experimenting with reading practices that take into account socio-political transformations. In fact, reading practices are central to the cultural wars in America that erupted during the 1990s and have continued to the present day. When governments, federal and state, seek to improve the education of children by inducing them to increase their quantitative reading of books so that they can be functional in the socio-economic system and find better jobs, it is clear that they are misreading children and will continue this practice, unless other social forces develop and demonstrate viable alternatives. There are many ways to read the world, and many new technologies and modes that we use to read texts of all kinds. There are many books that can help us, but they are not sacred and authoritative; the practices of print literacy are not the only useful activities that can enable us to foster critical thinking, sensitivity, pleasure, and civic responsibility. To quote Maryanne Wolf again,

> We must teach our children to be "bitextual," or "multitextual," able to read and analyze texts flexibly in different ways, with more deliberate instruction at every state of development on the inferential, demanding aspects of any text. Teaching children to uncover the invisible world that resides in written words needs to be both explicitly and part of a dialogue between learner and teacher, if we are to promote the processes that lead to fully formed expert reading in our citizenry. . . . My major conclusion from an examination of the developing reader is a cautionary one. I fear that many of our children are in the danger of becoming just what Socrates warned us against—a society of decoders of information, whose false sense of knowing distracts them from a deeper development of their intellectual potential.[26]

As I have indicated throughout this essay, the sincere fear noted by Wolf, the NEA, and other responsible adults has unfortunately been misread and manipulated frequently by federal, state, and municipal agencies and the press to create a myth about the BOOK and print literature. This misreading is apparent not only in America but in most of the English-speaking countries such as the UK, Ireland, Australia, and New Zealand. In their highly pertinent and provocative essay, "Adolescence Lost/Childhood Regained: On Early Intervention and the Emergence of the Techno-Subject," Allan and Carmen Luke argue

> that the crises of print literacy and their preferred ameliorative social strategies are being used as a nodal point in public discourse both to delay and sublimate the emergence of new educational paradigms around multiliteracies, around new blended forms of textual and symbolic practice and affiliated modes of identity and social relations, and to forestall a substantive debate over the implications such shifts might have for an aging, creaky, industrial, print-based schooling infrastructure. Our polemical position, then, is that the continued crisis in early print literacy has become a default stalling tactic by educational systems that are unable to come to grips generationally and practically with multiliteracies and increasingly alien and alienated student bodies.[27]

They argue, as many other critics do, that the new technologies and globalization have produced "new" young people whose pathways into the world for jobs and identity are not being addressed by parents and schools. They are not recognizing or do not want to recognize that the former traditional approaches to alphabetic literacy through reading print are not meeting the needs of young people who read texts much differently than the generations of teachers and educators who are teaching them. In *Literacy in the New Media Age*, Gunther Kress maintains,

The changes in the conditions surrounding literacy are such that we need to reconsider the theory which has, explicitly or implicitly, underpinned conceptions of writing over the last five or six decades. I have already said, insistently, that the major change is that we can no longer treat literacy (or "language") as the sole, the main, let alone the major means for representation and communication. Other modes are there as well, and in many environments where writing occurs these other modes may be more prominent and more significant. As a consequence, a linguistic theory cannot provide a full account of what literacy does or is; language alone cannot give us access to the meaning of the multimodally constituted message; language and literacy now have to be seen as the partial bearers of meaning only.[28]

The call or cry for a radical reformation of pedagogical approaches to the teaching of literacies with an emphasis on multimodality has motivated many educators and schools to develop early intervention programs based on the way that children use oral and written language and respond to the new technologies that prioritize the screen and images. Some of the early intervention programs are belated, led by adults still attached to policies of print literacy and alphabetic reading, and may be misguided by a concentration on traditional psychological views of infant development, as the Lukes point out. However, this is not always the case, and it is important to be discriminating in analyzing early intervention programs as Stuart McNaughton points out:

Psychologists working with social and cultural frameworks who are concerned with promoting early literacy development are more likely to ask a different question [than the Lukes assumed they do]: "How do socialization processes operating within and across settings provide channels for development, and given these how might these channels be enhanced for all children?" This is a question about how educational settings are structured and about the beliefs and values of socialization agents, as much as it is a question about identifying instructional mechanisms that are effective at a particular time.[29]

McNaughton puts his finger once again on the real problem in the discussions of children, education, socialization, the book, and literacy: value. Both the use and exchange value of children and books have been altered greatly by globalization. This has led, as I have argued, to a reconfiguration of children, reading, and books within the civilizing process that positions them to develop predispositions in everything they do, no matter what their class and ethnic background is or their gender, to view themselves as adroit consumers while becoming commodities themselves at the same time. The loyalty that children may have had or felt to a family or community is gradually being replaced by the market. Children respond more to brands and market forces than to social, educational, or political institutions. Adults stand perplexed because they have not yet fully grasped how and why children read the world differently than they do and respond to different reading matter through multimodalities that challenges their thinking. In short, we adults do not realize what we have produced in the name of progress because we misread the very nature of our relentless progress in the form of globalization.

If we truly value our children and their books and really want to learn what books and reading means today, we must stop misreading the current tendencies in our culture, alter our reading practices, and turn the tide of the reconfigured civilizing process, that has negated the promises of the Enlightenment, a formidable task, but one that is well worth the struggle.

Why Fantasy Matters Too Much   3

Young people today should be much better informed about the events of the recent past of our country. They should exercise their memories, understand in order to eventually oppose. To oppose identification. To oppose the belief that it is impossible to live in an economic system different from that in which they are living. To oppose the definitive victory of the cult of money and apparent capitalist efficiency. To oppose the loss of fantasy. But there is nothing definitive in history, and it is the prerogative of the young to imagine change.
Interview with the Italian pianist, Maurizio Pollini, "Esercizi di memoria,"
***Classic Voice* (2008)[1]**

In September, 1997, a fairy-tale princess and a holy saint, Princess Diana and Mother Teresa, died within a few days of each other. Millions of people openly and dramatically expressed their grief and mourning. Their pictures along with many different images of Diana and Mother Teresa were beamed all over the world through television and the Internet. The mass media carried all sorts of stories and acclaimed the two of them, the fairy-tale princess and the saint, so that little was left to the imagination. Fantastic spectacle was all that mattered.

We speculate with the fantastic. Fantasy is a celebrity and money-making machine. As a module in our brains, it has the capacity to transform plain junk into gold that glitters. Fantasy mobilizes and instrumentalizes the fantastic to form and celebrate spectacles which exist and have always existed—illusions of social relations of exploitation based on power. Spectacles violate and drain our imaginations by glorifying social relations of power that are made spectacular and involve the magic of fetishism. Generally, the results bring about delusion and acclamation of particular sets of social relations that are commodified, sold, and consumed. We acclaim commodities that we don't know, products that are not of our own making and that we consume mentally and physically. We reproduce images consciously and unconsciously that are not of our own making. The media and the corporate world occupy our psyches and manipulate our fantasies even when we dream. Our relations are mediated through fantastic spectacle and through fetish abetted by the latest technology that connects us while disconnecting us from our minds and feelings. Simultaneously, we seek to project our desires in the form of fantasies onto reality and endeavor to occupy a space in which our most profound wishes and desires can be realized. We seek cognition and recognition. In each instance—in the tension between corporate determination of the fantastic and individual projection of desire—we seem to anchor our understanding of reality in artworks dependent on the fantastic such as the Bible and fairy tales. Hence, Mother Theresa the saint. Diana the fairy-tale princess.

It is through fantasy that we have always sought to make sense of the world, not through reason. Reason matters, but fantasy matters more. Perhaps it has mattered too much, and our reliance on fantasy may wear thin and betray us even while it nourishes us and gives us hope that the world can be a better place. We have imagined gods, the kingdom of a single god, the miraculous feats of divine and semi-divine characters, and the commandments that have been established to lead us to the good life, if not paradise. It is through the fictive projections of our imaginations based on personal experience that we have sought to grasp, explain, alter, and comment on reality. This is again why such staples as the Bible and the Grimms' fairy tales have become canonical texts: unlike reality, they allegedly open the mysteries of life and reveal ways in which we can maintain ourselves and our integrity in a conflict-ridden world. They compensate for the constant violation of nature and life itself and for the everyday violation of our lives engendered through spectacle. They contest reality and also become conflated with reality.

But our fantasy and the fantasies that we conceive have become desperate, because they are outstripped by real existing conditions that instrumentalize them at every waking second of our day, and even when we slumber. It is a commonplace today that fiction, especially science fiction and what we label fantasy in the world of art, cannot keep pace with the devastating and disturbing fantastic of real occurrences, or what I call the incredible credibility of the real. Human-made robots defeat world champions in chess and may one day dominate their creators. Animals are synthetically cloned and created, and all sorts of murderous experiments are conducted on animals that are unimaginable. Virtual sex on the Internet and phone lines has become real sex in which no holds, or should I say, no positions, are barred. News telecasts, no matter how fantastic and spectacular, cannot keep pace with the rapid crimes, perversions, and inventions of live human beings that they seek to record and report. Television shows depend on our lust for celebrity that turns us into puppets of publicity. Space capsules circle Mars and Venus in ways never envisioned in science fiction. Unbelievable acts of ethnic cleansing and mass slaughter occur daily in Europe, Africa, and Asia that make films and books on these topics appear tame. Cult suicides occur in Canada, Switzerland, and the United States because followers seek passage to another world, not to mention the suicide bombers in the Middle East who seek their place in no place called heaven. Disturbed young men shoot harmless students at schools and universities in the States with weapons manufactured and sold over the counter and bought by anyone who wants to kill. Throats of villagers have been cut in Algeria in the name of Islam, while a writer by the name of Salman Rushdie has lived for many years under a death threat because he allegedly wrote words insulting Islam. The Catholic Church bribes and lies to ward off the accusations brought against the Church hierarchy for covering up the sexual abuse of its priests. Political dictators and their torturers who mutilated and still mutilate thousands of people in Argentina, Egypt, North Korea, and elsewhere continue to live comfortable if not luxurious lives. Sanctimonious presidents dress up in uniforms and suits in contrived official settings to celebrate nothing but their arrogance, lies, stupidity, and irresponsibility. Tears can be detected from a statue of the Virgin Mary in Italy. My own sober in-laws have seen a UFO hover before their eyes on a summer evening in Wisconsin. Strange diseases that devastate large populations keep appearing throughout the world without apparent remedies in sight. Identical twins raised hundreds of miles apart develop the same bizarre habits. Children are sold into prostitution throughout the world, or they are enticed by pornographers to perform licentious acts. Nothing seems left to the imagination in a film like *Eastern Promises* that endeavors to unveil the cruelty and barbarity of the Russian mafia in London, but this is something that cannot be grasped on celluloid. Politicians and corporate heads tell blatant lies and deal daily in all forms of corruption in front of the public to pursue racist and sexist policies and to keep their power, while cries of "the emperor is wearing no clothes" go unheard. We are all being surveyed, marked, and checked through complex technology in the hands of insensitive, ignorant, and puppet bureaucrats and police without our realizing it and without protection. Our everyday practices of work, buying food and clothes, attending school, and using objects in the household are conditioned by the spectacles of commercials and advertising that violate our inner and outer space. The fantastic in artworks seems inadequate to deal with the fantastic in our lives. The fantastic is embroidery and embroidered in our daily lives so that perversity and excess appear to be norms.

Hermann Broch, the Austrian writer, who fled the Nazis and sought a sanctuary in America, once asked, "Are we insane because we have not gone insane?" And this question is one to bear in mind when considering whether fantasy matters in our world. When the normal is so fantastically abnormal, what role can fantastic artworks play in our lives? Is the violence that we encounter in our everyday lives so much more fantastic than in literature, film, and the arts that we seek to consume the fantastic like harmless junk food as quick fixes and consolation? Can our joys really and realistically be enjoyed and nourished through the fantastic? Is there hope for the fantastic, much less hope for us to alter our social relations of exploitation and delusion?

There is no simple answer here. In fact, just as the function of the Bible as holy text filled with miraculous transformations and fantastic phenomena and just as the function of the classical fairy tale filled with utopian wishes have changed immensely in the last two thousand years, always dependent on the socio-cultural temper of the times, the very nature of the fantastic itself has been changed. In contrast to Tzvetan Todorov and Rosemary Jackson, who actually might have different notions of fantasy today after writing their seminal books *The Fantastic* in 1975 and *Fantasy* in 1981,[2] I do not think we hesitate or are taken aback when we read so-called fantasy literature or watch a fantastical film or see a fantastic painting or performance. Now, I think, we turn to the Bible and fairy tales and all kinds of fantastic artworks for diversion, what the French call *divertissement*, to take our minds off reality, to enjoy a moment of calm estrangement or titillation, to appreciate the extraordinary in the ordinary, to reassess our values and alternatives to determining social forces. Diversion does not necessarily contradict Todorov and Jackson, but it does bring into question the nature of the uncanny and the unexpected in all fantasy artworks. If nothing can be more uncanny, anxiety-provoking, bizarre, and incongruous than our everyday reality, then our turn to fantastic literature and artworks probably does not stem from our need for greater excitement and shock in our lives. We do not need fantasy to compensate for dull lives, but, I want to suggest, we need it for spiritual regeneration and to contemplate alternatives to our harsh realities. More than titillation, we need the fantastic for resistance.

But if fantasy is to provide resistance to real existing social conditions in the form of critical reflection and spiritual regeneration, we first must know what it is and how it operates in our brains and in the public sphere. We must also admit that there is only a vague consensus of what fantasy is, and this vague consensus is probably misleading and perhaps even contrived to be misleading. We must also concede that we shall never know the difference between reality and fantasy, and that this concession will prompt us to know how fantasy operates in our lives.

The Fantastic Spectacle

Let me pause here to cite a concrete example, a film that, I believe, presents an apt description of our current confusion about the meaning of fantasy and of our dilemma in a world determined in large part by the fantastic spectacle, and why we must try to be more clear and more critical about our use of the term. The film that I have in mind is an artwork of spiritual regeneration and critical reflection that uses fantasy to question the spectacle and expose the manner in which fantasy or, what in English should properly be called, the imagination, is instrumentalized. It is *The Truman Show*, produced in 1989 and directed by Peter Weir and partly based on Philip Dick's novel *Time Out of Joint* (1959). The film depicts the life of Truman Burbank, who, as an unwanted baby, is adopted by a television corporation and is selected to star in a documentary or "reality show" about the first year of the life of a child. When this show becomes very popular, it is continued and a large set is built on an island like an enormous cocoon in which Truman is encased without realizing that every second of his life is being filmed and telecast. He grows up on an island in a cozy town called Seahaven, unaware that the entire island is artificial and all the people on the island are actors, who pretend that they are either part of his family or part of his community. In other words, Truman lives in a bubble constructed by people working for a television corporation. His family and friends are all paid actors, chosen to dupe him. His daily life is watched or surveyed daily by millions of viewers. When he reaches the age of thirty, the same age that Christ went out preaching and the age of many protagonists in the fantastic novels by Kafka, he begins to have doubts about the reality of his existence and makes several futile attempts to discover how his life has been manipulated, and his community artificially created. Finally, he discovers the truth and wants to abandon the bubble, and when the director of the show admits the truth and offers him an opportunity to continue acting in the program that has been running for thirty years, Truman exits to step into reality, defying the spectacle of his life.

This brief synopsis does not do justice to the complex conception and production of the film. But it serves aptly, I think, to illustrate how we delude ourselves into thinking that we know what fantasy and reality are. The real director, Peter Weir and his co-workers, who conceived this film, used other artworks of fantasy to comment critically on how our daily lives are controlled and manipulated by fantasy, in this case, by a television show that plays with the life of the major protagonist in an experiment, not unlike that of Disney, to construct the perfect utopian community. Nothing is left to chance. The "manipulators" in the film—the director, crew, actors, and corporate executives—are represented as people who know the difference between reality and fantasy, and knowing audiences, too, are complicit with the speculation of a life. Yet, they are merely characters in a film created by real artists and technicians, who, it would seem, know the clear-cut difference between reality and fantasy and thus use the film to urge audiences to become more aware of how we all live in a bubble and to realize that our social relations are all mediated by spectacle. Yet, these real artists and technicians are dependent on their own mediated relations and the fantasy they created to critique the manner in which the imagination is being instrumentalized in contemporary American society. However, not only is fantasy shown to be an instrumentalized capacity in human beings, it is also a commodity that we as real viewers are expected to purchase and consume. As commodity, fantasy as film is obliged to play by the market conditions of the culture industry that undermines artful pro- duction, and thus the real effect of *The Truman Show*, the disenchantment of enchantment, intended to critique the culture industry, will be limited. The sub- versive truth of the film is thus subverted. But we must ask, is fantasy always a commodity? Does it always operate to delude? Is fantasy always manipulated and instrumentalized? Isn't there some hope for "enlightenment" in fantasy even if it is a commodity? Was fantasy always a commodity and thought of as a genre or special type of literature? After all, the trademark or rubric of fantasy in bookstores and publishing houses only became visible in the 1970s after the student revolution of the late 1960s declared, "More Power to the Imagination."

"Imagination," thought corporate executives and advertisers of the 1970s, "why not make that, too, into a commodity? After all, look at all those thousands of students carrying Hesse's *Steppenwolf* and Tolkien's *The Lord of the Rings* in their arms! Why not make their hope into a commodity? Disney has been making money off fantasy for years, why shouldn't we share in the profits?"

Defining and Distinguishing Fantasy

But, again, we must ask whether the imagination and fantasy can be completely commodified. Why do we attribute such great significance to fantasy if it generally deludes us? Or does it? To begin to answer all these questions, if they can be fully answered, we must carefully clarify the difference between imagination and fantasy because it seems that there is no difference at all. The word for imagination in French is *phantasie*, in Italian, *fantasia*, in Spanish, *fantasia*, and in German, *Phantasie*. In most European languages, fantasy means imagination. If we turn to *The Oxford Universal Dictionary*, we can see that there are several significant meanings historically attached to the word fantasy, which stems from Greek, Latin, and Old French and originally meant to show or to make visible. The meaning shifted to designate fantasy as the mental apprehension of an object of perception; it also came to signify a phantom or illusory appearance; a delusive imagination or hallucination; imagination or the process, the faculty, or result of forming representations of things not actually present; a supposition that does not rest on solid grounds; and a caprice.[3] No wonder we use the word fantasy in such different ways. Its meaning is loaded and overdetermined. All the more reason why it is more important than ever to be critical and judicious in our use of the term fantasy, and this is why I want to turn to Theodor Adorno's comments on fantasy in his book *Aesthetic Theory*, published posthumously in 1970, one year after his death. Indeed, he sheds light on the relationship between art and fantasy that might oblige us to be more discreet and to rethink what we mean by fantasy.

Adorno remarks that fantasy was closely associated with the originality of the artist and his or her capacity to invent or make something artistic out of nothing. Then he critically comments:

> This concept of fantasy was never essential to important artworks; the invention, for instance, of fantastic beings in contemporary plastic arts is of minor significance, just as the sudden intervention of a musical motif, though hardly to be discounted, remains powerless so long as it does not surpass its own factuality through what develops out of it. If everything in artworks, including what is most sublime, is bound up with what exists, which they oppose, fantasy cannot be the mere capacity to escape the existing by positing the nonexisting as if it existed. On the contrary, fantasy shifts whatever artworks absorb of the existing into constellations through which they become the other of the existing, if only through its determinate negation.[4]

Two aspects of fantasy are important for Adorno: fantasy as a capacity, that is, the module in the brain called imagination, which enables us to *transform* existing conditions into the negation of material reality; and fantasy as the result, the product of the transformative capacity of the imagination. As a product or thing, its quality as an artwork depends on its proposition, what it proposes, as an alternative to the existing state of things and how artfully it gives form to the negation of existing conditions. Adorno stresses that "fantasy is also, and essentially so, the unrestricted availability of potential solutions that crystallize within the artwork. It is lodged not only in what strikes one both as existing and as the residue of something existing, but perhaps even more in the transformation of the existing."[5] Transformation requires labor, mental and physical work.

> Not genetically, but in terms of its constitution, art is the most compelling argument against the epistemological division of sensuality and intellect. Reflection is fully capable of the act of fantasy in the form of the determinate consciousness of what an artwork at a certain point needs. The idea that consciousness kills, for which art supposedly provides unimpeachable testimony, is a foolish cliché in this context as anywhere else. Even its power to resolve objects into their components, its critical element, is fruitful for the self-reflection of the artwork: It excludes and modifies the inadequate, the unformed, and the incoherent. . . . What is bad in artworks is a reflection that directs them externally, that forces them; where, however, they immanently want to go can only be followed by reflection, and the ability to do this is spontaneous. If each and every artwork involves a probably aporetic nexus of problems, this is the source of what is perhaps not the worst definition of fantasy. As the capacity to discover approaches and solutions in the artwork, fantasy may be defined as the differential of freedom in the midst of determination.[6]

Adorno alludes to both the responsibility of the artist and the recipient of artworks by insisting on the importance of the critical consciousness of the artist and recipient, who both must refuse external pressures to form matter according to accepted conventions or to use the fantastic to reinforce the status quo. This does not mean that all art must be nonconventional and that artists and recipients must think out of the box. Rather, Adorno urges that fantasy be free to explore how people and art are determined and to propose possible solutions to the problems in which we might be enmeshed. All art must become, willy nilly, objectivized as things compelled to take a place in what Adorno called the culture industry. "If it is essential to artworks that they be things, it is no less essential that they negate their own status as things, and thus art turns against art. The totally objectivated artwork would congeal into a mere thing, whereas if it altogether evaded objectivation it would regress to an impotently powerless subjective impulse and flounder in the world."[7] All art, thus all fantasy, has to become animate and has to animate. "Aesthetic experience becomes living experience only by way of its object, in that instant in which artworks themselves become animate under its gaze. . . . Whatever in the artifact may be called the unity of its meaning is not static but processual, the enactment of antagonisms that each work necessarily has in itself."[8]

Adorno's reflections lead, I believe, to a different and discreet understanding of what we commonly call fantasy, especially fantasy that matters. First of all, it is clear that, for Adorno, there is no such thing as a genre called fantasy, nor can we categorize fantasy. To do this would be to undermine the very nature of fantasy. This point is made most succinctly by Lucy Armitt in *Theorising the Fantastic*:

Fantasy (at least in its most creative of guises) is, like all other literary modes, fluid, constantly overspilling the very norms it adopts, always looking, not so much for escapism but certainly to escape the constraints that critics like this [She is referring to Kingsley Amis.] always and inevitably impose upon it. . . . If we perceive genre as a category that "contains" (being entirely content-led), then the fact that the fantastic concerns itself with the world of the "beyond" (beyond the galaxy, beyond the known, beyond the accepted, beyond belief) should immediately alert us to the attendant difficulties it has with coping with limits and limitations.[9]

Indeed, all genuine artworks involve fantasy, the labor of the brain and/or imagination, and how to incorporate fantastic components into a work of art that negates what is externally expected of art in form and content. Every artwork must have some fantastic component, but not every art work is artistic. In fact much of what we call fantasy is predictable schlock and tritely conventional because it lacks critical reflection and self-reflection and appeals to market conditions and audience delusions. Those works are only significant because they reveal to what extent fantasy, the imagination, has become instrumentalized, and how the fantastic is being used to impose views, as impositions: 1. to profit from other people's needs and desires for spiritual regeneration and critical reflection; 2. to reconcile social, political, and aesthetic contradictions that are irreconcilable; 3. to project images that can be readily consumed and only promote the replication of the same images. Fantasy artworks of all kinds have become depleted of cultural substance because fantasy matters too much. Fantasy has too much potential to subvert and explore the differential of freedom. It must be subdued, controlled, channeled, and sublimated so that it cannot serve to negate the spectacles that blind us to social forces that determine our lives. The culture industry realizes the potential of the fantastic by commodifying it: fantastic elements are produced and reproduced to become important ingredients in the constitution of constant spectacles that impede cognition of the operative principles of the socio-economic system in which we live. Delusion has become the goal of fantasy, not illumination.

However, even if the fantastic serves to form permanent bubbles of delusion; society cannot be totally administered, and human beings cannot be totally manipulated and corroded, just as the imagination, i.e. fantasy, cannot be dominated by the logic of instrumental rationality. The more the fantastic, which matters too much for our survival as humane beings, is produced and reproduced, the fantasy as commodity awakens needs and desires that cannot be fulfilled by the culture industry and thus ultimately engenders resistance to the instrumentalization of fantasy and the fantastic. Commodified fantasy must produce fanatical heretics who demand alternate fantasies.

For example, there is a religious intensity I have noted in devout readers of fantasy literature or devoted viewers of fantasy films, and their devotion says something significant about the profound semiotics of the fantastic in literature and the films. This is not to say that all fantasy literature and films are religious or that reading fantasy literature or watching a fantasy film will always be some kind of holy cathartic experience. On the contrary, the experience is more often pagan delight or what the Germans call *Schadenfreude*, malicious joy, because we feel so helpless within the culture industry that systematically tends to deplete genuine pleasure. Nevertheless, there is a quality of hope and faith in serious fantasy literature and films that offsets the mindless violence and banality and contrived exploitation that we encounter in the computer games and spectacles of everyday life. If fantasy can be subversive and resistant to existing social conditions, then it wants to undermine what passes for normality, to expose the contradictions of civil society, to right the world out-of-joint in the name of humanity.

As fantasy, even the Bible thrives on subversion and documents why violence and suffering occur in the name of a dictator god, who appears to be just and moral, and in this documentation, the Bible proves to be a faulty text filled with absurdities and contradictions. It shows itself to be all too human, to partake of human experience. In fact, the disparate and desperate voices of the Bible have given rise not simply to immense scholarly and religious commentary (a fantastic hermeneutical undertaking in itself), but to more fiction that weaves the motifs and themes of the Bible in pursuit of the same questions that the Bible raised and could not answer. Here I am thinking of Joseph Roth's *Job* (1930). Written at the time when East European Jews still lived in impoverished shtetls and were threatened by pogroms, Roth sends a miserable and broken Russian Jew named Mendel Singer to New York, where a miracle restores a lost son to him. Then there is Archibald MacLeish's powerful drama *J.B.* (1958), which turns biblical boils into atomic disaster in a modern setting. Even Bernard Malamud's last novel, *God's Grace* (1982), a science fiction work, portrays a paleologist Calvin Cohn as the lone survivor of the ultimate nuclear devastation who debates God's will while seeking to civilize chimpanzees on an island in the "new world." Ultimately, the chimpanzees eat Cohn. In a similar vein, Mario Vargas Llosa wrote a novel of magical realism, *The Storyteller* (1989), in which the branded Saul Zucatas joins a tribe of Amazonian Indians who represent to him a lost wandering Jewish tribe at the mercy of the violent force of civilization. We relate to Mendel Singer, J. B., Calvin Cohn, and Saul Zucatas through the Bible and through the fantasy of their authors, who resist the tendencies of social reality in their fantasies and the fantastic.

Job is but one strand of the Bible that enters fantasy literature because, like the myth of Sisyphus, it is a remarkable story about the absurdity and injustice of suffering, and it is also a testimony to the strength and courage of humankind. No matter how dark and sinister those forces that violate our lives are, the fantastic forms and motifs in artworks suggest that we can discover our own human powers to resist such violence, not by imitating the gods and the devils, not by playing with other people's lives. The fantastic leaves traces of human resistance and proposes alternatives that free the mind to contemplate possible future projects in which desire may be fulfilled. Desire forms the basis of daydreams and all forms of popular culture that, even in their inarticulate and limited forms, cry out for fulfillment. Desire demands utopian projects, tiny and magnificent.

The fantastic is not only a projection of fantasy/imagination but also of rational critical consciousness. As Adorno remarked, there can be no separation of the intellect and the sensual when we talk about the fantastic, for fantasy negates what is corporeally experienced and sublates what must be carried on as a necessary ingredient in the formation of a transformed condition with utopian potential. Ernst Bloch, the great German philosopher of hope, a good friend of Adorno, maintained that the best of artworks and even the worst often contained traces of anticipatory illumination that shed light on a way forward toward a utopian society. Utopia cannot be defined, but it is constituted by fantastic elements in life and art that embody the daydreams of a better life, that is, a different life. A better life can only distinguish itself from what it negates in its differential freedom that is provided by the fantastic. It is through difference that the fantastic provides resistance and illuminates a way forward. It shows what is missing in our lives and refuses to compensate for the lack by proposing solutions and providing categories through which we can define people and situations. The fantastic offers glimpses and markers that recall the original meaning of fantasy, the capacity of the brain to show and make anything visible, for without penetrating the spectacle that blinds us, we are lost and lose the power to create our own social relations that are not based on exploitation.

The Fantastic in Children's Literature

If the fantastic refuses to define itself or to be defined as the genre of fantasy, it does so because it is in every genre that matters. It endorses every artistic mode of expression and inspires the forces of confrontation in every cultural field of production. In children's literature, the fantastic almost matters too much, and there is a danger that it embroiders too many works without substance without resisting the forces that have reconfigured children into consummate consumers. At the same time, some of the most unusual books have been produced in the field of so-called children's or youth culture that includes picture books, comic books, graphic novels, television programs, and film, and I would like to discuss briefly some of the diverse modes of the fantastic employed by writers and artists to induce effects intended to create difference and reveal the extraordinary in the ordinary. My focus is on the visual because I believe books, film, television, and the Internet have increasingly made greater use of the fantastic images and illustrations to comment on the spectacles in our lives or to collaborate with them. I am using the terms children's literature and youth culture with caution, because there is no such thing as a well-defined children's literature or youth culture with borders and limits to enclose the young or to keep out predators that governments and corporations have sought to construct. The fantastic blurs the lines between commodities produced for children and for adults and between boundaries built by governments and corporations. Resistance is thwarted and created at the same time by the fantastic. In fact, adults are intricately involved in every aspect of children's literature and youth culture, while their lives are managed, constricted, and incorporated into the culture industry.

My examples of the fantastic in children's and youth culture are not intended to be models of the perfect use of the fantastic, rather they are personal choices of works that have struck my imagination. In each case I want to focus on how the fantastic can foster alternative thinking and viewing and negate spectacle and delusion. It should be borne in mind, however, that the fantastic, while conveying the fantasies and intentions of the artist, is not defined by its telos and is not always ironic or subversive. Its effect cannot be totally predetermined or determined, except to say that a reader and viewer will always be impelled by the dynamics of the fantastic to reflect seriously and imaginatively about the customary ways he or she engages with the world. The quality of the fantastic depends on whether it enables the reader/viewer to see and grasp the social and political mediations that produce the spectacular. Hope for change can only be created if the fantastic illuminates and exposes delusion.

In their important study, *How Picturebooks Work*, Maria Nikolajeva and Carole Scott remark,

> If words and images fill each other's pages wholly, there is nothing left for the reader's imagination, and the reader remains somewhat passive. The same is true if the gaps are identical in words and images (or if there are no gaps at all). In the first case, we are dealing with the category we have named "complementary," in the second, "symmetrical." However,

as soon as words and images provide alternative information or contradict each other in some way, we have a variety of readings and interpretations.[10]

Nikolajeva and Scott proceed to discuss how counterpoint between textual and iconic narrative creates tension, and it is often through the ironic juxtaposition of word and image, word and word, and image and image that the reader becomes aware of incongruous and bizarre formations. Regardless of whether the reader is a child or adult, the fantastic in picture books fails when it is merely descriptive, complimentary, decorative, or titillating. It succeeds best when it provokes the reader to stand back, take a second look, doubt, and reflect. Often image and text resist one another. The resistance to convey direct meaning and draw literal parallels with reality is at the heart of the design in picture books that make effective use of the fantastic to provide resistance to reality and that show how reality can be transformed.

For instance, Peter Sís, the Czech-American illustrator, is fond of creating extraordinary worlds out of ordinary occurrences in his picture books. In *Madlenka* (2000) the story begins simply by announcing that a little girl named Madlenka, who lives on a block in a house in the universe on a planet on a continent, discovers that her tooth is loose, and she runs out into her neighborhood to spread the news. At each stop she meets someone from another country, the French baker, the Indian news vendor, the Italian ice cream seller, the German lady at her window, the American grocer, and the Asian shopkeeper. Each visit turns into an exotic journey to another country until Madlenka returns to her parents and tells them that she went around the world and lost her tooth. Sís employs pointillism, brightly colored scenes, cross-hatched black and white backgrounds, cutouts, and unusual typography to transform an ordinary event in a young girl's life and an ordinary walk in a New York neighborhood into a rich, dramatic, multi-cultured discovery of the world. In a more recent work, *The Wall: Growing Up Behind the Iron Curtain* (2007), Sís introduces readers into another world which he experienced as a young boy and fled as an adult. In this remarkable autobiographical picture book that reads like a graphic novel, Sís again uses intricate black and white points to depict personal and political events through images that reflect the drab and oppressive conditions in Czechoslovakia from 1945–1991 with red marking the taint of communism. Interspersed are colorful figures, maps, and photographs, projections of a desire for greater freedom. The typography of his text continually changes fonts and placement on each page. In the afterword, his last paragraph reads:

> Now when my American family goes to visit my Czech family in the colorful city of Prague,
> it is hard to convince them it was ever a dark place full of fear, suspicion, and lies. I find it
> difficult to explain my childhood; it's hard to put into words, and since I have always drawn
> everything, I have tried to draw my life—before America—for them. Any resemblance to the
> story in this book is intentional.[11]

And, of course, the images throughout the book are playful comic depictions
of his life story framed by two life-size self-portraits with him in the same pose as a
baby at the beginning and as an older man at the end. In the first image, the smiling
blue-eyed baby is nude and holds a red pencil in one hand and a piece of paper
with a red mark on it in the other. In the second the blue-eyed smiling man is
dressed and has whiskers. He holds a red pencil in one hand and a piece of paper
with a red question mark on the paper in the other. Below we read, "As long as he
can remember, he will continue to draw."[12] Indeed, his drawings mark the importance of the fantastic to articulate his desire for freedom of expression and to write
and draw his life the way he imagines it as a life of resistance.

Though his style is different from that of Sís, David Maccaulay shares the same
artistic vision insofar as he seeks to stimulate readers to revise their notion of a
picture book, architecture, and narrative by making full use of their imaginations.
Most of his work consists of black pen and ink drawings that are concerned with
portraying the cultural history of how buildings and machines have been constructed. *Cathedral: The Story of Construction* (1973), *Pyramid* (1977), *Unbuild-
ing* (1980), *Mill* (1983), *Ship* (1993), and *Mosque* (2003) render the process
behind the visible structures and machines and to what purpose the fantastic has
been put to use in architecture. His most unusual and fantastic book, however, is
Black and White (1991) in which nothing is black and white, and everything seems
to be mismatched. The picture book contains quadrants drawn in different styles
on two-page spreads, and each quadrant tells a different story throughout the
book. The images of the two stories on the right side are often without text. One of
the stories on the left side is sketched as scenes from a comic book or graphic
novel. When there is text, the typography keeps changing and eventually splices
into words that appear torn from a book. Each of the stories has a title: "Seeing
Things," "Problem Parents," "A Waiting Game," and "Udder Chaos," and the titles
allude to what qualities are necessary to understand the events as one story spills
into the frame of another story and intermingles with it. Patience and discerning
vision that allow the imagination to play with the words and images are necessary
to grasp the problems that are caused by a masked thief, a delayed train, and
parents, who appear to be strange in the eyes of their children. In the end the
arrival of the train signals a departure for another series of events. The reader is

freed from all conventions of reading and seeing to imagine how incredible ordinary experiences are, not unlike the experiences that Madlenka felt as she wandered about her neighborhood.

The Russian-American illustrator Vladimir Radunsky makes full use of one of his own ordinary experiences, an encounter with a bronze statue in Brussels, that generated his book *Manneken Pis: A Simple Story of a Boy Who Peed on a War* (2002). Radunsky retells a Belgian legend using collage, pastel water colors, unusual typography, and figures that criss-cross two-page spreads. The images are drawn in the manner in which a young boy or girl might sketch, and the story is a charming ironic tale about a boy who becomes so scared about the war in his town that he has to pee, and he pees from the top of the building on both sides until everyone stops fighting. The people are so happy that, in the end, they erect a statue in his honor. Of course, this provocative fantasy picture book has not had wide distribution in America or other countries because it breaks taboos. Radunsky prompts children and adults to pee on reality, but he also encourages creative play. In one of his most recent works, *Le grand Bazar* (2006), a brilliant work, which unfortunately has not yet appeared in English, Radunsky has produced a book that is to be taken apart and recreated by "readers from 5 to 105 full of imagination."[13] For instance, at the beginning of the book he writes that everyone has at one time or another scribbled on a photo in a magazine, journal, or newspaper and changed the image. So, he provides seven pages of postcards with images and photos, two of the same sort, and he encourages readers to use a pencil, crayon, or pen so that they can change the image any way they desire and then send to anyone they desire. He also suggests that readers can keep one of a pair untouched so that they can see a before and after picture. In another section of the book he provides comical scenes of two children, their parents, and their pet slipping on toys, falling off chairs and stools, and crashing to the ground. In the last scene, reminiscent of Chagall, the family flies through the air away from their house. In this section readers are asked to provide the text to the story as many times as they want. In yet another part of the book, he provides the text about a terrible injustice that happens one morning in Paris and prompts his readers to provide the illustrations. There are also cutouts of figures on glossy paper along with letters of the alphabet so that readers can assemble collages. For Radunsky it is the fantasy of the readers that matters most, and as an artist, he uses the fantastic to break with conventions of the traditional book that, he suggests, can be re-created in a way that enables the readers to project and realize their own fantasies. At the same time, he shares his own writing and images that he hopes will be re-utilized to ignite the imagination of the readers.

Imagination is also at the center of Neil Gaiman's *The Wolves in the Walls* (2003), illustrated as a type of graphic novel by Dave McKean. The droll story concerns a young girl named Lucy, who hears noises in her home coming from inside the walls. She and her pig puppet believe that the noises are made by wolves, but her mother, father, and brother dismiss her and believe that she is imagining things. However, wolves do indeed come out of the walls and invade the house forcing the family to flee. After they are settled outside and resume their daily activities, they gather to discuss where they should make their next home until Lucy insists that they return home and live in the walls as the wolves had done. Indeed, they do this, but they cannot stand the way the wolves party and destroy their home. So they come out of the walls and threaten the wolves who run for their lives and disappear. All seems to end happily until Lucy says to her pig puppet that she hears elephants in the walls of the house. Her imagination will never stop just as the story can never end, and McKean's illustrations make use of puppets, photographs, maps, ink drawings, different shades of color as the settings change, and diverse fonts for the typography. Gaiman's ironical narrative begins with ordinary events, a mother making jam, a father playing his tuba, and a brother involved in video games, and perhaps because Lucy is bored and ignored, or perhaps because Lucy has a fervent imagination, she hears noises in the walls: "They were crinkling noises and crackling noises. They were sneaking, creeping, crumpling noises."[14] The noises erupt causing Lucy and her family to begin an imaginary journey to confront an invasion that has disrupted family life and will continue to do so. What the wolves represent—and what the elephants might represent—never becomes clear, except that they are intruders and can only be resisted by the imagination.

McKean has poignantly illustrated another unusual work that deals with the significance of the imagination for resistance and survival. This one is a graphic novel, written by the gifted British writer David Almond, supposedly for middle readers, and it is called *The Savage* (2008). The narrative framework of this book is highly original: the story is narrated by a young boy named Blue Baker, about nine or ten years old, who recalls a traumatic period in his life when his father died suddenly from a heart attack. In order to deal with the loss, Blue recalls, he began writing in an old notebook about a savage boy who couldn't talk, lived in the woods, and killed and ate anybody or anything that came within his vicinity. When Blue quotes from his notebook, we begin reading a story-within-a-story, and the grammar and spelling reflect the "ungrammatical" and sensitive mind of a wounded boy. In addition, the mind's projections are reflected in the images drawn by McKean in shades of green and blue. The fantastic figure of the savage, depicted by McKean, vividly reveals how Blue used and still uses his imagination to over-come his deep anger about his father's death and the mockery of Hopper, a bully, who constantly threatened and mocked him. To Blue's surprise, Blue reports in the frame narrative, the savage, whom he had created, came alive but refused to eat him and his little sister when they entered the woods. Instead, Blue befriended the savage, whom he had created as his alter ego, and in turn, the savage eventually terrified Hopper without killing him so that the bully eventually left Blue in peace. Moreover, Blue discovers that the savage had drawn pictures of Blue and his family in a cave long before Blue had begun writing about the savage. It is through the use of his imagination in writing and reading that Blue realizes the savage was in his own heart and will remain there. The fantastic shows him the way home while resisting social and personal forces that were depressing and disturbing him.

This is also the case in Shaun Tan's stunning graphic novel, *The Arrival* (2006), a book without words that is strangely universal in its appeal and subject matter. Strange and estrangement are the only words that can aptly describe this book. It took Tan, an Australian illustrator, more than five years to complete this work, and when one views the intricate designs and images, it is clear why he needed so much time to fully realize his vision. Tan's illustrations evoke a story rather than tell one. It is a tale of emigration and immigration that millions of people have experienced in diverse ways, and the experience of leafing through *The Arrival* recalls millions of stories and encounters that emigrants encountered and still encounter. The plot is simple, but the images are complex and demand careful attention, reviewing, contemplation, and even more reviewing. The action begins in an industrial city some time at the beginning or middle of the twentieth century. A man in his forties must separate from his wife and daughter, about eight or nine years old. Apparently, he cannot find employment and has decided to travel to a distant country. They accompany him to a ship. Along the way the threatening spiked tail of an oppressive dragon haunts them. In the second part of the book that depicts the voyage on a crowded ship, the images turn from stark realistic pictures of the crowded conditions on the ship to incredible and bewilder-ing depictions of a gigantic harbor city that resembles New York and Ellis Island, but the images are bizarre and baffling and are transformed by huge birds, towers, temples, inscrutable signs, strange letters, and baffling numbers. The machines, articles, creatures, and peoples are all confusing. Daily life appears to be a montage of things, and the anonymous man cannot at first comprehend how to make his way through the wondrous labyrinth of a city. Nothing functions in the way to which he was accustomed. He has a great longing for his wife and daughter. He cannot communicate with anyone. However, he does not give up hope. He finds a single barren room that is also occupied by a weird animal that follows him around. Gradually, he meets people who tell them their stories of desperate survival. Seasons change. He begins working. Eventually he has enough money to send for his wife and daughter. The world around them remains totally strange and strangely familiar. They are together despite or to spite the confusing world that could have kept them apart.

Tan's silent book is a story of hope without an ending. The illustrations are similar to photographs turning brown. They are in hues of black and brown. The inside front covers and inside back covers show fifty passport photos of people of different ages from fifty different ethnic backgrounds and cultures. In many ways, given the problematic way in which immigration and immigrants are being discussed and treated in our globalized world, Tan's book recalls how the world—how most developed countries—has been built and developed by immigrants who arrive in a place that they look upon as utopia only to learn that their aspirations will be challenged. We don't know what will happen to the anonymous man and his family, even though they are happy to be reunited. We do know, however, that the family will not always be as happy as it is pictured at the end of the book. The arrival is just the beginning, and the arrival for immigrants in today's globalized world does not augur acceptance or acculturation.

Intrusion, disintegration, and threats to the harmony of the family and community appear to be common themes in our postmodern world. Numerous other genres, receptive to the modality of the fantastic, reflect this disturbing trend toward disintegration of family and community and the cultural wars surrounding it. The heroes in the field of comic books and graphic novels are no longer Captain Marvel, Superman, Wonder Woman, Batman, and others who work with government to tame the forces of evil. Instead, they are often mutants like the X-Men, who try to restrain politicians, the military, and police from establishing neo-fascist regimes or from destroying the world. Or they are outsiders and refugees who endeavor to maintain a sense of community in an unwelcoming atmosphere. One of the more interesting series of comic books that deal with the topic of the besieged community of refugees is *Fables*, which began appearing in 2002, and now includes over 60 issues of stand-alone comics and composite graphic novels. Conceived by Bill Willingham, the series begins with the premise that numerous characters from fairy tales, legends, myths, and folklore have been compelled to leave the lands of their origins, or Homelands. They do not know their mysterious enemy called the Adversary, except that he has taken over their homelands. So they migrate to New York City and form a clandestine community called Fabletown. However, many of them have difficulty adapting to the contemporary world, and their community is dysfunctional. The first five episodes, gathered in a trade paperback titled *Legends in Exile* and illustrated by Lan Medina, Steve Leialoha, and Craig Hamilton, concern the alleged murder of Rose Red, whose body is missing from her devastated apartment that has a warning written in blood on a wall: "No More Happy Endings." Actually, there will be a happy ending because Bigby Wolf, security officer of Fabletown, discovers that Jack the Beanstalk and Rose Red concocted a scheme to make it appear she had been murdered because they were in need of money. During the investigations we learn that King Cole is the incompetent head of the Fabletown community; Snow White is the intrepid director of operations, trying to hold the fairy-tale and legendary characters together; Prince Charming is a philanderer; Beauty and the Beast are having marital problems; Bluebeard is a wealthy baron and philanthropist; and a talking pig escapes the Farm in upstate New York where non-human characters from fables must live.

At the heart of Willingham's concept is the subversion of the traditional function and notion of popular genres like fairy tales, legends, nursery rhymes, and fables. Each character retains some of his or her original personality but seeks to reform or is reformed in the contemporary setting of New York. Thus, the big bad wolf is ironically Bigby Wolf in charge of security, and Bluebeard a magnanimous rich gentlemen. However, at any time, they can transform themselves or break out into their original identities and become savage. Snow White, who appears as the super management director, keeps trying to clean up the mess in the secret community of Fabletown. Reconciliation of conflicts appears difficult, even though every long episode has its conclusion. The prose and plot of the episodes are not complex and unusual. At most there is a cute ironic play with traditional genres. The resistant quality of the fantastic is minimized, as it generally is in most popular forms of art such as comics and graphic novels, to have a large appeal.

This is also the case in Linda Medley's *Castle Waiting* (1996), which, like *Fables*, uses the fantastic to subvert the classical fairy tales. She self-published her graphic novel with black and white ink drawings in 1996 and has intermittently produced comic book sequels and graphic novels that focus on different characters who come to inhabit the castle that Sleeping Beauty abandoned after she had been wakened by a prince. Although the castle has deteriorated and is inhabited by bizarre poltergeists, it serves as a refuge for various fairy-tale and legendary characters who arrive and tell all about their trials and tribulations. The castle is generally run by a gentlemanly stork named Rackham, after the well-known Victorian illustrator, and there are strange bearded nuns, humorous animals, and a mysterious pregnant woman who inhabit the place. Medley's contemporary

American slang is in stark contrast to the depiction and setting of the characters in the distant past, while their troubles are very similar to the conflicts in the contemporary world. It is only in a retreat, Medley suggests, that a true community, albeit one that allows for great diversity and tolerance, can be found. In this regard her fantastic projection of family and community differs greatly from the conflict-ridden community in *Fables* and is more like the mutant school in *X-Men*, where people who differ from the norm must live on the margins of society in a sanctuary.

And perhaps this is the only place that people in contemporary American society can find sanctity and sanity. Whereas the fantastic is frequently employed in all forms of popular culture to project utopian possibilities for developing a humane community in which differences among people are resolved through mutual support, the fantastic also serves to provide a persistent critique of the norm that appears to be so perverse and incongruous that the only hope for spectators, young and old, is laughter—and I would suggest, a laughter that does not necessarily provide relief or hope for a better world. In certain animated television series such as *The Simpsons*, *Southpark*, and *Family Guy* the dysfunctional families and communities are exaggerated depictions of the changing relations in American society that indicate how bedeviled we are by our contradictions. Irreverent, ironic, and relevant critiques of American quotidian life are created through the behavior of characters who represent family and community gone amuck. Whereas many writers and artists have employed the fantastic to suggest alternatives to decadence, that is, societies in decline, there is clearly a strong dystopian tendency in popular culture for young people suggesting that social conflicts and injustice may never be resolved, and that the outcome to the struggles may be neo-fascist societies as projected in the famous works *Brave New World* (1932) by Aldous Huxley and *Nineteen Eighty-Four* (1949) by George Orwell.

In more recent years writers, who have sought to address young readers in dystopian works, such as William Sleator in *House of Stairs* (1974), Lois Lowry in *The Giver* (1993) and *Gathering Blue* (2000), Nancy Farmer in *The House of the Scorpion* (2002), and Susan Cooper in *Green Boy* (2002), have interrogated the pursuit of the perfect society in the name of progress through fantastic projections. This is where the dystopian factor plays a role, for the pursuit of perfection, the perfect place and society, or even the dissemination of democracy and Christianity, can also lead to rigid if not totalitarian societies. Much of what we cite as progress, especially technological progress, has a double edge to it. The cloning of vegetables, animals, and humans that may help overcome hunger and disease may eventually lead to the mechanization of the natural and human world as we know it. The advances in communication may lead to miscommunication, disconnection, and alienation. One could argue that the great drive of human beings to establish fairer, more socialist and democratic societies has led to perverse societies, what we might call negative utopias, or what is projected as dystopias in literary works for young and old readers as well as in films such as *The Matrix* (1999).

Two important examples are Farmer's *The House of the Scorpion* and M. T. Anderson's *Feed*. Both works are dystopian novels in which a young boy realizes that his life is not what it seems and that he is being controlled by forces linked to the corporate world run by hegemonic groups dominating the government, business, and military. In *The House of the Scorpion*, the action takes place in the future in the country of Opium, located between America and Mexico, which is now called Atzlán. Matt, the major protagonist, comes to realize that he is the clone of a drug lord named Matteo Alacrán, who uses eejits, people with computer chips implanted into their brains, to work on his farms. As Matt grows, he realizes that most of the eejits are illegal immigrants who have tried to cross Opium from Atzlán to America and have been caught and transformed into zombies. Once Matt grasps their situation and his own, he manages to escape to Atzlán, where he encounters other difficulties in an orphanage that pretends to be communist while exploiting the orphans. Eventually, Matt learns that his mother, aptly named Esperanza, is living in America and fighting for the rights of clones. With the promise of her help, he returns to Opium with the intention of shutting down the drug trade and transforming the eejits back into human beings. While there is some hope in this dystopian novel, it is clear that Farmer's major political purpose in her use of the fantastic is to expose the collusion between politicians and criminals and how new technological inventions are being abused to transform humans into automatons. Given the forces in control of America and Aztlán, it is not clear whether Matt will have any success in "re-humanizing" the small country of Opium, much less himself.

But Farmer's science fiction work is optimistic compared to Anderson's *Feed*, which offers a more disturbing fantastic projection of the future, indeed, a very near-future. Here, too, computer chips, corporate greed, and corrupt governments play a major role, and here, too, we see the destruction of human beings through technology controlled by the government and corporations through the perspective of a teenage boy named Titus. Feed is a computer chip that is planted in human beings and is effectively used to socialize young people, control their thoughts, and basically prompt them to consume products of the culture industry. Titus, who is totally configured through a computer network, falls in love with a young woman named Violet while on a trip to the moon. It is also there that a man, who belongs to a group of resisters in the Coalition of Pity Party, an anti-feed group, hacks into their feeds so that they can begin thinking for themselves. But once they return to earth, their feeds are restored except that Violet begins to die due to malfunctions in her computer chip because it had been too cheap and had been implanted late in her young life when she was seven. Titus disassociates himself from Violet, out of fear that she is revealing the truth about the technologized consumer culture, but he cannot fully wipe her from his mind and the realization that the socio-economic system is causing pollution and probably the total collapse of America.

Anderson has a great gift not only for describing a transformed highly technological and consumerist world, but also for inventing a new jargon and vocabulary that the young people use to describe their experiences. In Anderson's "brave new world" of America, very few people own their own thoughts, language, and feelings. Most people are estranged from one another and totally dependent on machines of one kind or another. The future is a horrible nightmare that is, it seems, approaching us faster than we realize. Like many other concerned writers and artists, Anderson believes that fantasy matters, perhaps too much, or that it matters so much that the battle for humanity will depend on how fantasy is used in the culture wars. In an interview with Joel Shoemaker in 2004, he remarked,

> We live in a culture of corporate-sponsored narrative, which is a culture of underwritten endumbening. In an attempt to reach an ever wider audience, television, movies, magazines, and even publishers rely on three elements pernicious to complicated narrative: first the sapping of particularity (for fear that eccentricity will frighten off potential viewers, or more dangerously, encourage the splintering of mass demographics); second, the simplification of narrative (because of an assumption that the bulk of people want to hear over and over again the stories they have already heard); and third, the pursuit of anything, be it tumbling helicopters or showering cheerleaders, that might constitute "action." This creates a vicious cycle, however. As children are raised on simpler and simpler narratives, they become acclimated to that banality, and grow distrustful of anything that deviates from it.[15]

Anderson's work is a pertinent example of how the fantastic can be used to explore how the fantastic is being exploited. It brings us back to Philip Dick's *Time Out of Joint* and Peter Weir's *The Truman Show*, works that illuminate the processes and operations developed by hegemonic groups such as the government, the culture industry and its corporations, the Church, and educational institutions to create fantastic spectacles that blind us from the seeing the pollution, corruption, and other abuses that they cause. We eat, drink, and consume the fantastic as spectacle from morning to night. If there is such a grand thing as "fantasy" and if it matters, then we must investigate what it is and what we mean by it. We all have fantasy, and through fantasy we seek to encounter the voids in our lives by generating visions of how we want to live and realize whatever potential we have. In most cases these visions do not correspond to the dominant "norms" and ideologies of our society and, therefore, they must be brought into line so that our socio-economic system runs smoothly. Our fantasies must be channeled through the spectacular to curb our critical thinking and creative work. Fortunately, we have not reached the point where we all live in bubbles like Truman, or where we all have chips implanted in our brains. We are not yet totally controlled by hysterical spectacles of terror and the apocalypse. We can still make many choices as to how we can shape the visions of our fantasies and what types of fantastic products we want to consume, share, and use. Fantasy involves a certain amount, if not a great amount, of conscious choices and citizen responsibility, not censorship and conformity or even consensus. In a recent interview that appeared in *The Rake*, Steven Heller, author of *Citizen Designer: Perspectives on Design Responsibility* and co-director of a design program at Manhattan's School of Visual Arts, remarked,

> If you are in a profession that both uses and abuses resources, be aware of what you are doing. I think that's the first step in design citizenship. From there one has the freedom and responsibility to decide how one's talents are used. To knowingly hurt others through one's work or wares is irresponsible, if not criminal. So don't do it.[16]

Fantasy matters because it can enable us to resist such criminality, and it can do so with irony, joy, sophistication, seriousness, and cunning. Whether the fantastic works that we realize become works of art will depend obviously on our talent but also on our refusal to become complicit in criminal operations of the culture industry.

The Multicultural Contradictions of International Children's Literature: Three Complaints and Three Wishes

4

> The subject of books available in English translation usually resolves itself into a question: why are there so few of them?
>
> Because there are: disgracefully few. Shamefully few. And fewer than there used to be, too, at a time when publishers are putting out more books than ever. Only about 3% of the books on the UK market are translations, compared with about 23% in France. It's as if something has happened to our understanding of the world, making it narrower and less interested in the experience of elsewhere. . . .
>
> Some commentators say that it's paradoxical to find so little interest in literature from abroad in this age of globalization, but perhaps that's the very problem: globalization is a phenomenon that's driven by money and business, not by culture and curiosity.
>
> Philip Pullman, "Introduction," *Outside In: Children's Books in Translation*[1]

As I have now reached the ancient age of seventy, I feel more and more that I am entitled to complain and grumble about the perversity and banality in our world, especially when I write about children's literature, because there is a tendency for the reading public to rejoice and celebrate all the dazzling qualities of this literature and all the good it does, especially after we have entered the Age of Harry Potter when it is now generally believed that miraculous changes have been brought about by this series of novels and that they will continue to affect us supposedly for our good. Since I have already complained long and loud about the myths and misreadings of the Potter phenomenon[2] and was correct to complain, I think I should now be granted at least three more complaints about multicultural literature in America and its contradictions and with my complaints, three wishes—wishes that I hope will make my complaints disappear.

Three Complaints

Now a complaint is an interesting term. We generally associate it with a kind of legal allegation filed against a party who has caused us some difficulty. But it is also an expression of grief, pain, or resentment. Finally, it can simply be an ailment of some kind, and my complaints, I believe, fit the last category, and I am hoping, if my wishes are granted, I'll find myself cured from future complaints, and finally, I'll be able to enjoy old age.

My first complaint is caused by intolerance. As I said above, the older I get, the more I grumble and the more intolerant I become. I used to think that Brian Alderson, the superb British scholar, was the most fierce and fearful grumbling critic in the field of children's literature. Hard to please, demanding, knowledge-able, satiric, and insightful, Brian is not an easy-going colleague, and I worry whenever I hear that he might be chosen to review one of my books or he might appear on a panel with me. I admire him for his outspoken views and devotion to children's literature of high quality. But I also feel at times that he is a grumbler, a complainer, a moaner, and a grumpy old man. Now I find, as I have grown older, that I may be following in his footsteps, for I am going to grumble and bark, demand and provoke, and I am going to insist that I am entitled to this privilege. Even though I may not be as incurably astute and sensitive as Brian Alderson, I am suffering from a certain intolerance of the banality in the field of children's literature and its criticism.

My second complaint concerns my inability to deal with ignorance. I am suffering first of all from my own ignorance for which I often compensate by trying at all costs to be somewhat knowledgeable and realizing I can only be a kind of dilettante. Often I make some outlandish remarks that I hope other people will tolerate. Since I have written on German, French, Danish, and Italian children's literature, many people assume that I am knowledgeable about developments in these countries. Now it may be true that I have followed certain tendencies, mainly in the area of fairy tales and fantasy literature, in these countries, but I am woefully incapable of summarizing the most important trends or even alluding to the very best works of key authors and illustrators in the last ten or fifteen years. Come to think of it, though I have edited *The Oxford Encyclopedia of Children's Literature* (2006) and try to keep up with the more innovative writers of children's literature in America and the UK, I think I would have to plead ignorance if one were to ask me to depict the most significant currents in the different genres of American and British literature during the past fifty years. There is such an overwhelming production of experimentation and extraordinary writing and illustrating in the field of children's and young adult literature in North America and the United Kingdom that you would have to be some kind of fantastic computerized reading robot to consume and catalogue all the works that might constitute valuable and meaningful reading materials for young readers. Whenever I travel in America, for example, I continually learn about new and young writers, artists, and storytellers, well-known regionally or locally, but barely mentioned in the national press, and perhaps in danger of fading into obscurity. My personal library is filled with obscure authors and illustrators whose works I have devoured with great enthusiasm and would love to share with a larger public. My library also *lacks* numerous contemporary works that I should know but don't, either due to ignorance or lack of time and interest. Curiously, and this is part of my complaint, my own ignorance makes me aware of how ignorant the general public and media are about the condition of children's literature in America and in the world, not to mention multicultural literature. Sometimes I feel it is insufferable when I read or hear anything about the necessity to develop multicultural programs of literature for young people when those people proposing the programs have not reflected about the impossibility of accomplishing this goal when our young people are ignorant about their own culture.

My third complaint is connected to globalization. Don't ask me to define this term, but I am suffering from it, as are most of you. Thousands of scholars are using it now in positive and negative ways. All I can say is that it is a sickness that troubles my soul. Zygmunt Bauman, a British sociologist, whom I greatly admire, has perceptively written:

> Globalization divides as much as it unites; it divides as it unites—the causes of division being as identical with those which promote the uniformity of the globe. . . . An integral part of the globalizing processes is progressive spatial segregation, separation and exclusion. Neo-tribal and fundamentalist tendencies, which reflect and articulate the experience of people on the receiving end of globalization, are as much legitimate offspring of globalization as the widely acclaimed "hybridization" of top culture—the culture at the globalized top. A particular cause for worry is the progressive breakdown in the communication between the increasingly global and extraterritorial elites and the ever more "localized" rest.[3]

One might ask how do Bauman's remarks about globalization pertain to do children's literature? My response is that we cannot grasp the state of children's literature, especially the state of international and multicultural children's literature, without understanding globalization processes. And Bauman, along with Joseph Stiglitz,[4] is one of the most astute critics of how globalization operates. For instance, one major point he makes throughout his book, *Globalization: The Human Consequences* (1998), is that the new technologies of advanced capitalism have fostered ever new mergers and conglomerates that determine the production and distribution of culture throughout the world. Those cultural products that dominate the market—let us say the Disney works or even the Harry Potter books—will bring about a sense of global unity that benefits elites who can transcend space and time and enjoy great freedom of movement. However, these same products leave the majority of people, who cannot move with ease, without a sense of their own local culture, and in reaction they will turn toward more fundamentalist cultures of their own localities and refuse to interact with the imposed culture. Cut off, these people will cut themselves off from the global television and mass-mediated cults of the West, largely America. International understanding becomes less possible. Bigotry and intolerance spread through fear and anxiety. What is acceptable for American children and appropriated by the American conglomerates as good international children's literature will have no relevance for children and adults in the Middle East, Asia, Africa, or South America. Nor do most of these works shed light on other cultures, particularly the great diversity within nations and the problems that these nations have. Whatever we receive or acknowledge as "good" children's literature from foreign countries are basically products from elites of these countries that are geared toward a capitalist market. Anyway, American and British publishers rarely translate books from foreign countries. Writing in 1998, Carl Tomlinson put the number of translated books for children in America at about 1.2 percent and in the UK at about 3 percent.[5] But, if you go into any bookstore in Europe, the bookshelves in the children's literature sections will have an extraordinary amount of works translated from the English, ranging from 25 percent to 35 percent of books published for children. The communication between us and others, the others and us, is hindered by the very processes of communication and mediation that we have established to link us in the global culture industry which operates to blind us as we try to open our eyes. So, I think anyone can understand why I am complaining about globalization.

Three Wishes

And now that I have listed my three complaints, it's time for three wishes.

My first wish is for greater critical and self-reflexive collaboration among writers, illustrators, publishers of children's books on an international scale, and greater cooperation with teachers and librarians. Let me present two examples of what I mean, and why these examples, though wonderful in intent, fall somewhat short of what I mean by critical collaboration. In 1986 Mitsumasa Anno published a book with Dowaya in Tokyo and Hamish Hamilton in London under the title *All in a Day* (1986). In his "Introduction," he states:

> This is a book which I made with picture book authors from eight different countries. The story starts at midnight, Greenwich Mean Time, on the last day of the year.
> Because there is only one moon its shape is the same wherever you see it. But the moon which you see in Tokyo, Japan, and the moon which you see in Sidney, Australia, face in opposite directions. The half moon you see from Kenya looks as though it is lying down. So the half moon there looks like a boat when it is setting.
> This book shows differences in language, time and season. But it does not explain why these differences exist. I hope that when children all over the world think about these differences, they will be surprised and excited.[6]

The illustrators are Raymond Briggs, Ron Brooks, Gian Calvi, Eric Carle, Zhu Chengliang, Leo and Diane Dillon, Akiko Hayashi, and Nicolai Y. Popov, representing the UK, America, Australia, Brazil, China, Kenya, Japan, and Russia. Each double page spread contains eight illustrations depicting the activities of children at different times in different cultures at the beginning of a New Year. The story, if one can call it one, is narrated by a stranded boy on an uninhabited island, and it is inserted horizontally between the rows of pictures and illustrated in pastel water colors by the ironic Anno. The stranded boy, who has an SOS sign hanging from a palm tree and a dog to keep him company, relates what his friends are doing at given times of the day while he sends out a dove for help. On the final page the boy is about to be rescued, and his friends continue to carry out their daily activities on January 1 and 2. The emphasis in the book is on difference—different perspectives, different illustrative styles, different customs, different physical types. The images are serene. There is a general mood of optimism as the New Year is about to begin, and each scene, carefully and allegedly illustrative of a particular culture, is stamped by the unique personality of the illustrators who envision what children do to celebrate the New Year in diverse cultures. There is a sense of joy in each scene and in the rescue of the stranded boy who is looking the wrong way at a picture of a ship while a real ship is on its way to save him.

Such a book is exemplary in the manner in which author/illustrators have collaborated to convey the meaning of difference in time, space, and customs. There are other more traditional collaborative books that are also important models such as *The Oxfam Book of Children's Stories: South and North, East and West* (1994) edited by Michael Rosen and published in America and the UK. It contains twenty-five stories from such countries as Cyprus, Bolivia, Bangladesh, Indonesia, Greece, Vietnam, and Zimbawe, and they are illustrated by such gifted artists as Nicola Bailey, James Marsh, Helen Oxbury, Michael Foreman, and Satoshi Kitamura. Most of the stories are folk tales and fables with some more contemporary narratives included. All the tales have one or two striking illustrations that exhibit the insights that the artists have into the stories that were collected by Oxfam social workers who first heard them from people they work with in different countries around the world. Oxfam is short for the Oxford Committee for Famine Relief founded in 1942, and there is a statement at the end of the book about the purpose of Oxfam in publishing it:

> The collection of stories can open windows into other cultures and lives. With the rapid growth of international travel and world wide communications the world is shrinking, and we share experiences with more and more people. Through this book we can share stories from other cultures, but there are other experiences that we would probably not choose to share.
>
> Every day millions of people in many countries go without things we in developed countries take for granted: food, shelter, water, education, health, care, and the right to make decisions about our own lives. For many people things are getting worse, not better. Oxfam is helping people break out of their poverty by supporting them in efforts to make changes that will last.[7]

The collaboration in the Oxfam book is based on the cooperation of children, social workers, illustrators, teachers, and writers who contributed different versions of the stories that were edited by Rosen. Each story provides a brief glimpse into the customs of diverse cultures. For instance, "Why Do Dogs Chase Cars," illustrated by Michael Foreman, is a comic anecdote about how differently animals behave toward cars in West Africa. "Pedro and his Dog" concerns a city boy in Bolivia who spends his summer vacations on a farm in the Andes mountains. When Pedro takes a friendly dog from the farm, the dog cannot adapt to the city, and Pedro must learn to understand why the dog runs away and returns to his native setting, so to speak. A tale about freedom and respect for foreign cultures.

Indeed, both *All in a Day* and *The Oxfam Book of Children's Stories* enable readers to gain *some* understanding and respect for Otherness and the diversity of cultures. However, despite the remarkable quality of these books and the cooperative efforts, I believe that they are too rosy and avoid depicting unpleasant incidents and situations, and that they are politically negligent. For instance, millions of children in the countries represented by the illustrators in *All in a Day*, including America, do not cheerfully celebrate the New Year. More than likely they are "stranded." They live in poverty, experience abuse and deprivation, and are concerned primarily with survival. Their desperate stories are rarely heard in the realm of children's literature. We are still not collaborating enough and not producing books in our collaborations that focus on major conflicts within and between cultures, why they come about, and what alternatives there are to resolving the misunderstandings that seem to endure. It is not enough today to publish optimistic stories that give superficial glances into other cultures and then to believe our children will have a better understanding of the world. Critical collaboration means bringing together educators and artists of different countries and seeking to conceive of books that educate children about the real causes of exploitation, bigotry, sexism, racism, and war. The real causes, in my opinion, have a good deal to do with the intolerance of organized religions, the consumerist ideology fostered by international conglomerates, militarism, and machismo that emanate from patriarchal cultures, violence that emanates from cultures that celebrate competition, achievement, and celebrity cults, racism in almost all nations of the world, and colonization. I could continue to list many other "evils" that are not being addressed in the books that we produce and in the organizations that we form. But I do not want to appear as a righteous preacher, nor do I want to make it seem as though people involved in children's literature are not concerned about these topics and are not attempting to undertake projects to confront them. I do, however, want to assert that we are not bold enough and that we, especially in America, are not political enough. Certainly, our editors and publishers who must answer to the conservative executives in their corporations are very unwilling to criticize the forces that feed them and at the same time contribute to the dilemmas such as poverty, war, racism, and exploitation that we are facing worldwide. Their unwillingness or hesitancy must be recognized and criticized, and we must, I sincerely believe, establish collaborative projects in the domain of international children's culture that will engender collaborative artworks that approach conflict from different perspectives ranging from pessimistic to optimistic. We need books that will stimulate the young in all cultures to grasp why it is that we do *not* understand other cultures and why we cannot pretend that it is easy to understand other cultures. We need books that will expose the complex nature of domination and intolerance and teachers and writers who will work together to conceive and design all forms of artworks, particularly artworks where children are deprived of books, to foster mutual understanding of differences and a comprehension of the powerful forces conditioning children to fear the unknown.

This leads me to my second wish, and it is a wish for wisdom, not just for myself. I want the entire world to wise up and to know just how creative, compassionate, talented, and fascinating people who live in other cultures are. My wish for wisdom is also a wish to end ignorance and the fear of the unknown that often leads to mass hysteria. One way to do this is to make books from other cultures more available and more accessible and to educate the educators how to mediate cultural difference in honest and frank ways. Here I want to speak specifically about a great problem that we have in America—one that also exists in the UK. It involves our hubris and our wealth and enormous geographical size and diversity despite a national trend by conglomerates toward homogenizing our tastes and leveling our differences.

As I have already remarked, America and the UK do comparatively speaking very few translations of books for children from other cultures.[8] One need only visit American and British bookstores—and here it is difficult to speak about bookstores for children but rather markets or chain stores—to realize there are very few if any books by foreign authors available. On the other hand, if you visit a bookstore in France, Germany, or Italy, countries with which I am most familiar, there will be numerous books by American and British authors for all age groups— and I am not just speaking about the Disney products and traditional classics. How, I ask myself, can American children (and adults) develop any sort of understanding about people in other cultures if the books from other cultures are not translated and then taught by educators who know something about these cultures or are curious enough to learn about these cultures? We can beg this question by replying:

- We produce hundreds of multicultural books in America today. Admittedly most are produced by our own authors, who are well-intentioned and are always appropriating from an American perspective in their adaptations of stories from other cultures, but we are concerned and are productive.
- Our country is so large that we have enough difficulty dealing with regional differences or urban/agrarian differences, not to mention urban/suburban differences and ethnic conflicts.
- We need to focus more on ethnic differences and multi-national topics within our own nation before we deal with international conflicts.
- There are now universal problems that everyone faces in the world, and there is no great need to translate books when our own authors and illustrators are so talented and are dealing with these universals.

- Our teachers—not to mention our parents—are not educated or trained sufficiently to discuss translations of books from other cultures. Most do not speak or read a foreign language. Most are more concerned about discipline in the classroom and creating a decent atmosphere where basic skills can be taught.

There is some truth in all these replies, but if we accept these replies and do not question the rationalizations and try to change the conditions that cause myopia, we shall contribute to the worst aspects of globalization, namely isolation and separation, and we shall remain ignorant about other cultures and the artworks that are being produced in other cultures. Unless we hear the voices of other writers (even in translation) and see the images of different illustrators, we shall not be able to grasp how and why foreign cultures have unique ways of doing things and different opinions about America and their own customs and identities. Even here, there is a problem, for those authors who might be translated tend to represent the educated elites of their cultures and do not give us a full picture of the countries they represent. Nevertheless, their works are valuable because they do endeavor to grapple with local and particular problems, issues, and customs that shed light on their cultures and can make us cognizant about differences and problems of communication. And, in literature for the young, they provide great opportunities for understanding their cultures, their difficulties, and the gaps in communication with great innovation and artistic experimentation.

In Search of Books from Other Cultures to Bridge Our Gaps

Wishing for more insight and wisdom, I want to discuss some works by authors and illustrators from Germany, France, and Italy, who are not well-known if they are known at all in America. Almost all these authors are "household" names in their respective countries, and our ignorance of their works points to a great lack in our knowledge and wisdom. Again I want to insist that I am arbitrarily discussing authors with whom I have become acquainted by chance, and that I do not have either a comprehensive or incisive knowledge of literature for the young in these countries. For those people who want to obtain a general background, I suggest that you look at the *International Companion Encyclopedia of Children's Literature* (1996), edited by Peter Hunt,[9] *Zauberkreide: Kinderliteratur seit 1945* (1994) by Gundel Mattenklott,[10] *Literatur für Kinder und Jugendliche: Eine Einführung* (2000) by Hans-Heino Ewers,[11] *The Changing Face of Children's Literature/Livres d'enfance, livres de France* (1998), edited by Annie Renonciat,[12] *Jeux et enjeux du livre d'enfance et de jeunesse* (1999) by Jean Perrot,[13] *La letteratura per l'infanzia* (1995) by Pino Boero and Carmine De Luca,[14] *Comparative Children's Literature* (2005) by Emer O'Sullivan,[15] *Outside In: Children's Books in Translation* (2005), edited by Deborah Hallford and Edgardo Zaghini,[16] and *Beyond Babar: The European Tradition in Children's Literature* (2006) by Maria Nikolajeva.[17] All these works provide cultural-historical parameters for understanding the unusual development of children's literature in Germany, France, and Italy. Since my proclivities and taste tend toward an appreciation of fantasy literature with substantive social and political implications, I shall refer to a couple of books, generally fairy-tale books that I wish might be translated, and then I shall focus on an important contemporary author in each country, whose works I wish would be translated. It should be noted that I would have liked to have included more works by women authors and to discuss the different ways that gender roles are represented in European children's literature, but space constraints have limited my choices as well as my focus on fantasy and fairy tales.

Bearing in mind that, from 1945 until 1989, Germany had a rich tradition of children's literature in two different political entities, the Federal Republic of Germany and the German Democratic Republic, and that there are also many notable Austrian and Swiss authors/illustrators who produce books for the young—not just Christine Nöstlinger and Lisbeth Zwerger in Austria—I want to mention three authors of fairy-tale works that deserve translation. The first book is Janosch's *Janosch erzählt Grimm's Märchen* (1972), which was translated into English as *Not Quite as Grimm* in truncated form by Patricia Crampton in 1974 and was distributed mainly in the United Kingdom. Subsequently Janosch revised and expanded his edition of tales and republished the book with his illustrations in 1991. Not only are his tales extraordinary critiques of the Grimms' tales, what one might call fractured fairy tales, they also include his provocative black and white ink and water-color illustrations that complement his revisions of the Grimms' stories. Janosch revitalizes the Grimms' tales by setting them in the present and testing the applicability of their moral messages for our times. Similar to Janosch's work and undoubtedly influenced by him is the Swiss author Franz Hohler's book, *Der Riese und die Erbeerkonfitüre* (1993) illustrated by Nikolaus Heidelbach. Like Janosch, Hohler turns the fairy-tale tradition upside down with thirty-one highly ironic stories, and they are accompanied by Heidelbach's surrealistic images. Incidentally, Heidelbach is famous for his highly controversial and provocative images of the Grimms' fairy tales,[18] and the collaboration between him and Hohler has led to one of the more unusual fairy-tale books published during the 1990s.

More serious than the fairy tales of either Janosch or Hohler is the work of Rafik Schami. Born in Damascus, he immigrated to Germany in 1971 at the age of twenty-six, and, since 1982, he has published several collections of fairy tales based on the Syrian oral storytelling tradition and contemporary fantastic narratives. One of his best collections is *Das Schaf im Wolfspelz* (1986), in which the title story tells about a sheep, who covers itself with a wolf's skin and goes into the woods to join the wolves. At first the sheep has difficulty learning how to howl with the wolves, but it soon learns to act and behave like a wolf and even thinks that it is a wolf. However, the wolves finally discover who the sheep really is when a dog accidentally tears off the wolf's skin from the sheep. The wolves devour the imposter, and the dog and his master are glad that there is one less wolf in the world. Some of Schami's tales are beginning to appear as picture books in America,[19] but his more ironic and sophisticated tales, intended for crossover audiences, have not seen the light of translation.

None of Kirsten Boie's works have been translated either. One of the most gifted of the contemporary writers for young readers in Germany, Boie is adept at writing highly realistic novels and fantasy. For instance, *Erwachsene reden. Marco hat was getan* (*Grown-ups talk. Marco Has Done Something*, 1994) is based on a real incident—the burning down of a house in which Turks are living. In her narrative the 15-year-old Marco, who lives in a small town in Germany and is receptive to neo-Nazi propaganda, takes his revenge for flunking a course by setting fire to a house inhabited by Turks understood as foreigners, aliens, the other. Two children are killed, and the incident is a national scandal. Boie's framework for her narrative is set by interviews with thirteen people (the mayor, minister, friends, social worker, teacher, neighbor, etc.) who associated with Marco, whom we discover is somewhat spoiled, arrogant, charming, lazy, ignorant, and offensive. (The frame is similar to the Max Frisch's famous play, *Andorra*, 1961, which dealt with anti-Semitism and fascism.) Moreover, we learn a great deal about the failings of the grown-ups and the provincialism of idyllic small town life in Germany. Boie ends her novel by giving Marco the last word:

> Marco says, that's not the way he wanted it.
>
> I just wanted to give them something to think about. Get them scared. They should finally realize that nobody likes to see them around here.
>
> Marco says, everyone thinks the same way. Marco can name names of grown-ups who talk just like him. But they don't have any courage. . . .
>
> Marco's sorry that it had to be two children who got caught. They could have perhaps had a beautiful life in Anatolien [Marco's pejorative term for a city in Turkey]. If they had stayed in Anatolien, nothing would have happened to them. But Marco doesn't understand all the fuss. It's not that everyone is now acting as if they love Turks. When he hears the

claptrap now he feels like throwing up. They all talked completely differently before this. It's naturally bad luck for the children.

But Marco doesn't feel that he's really guilty in any way.[20]

The open, somewhat pessimistic ending of this novel is offset by another one of Boie's novels for slightly younger readers, *Abschiedskuss für Saurus* (*A Kiss Good-bye for Diny*, 1994). Here a young boy of about ten named Malte flees into a park to escape a fight with Olaf, whom he has gotten into trouble and who is terrorizing him. By chance Malte discovers a dinosaur named Saurus, who has somehow mistakenly returned to earth and has forgotten how to wish himself back to his homeland. In his quest to save the friendly dinosaur, Malte enlists the help of his friend Rike and his enemy Olaf, and though he loses the loveable Saurus, he gains confidence in himself and learns how to resolve a conflict to which he contributed. Boie has written other works dealing with the different terrors that children face inside and outside of schools such as *Nicht Chicago. Nicht hier* (*Not Chicago. Not Here*). They all recount very specific problems that children of different ages encounter in Germany, and at the same time, they speak to young readers throughout the world and enable them to grasp similarities and differences from a German author's perspective.

In France, too, there are contemporary writers whose works revolve around particular French conflicts and transcend them at the same time. But first, a brief word about Pierre Gripari (1925–1990), well known in France but practically unknown in America. He wrote three important fairy-tale collections *Contes de la rue Broca* (*Tales of the Rue Broca*, 1967)—the only one of his books translated into English[21]—*Contes de la rue Folie-Méricourt* (*Tales from Folie-Méricourt Street*, 1983), and *Patrouille du conte* (*Fairy Tale Patrol*, 1983) that are even more radical and subversive than the tales of Janosch. In particular, *Patrouille du conte* concerns eight children on a politically correct mission in the Kingdom of Folklore to change the sexism, bigotry, and violence of the classical fairy tales. However, once they begin their campaign in the name of humanitarianism through prohibitions, they unleash even more violent behavior that suggests to readers how difficult it is to accomplish revolutionary change. (Incidentally, there is another more recent book about the difficulties in the realm of fairyland, Christian Oster's *La grève des fées* [*The Strike of the Fairies*, 2001], but it is not as poignant and original as the work by Gripari.)

Another author, Jean-Claude Mourlevant, is, in my opinion, as poignant and certainly more poetic than Gripari. Mourlevant's novel *L'enfant Océan* (*The Pull of the Ocean*, 1999) is based on Charles Perrault's "Little Tom Thumb," and it is a remarkable realistic narrative about child abuse—that is, if it is proper to use the word "remarkable" in this instance. I meant that it deserves to be noted for its unique narrative structure and sensitive portrayal of a social problem that continues to haunt most countries throughout the world. Similar to the device that Kirsten Boie used in *Erwachsene reden*, Mourlevant strives for multiple perspectives about the case of the disappearance of Yann Doutreleau. A social worker, Yann's parents, his six brothers, a baker, a policeman, a truck driver, an unemployed worker, a wealthy industrialist, and other people comment on the flight of Yann and his brothers from Central France toward the Atlantic Ocean. The story is simple: Yann's parents are poor, uneducated farmers who maltreat their seven sons, three sets of twins plus Yann, a 10-year-old, the youngest in the family. The boys are malnourished and treated harshly by both mother and father. Yann himself is so neglected that he is a runt and resembles Tom Thumb. Among the boys he is the only one to stand up to his parents. He is the smartest and the most resilient. His great passion is school, and when his father throws his school books and bag down a well, Yann causes trouble at school and is brought home on a rainy night, disheveled and distraught. That night he overhears a conversation between his parents, and he wakes his brothers and tells them that their parents are about to kill them and they must escape to the ocean, their only hope. Trusting Yann and fearful for their lives, they follow him into the woods and manage to make their way to Bordeaux and to the Atlantic Ocean, where they become trapped in a large house on the beach. The only escape is through a phone that they discover, and they reluctantly call their parents, who inform the police about the whereabouts of their sons. The police rescue the boys, but Yann is missing. Everyone believes that he has drowned in the ocean. However, Yann secretly informs one of his brothers that his parents had never intended to kill them. They were going to kill the seven kittens that had just been born in the barn, not their sons. Yann had known this all the time, but he also knows how brutal his parents are. His confession is meant to ease the return of the sons to the parents, but Yann refuses to return and is last seen by a watchman on a bridge. The boy is gazing at the ocean to the west with a smile on his lips.

Yann's story is a narrative of survival with hope, and Mourlevant manages to document the boy's life history with short terse poetic accounts by witnesses to his struggles. He blends the documentary and the poetic in a brilliant reinterpretation of Perrault's seventeenth-century tale that deals with abuse and abandonment of children in hundreds of other tales such as "Hansel and Gretel." The descriptions of brutal mistreatment and misunderstanding are matched in this narrative by the compassion shown by the brothers and the decent treatment they receive on the way to the ocean—their symbol of hope.

It is hope that stamps most of the work by Gianni Rodari (1920–1980), and I want briefly to mention his significance in Italy as a kind of plea for more due recognition and translation of his works. Rodari is considered by Italians to be the most gifted and popular writer for children in Italian history. Yet, only four of his books were translated by British firms into English in the late 1960s and 1970s, and even these works never made their way to the American shore. His only work in print to-date is my translation of *Grammatica della fantasia* (*The Grammar of Fantasy*, 1993), and this is a theoretical study, not one of his usual or should I say unusual works of fiction. Here I want to mention just one of Rodari's books *Tante Storie per giocare* (*Many Stories for Playing*, 1971), one that I have just finished translating, because it is related to the innovative work of Janosch, Hobel, Schami, and Gripari. This collection employs a narrative form that calls upon children to become productive creators of the stories themselves, and it begins with an ironic introduction as if the book were to be used like a machine or instrument:

Instructions for Use

These stories are being published by the kind permission of RAI - Radiotelevisione italiana. In fact, they stem from a radio broadcast with the exact title, "Many Stories for Playing," and they were broadcast in 1969–70.

The same stories appeared later in the journal, *Corriere dei piccoli*.

Each story has three different endings, and the readers can select the one they prefer.

At the conclusion of the volume the author has indicated the ending that he prefers.

The illustrations form part of the game because they suggest other conclusions. At the end of the book there is also a list of proposed endings by the illustrator.

The readers are to read, look, and reflect and, if they do not find an ending to their liking, they are to invent one, write one, or draw one themselves.

Enjoy![22]

For example, one can enjoy how the Pied Piper arrives in Rome and tries to undo pollution by leading all the cars like rats into the Tiber River, or one can enjoy how Pinocchio becomes the owner of a lumber mill by continually sawing off his wooden nose that keeps growing back. Then, like a greedy capitalist, he sells the wood, exploits his workers, and makes huge profits. The stories in *Tante Storie per giocare* are not only highly entertaining, but they reveal just how much Rodari depended on his active work with children for stimulation and how he reflected on this work constantly and intensely up to his death. Not only did

Rodari write provocative tales, but he also wrote novels, fables, riddles, and poems. Indicative of his stance toward children is the following short poem:

Lettera ai Bambini

È difficile fare
le cose difficili:
parlare al sordo,
mostrare la rosa al cieco.
Bambini, imparate
a fare le cose difficili:
dare la mano al cieco,
cantare per il sordo,
liberare gli schiavi
che si credono liberi.[23]

A Letter to Children

It's difficult to do
difficult things:
speak to a deaf person,
show a rose to a blind person.
Children, learn to do
those things difficult to do.
Give a hand to a blind person,
sing for a deaf person,
make the slaves free,
who think they are free.

Rodari's influence on contemporary Italian writers is enormous, and it is particularly apparent in the works of one of the most gifted writers in Italy today, Roberto Piumini. Like Rodari, Piumini is highly versatile. Trained in the theater and communications, he has acted and created radio and television programs for children. In the course of the past thirty years he has written well over 200 books (fairy tales, legends, novels, nursery rhymes, poems, ballads, plays) for young readers of different age groups. He has also published two novels for adults and translated Shakespeare's sonnets into Italian. In America, four of his minor works have been translated into English—*The Saint and the Circus*, *Mattie and Grandpa*, *The Knot in the Tracks*, and *The Store*—and they are all out of print. One of most recent books is *Doctor Me Di Cin* (2001). While these books are delightful, they really do not give the American reader an idea of how talented and innovative Piumini is as a writer. Therefore, I should like to discuss one of his more recent experimental crossover books that I personally consider a profound contribution to literature in general.

Lo Stralisco (1993) is a poetic novel about a Turkish painter named Sakumat, who lives in a fictitious city Malatya in a rocky valley. Famous for his imaginative landscape paintings, Sakumat receives commissions all the time from wealthy patrons. One day a messenger from the Ganuan, Lord of the realm of Nactumal in the North, knocks on his door and requests that he travels immediately to Nactumal for an important commission. The messenger informs him that he will be most generously rewarded for his efforts. At first, Sakumat declines, but then he reflects for a moment: he is curious to find out why such a powerful and proud lord wants him to paint something. So he makes a long and arduous trip to Nactumal and discovers that Ganuan has an 11-year-old son named Madurer, who has a mysterious illness. He cannot go outside the palace because he is allergic to many different things and could easily die. So Ganuan would like Sakumat to paint the walls of three different rooms according to the desires of Madurer, that is, he would like Sakumat to bring the outside world inside to Madurer. After meeting the tender and frail Madurer, Sakumat accepts the commission, and using the inspiration and imagination of Madurer, Sakumat paints glorious landscapes on the walls and also teaches Madurer how to paint. At one point, Madurer invents the magical flower *lo stralisco* on the wall that glistens in the dark as a flower of hope. But despite the love that develops not only between Sakumat and Madurer but also between Sakumat and Ganuan as brothers, Madurer dies a year after the walls have been painted. Ganuan offers Sakumat a place to stay and a good deal of wealth. But Sakumat refuses and returns despondently to his home. He refuses to accept any more commissions to paint and appears to have lost the desire to paint. Finally, he leaves his home and travels to a small village on the seacoast where he spends the rest of his life peacefully as a fisherman.

There are many relevant themes in this novel for young people: the meaning of art and the artist, the love of father and son, the purpose of the imagination, brotherhood, contact between inner and outer worlds, and the philosophical concept of hope. Piumini's clear, simple, and poetic language evokes an atmosphere of great kindness and generosity that one rarely finds in contemporary society. The relationships formed through the artistic sensitivity are compassionate and deep, and despite Madurer's death, the reader is not left with a sense of despair but with great respect for the transformation that Sakumat has undergone as a human being.

Piumini's novel is a narrative of hope, and it is this story of hope that leads me to ask for my last wish, which is for hope. To end my grumbling, my ignorance, and skepticism, I could use much more hope so that I can feel that all our efforts are not in vain, that we (writers, artists, librarians, teachers, young people) can succeed in creating a children's literature that bridges cultures. Speaking as an

American and about the role that American corporations play in the culture industry, I believe that there is a grave danger that the American globalizing tendencies
have a colonizing effect that could hinder if not prevent a mutual sharing of
relevant cultural works from other cultures within and outside America. Therefore,
when I speak of hope, I am not speaking of some metaphysical philosophical
concept, but the hope that Paulo Freire speaks of in *Pedagogy of Hope* (1997). I am
speaking of a hope that stimulates critical thinking and concrete action, for we can
glimpse alternative possibilities to the "evils" in the world once we realize what
these evils are. *Great children's literature is great literature.* It is frank, honest,
aesthetically pleasing, and eye opening. It can generate images of hope even when
formed in the darkest of all narratives. Philip Pullman has made this eminently
clear in his inspiring trilogy *His Dark Materials*, which encompasses different
worlds and moves back and forward in time so that readers can glean what lies
beneath the negative forces robbing the young of their unique essences. There is
nothing mysterious about what saps life from our young, and if we are to stop the
waste, then we need strong international collaboration, more equal production of
books and other cultural artifacts that confront the waste, and more and more hope
to keep us reading the world to bridge worlds and resolve conflicts that are not
impossible to resolve. As Rodari might say in a letter not to the children but to us:

> Grown-ups,
> if you are really grown,
> open your eyes,
> confront the lies,
> don't give up hope,
>   hold out your hand,
> embrace the world,
> reach for the skies.
> It's never impossible
> to do the impossible.

What Makes a Repulsive Frog So Appealing: Applying Memetics to Folk and Fairy Tales 5

Though most readers of the Brothers Grimm tale "The Frog King, or Iron Heinrich" call this story "The Frog Prince" and do not know much about the history behind the evolution of this tale, that is, how the tale evolved from the oral tradition to become a literary classic, almost everyone knows—even those people who have never read the tale—about the aggressive, nasty, disgusting, talking frog, who wants either to sleep with or to be kissed by a beautiful princess. And almost everyone knows that the prince/king needs to be magically transformed to get what he wants—even if it means he must sometimes be slammed into a wall or have his head cut off instead of obtaining permission to sleep in the princess's bed or to receive a kiss. The slimy, repulsive reptile is not what he seems to be; his attempts to coerce the princess to have sex with him fail until he shows his "true" colors. Only when he is handsome and wealthy and suits the mating standards of the princess does he succeed in bedding and wedding her. He passes the test as appropriate bridegroom suited for a lovely princess.

"The Frog Prince"—and I shall call the tale by its more popular title—is known and beloved throughout the world in many different variants. In fact there are probably thousands of versions in diverse languages; the tale has been adapted and disseminated through poems, illustrations, radio, film, cartoons, photographs, postcards, CDs, DVDs, toys, posters, paintings, clothes, plays, and the Internet.[1] We love the lascivious frog who magically turns into a prince. Perhaps love is too strong a word. Let us just say that we have a fatal attraction to the enchanted repulsive frog, and we don't know why.

What is interesting about "The Frog Prince" and most canonical fairy tales in the western world is that we have no idea why we care about them, know them so well, are attracted to them, and are apt to pass them on to other people without a second thought. Certain fairy tales have become almost second nature to us, and it is not simply because they have become part of an approved hegemonic canon that reinforces specific preferred values and comportment in a patriarchal culture— something that they indeed do—but they also reveal important factors about our mind, memes, and human behavior, especially mating strategies and courting prac- tices, that can be traced back hundreds if not thousands of years in different societies, and I want to try to explain this appeal through the use of memetics, relevance theory, and evolutionary psychology.

But before I do this, I should like to comment briefly on the Brothers Grimm and their different versions of "The Frog Prince" to demonstrate how they artistic- ally shaped, prepared, and stabilized the tale so that it embodied the qualities that made it memetic, and by memetic, I am referring to Richard Dawkins' notion of meme, which is a cultural artifact that acts as a cultural replicator or cultural adaptor and manages to inhabit our brains and to become so memorable and relevant that we store it and pass it on to other humans. A folk or fairy tale that becomes a meme is a communication that indicates something significant about our genetically and culturally determined behavior and our interactions with our environment within a historical process that enables us to adapt to the changing world. In the case of "The Frog Prince," the information conveyed by the narrative, symbols, and icons is related to changes in our innate mating behavior that has been modified by particular cultural transformations. Some memeticists might argue that the tale itself as meme seeks to propel us to disseminate it willy-nilly. *But not every folk or fairy tale is a meme or can become a meme*, and my definition of a folk/fairy tale as meme departs from the more orthodox and restricted definitions of the term.[2] I argue that only when a tale makes itself or is made relevant through human agency and fulfills certain basic needs of people will it become a meme within a pool of memes or memeplex; once it retains a place within a module of our brain, it provides information vital for adapting to the environment, and, in the case of "The Frog Prince," vital in the process of sexual selection, reproduction, and the evolution of culture.

The Grimm Versions

Though "The Frog Prince" is the most famous variant of a tale type catalogued by folklorists as ATU 440: Frog King or Iron Henry, related to the Beast/Bridegroom

Figure 1 German nineteenth-century picturebook of "The Frog King." The illustrator is Grimmer.

narratives,[3] it is not commonly known that the original title of this tale type in the Grimms' Oelenberg manuscript of 1810 was "The Princess and the Enchanted Prince,"[4] and indeed, if I could rewrite the title, I would place the emphasis on the princess as protagonist and call the tale, "How and Why a Princess Selected Her Mate." (It will become clear later why I prefer this title.) What is important to know at this point is that Wilhelm Grimm wrote down this tale after hearing it told by one of the female members of the Wild family in Kassel some time between 1808 and 1810. Then, in 1812, when the brothers decided to publish the collection of tales that they had gathered and heavily revised, "The Princess and the Enchanted Prince" was given the title "The Frog King, or Iron Heinrich," and was considered so significant that it was honored with the first place in their collection and remained in this place through the seven different editions that the Grimms published during their lifetime. Moreover, the Brothers even published a variant in the 1815 second volume of the first edition which they called "The Frog Prince" and deleted it in the second edition of 1819 because they incorporated elements of this tale in "The Frog King," which they retained and kept changing until the final edition of 1857.

After this final edition and the deaths of the Grimms, "The Frog King" continued and continues to be the very first tale one reads in all the complete collections of the Grimms' tales, no matter what the language in which the text is printed, and it has seeped into our consciousness in many respects as the model Grimm tale in style, form, and content. Indeed, Wilhelm labored over this tale for almost forty years so that it became more and more embellished and communicated a moral message that advocated the restoration of the patriarchal word and world order to which young women were to subscribe. Therefore, it deserves special attention, and it is indeed fascinating to compare the evolution of the text from its inception in the 1810 manuscript to the final printed form in 1857. Let us examine the initial scene of the 1810 manuscript, the 1812 printed text, the 1815 variant, and the 1857 final text.

The Princess and the Enchanted Prince (1810)

The youngest daughter of the king went out into the woods and sat down by a cool well. Soon after she took out a golden ball, and as she was playing with it, the ball suddenly rolled into the well. She watched as it fell deep into the water and stood sadly by the side of the well. All at once a frog stuck its head out of the water and said, "Why are you lamenting so?"[5]

The Frog King or Iron Henry (1812)

Once upon a time there was a princess who went out into the woods and sat down by a cool well. She had a golden ball that was her most cherished plaything. She threw it high into the air and then would catch it and enjoyed this very much. One time after she threw the ball high into the air, she stretched out her hand and curled her fingers, ready to catch the ball. However, it bounced on the ground right by her and rolled and rolled until it fell into the water.

The princess watched it fall and was horrified. The well was so deep that it was impossible to see the bottom. Then she wept despondently and began to lament: "Oh! If only I had my ball again! I'd give anything to get it, my clothes, my jewels, my pearls. Anything in the world!"

Just as she was grieving, a frog stuck its head out of the water and said, "Princess, why are you grieving so bitterly?"[6]

The Frog Prince (1815)

Once upon a time there was a king who had three daughters. In his courtyard there was a well with beautiful clear water. On a hot summer day the oldest daughter went down into the courtyard and scooped a glass full of water from the well. However, when she held it up before the sun, she noticed that it was musty. Since this was so unusual, she decided to dump the water back into the well. Just as she did this, a frog stirred in the water and stuck its head into the air. Finally, it jumped on to the edge of the well and said to her:

> "Whenever you decide to become my sweetie,
> I'll give you clear water, clear as can be."[7]

The Frog King, or Iron Heinrich (1857)

In olden times, when wishing still helped, there lived a king whose daughters were all beautiful, but the youngest was so beautiful that the sun itself, which had seen many things, was always filled with amazement each time it cast its rays upon her face. Now, there was a great dark forest near the king's castle, and in this forest, beneath an old linden tree, was a well. Whenever the days were very hot, the king's daughter would go into the forest and sit down by the edge of the cool well. If she became bored, she would take her golden ball, throw it into the air, and catch it. More than anything else she loved playing with this ball.

One day it so happened that the ball did not fall back into the princess's little hand as she reached out to catch it. Instead, it bounced right by her and rolled straight into the water. The princess followed it with her eyes, but the ball disappeared, and the well was deep, so very deep that she could not see the bottom. She began to cry, and she cried louder and louder, for there was nothing that could comfort her. As she sat there grieving over her loss, a voice called out to her, "What's the matter, princess? Your tears could move even a stone to pity."[8]

There are several important observations to be made about the Grimms' editing process largely supervised by Wilhelm Grimm beginning with the second edition of 1819.

1. The tale almost doubled its length by the 1857 edition.
2. The descriptions grow more lavish; the characters are fleshed out; the transitions are more fluent; the style is more florid and artistic.
3. The initial phrase in the final text of 1857 is not "Once upon a time," but "In olden times, when wishing still helped," and this elegant beginning, which introduces us to a princess whose beauty amazes even the sun, indicates how carefully Wilhelm Grimm tailored the tale to meet the reading expectations of an educated upper-class audience. Accordingly, he de-eroticized the story he heard (and probably other variants as well) so that the princess appears to be a child, and the frog never enters her bed. The strong woman's perspective is modified by the introduction of a severe father figure who represents the moral code of the Grimms.
4. Though the text of 1857 stabilizes the story in the form that Wilhelm Grimm wanted it to be conveyed, this is not a stable or static text. It is what I call a flexible text that was developed in writing from oral storytelling and was constantly changed in print by one editor to incorporate other oral and literary versions.

Both Wilhelm and Jacob were inclusive and sophisticated editors; that is, they tended to modify the tales they published by including motifs and components of variants that they collected from friends, colleagues, and informants, and they grew to appreciate the deep historical roots and the common features that their tales shared with stories throughout the world. Like other tales in their collection, "The Frog King" has an extraordinary capacity to appeal to and attract readers and tellers because it was constituted by and cultivated through a constant exchange of oral and literary articulation and communication. The artistic shaping of the tale by Wilhelm enabled it to become more relevant, memorable, and accessible so that it could be disseminated more readily not only in Germany, but throughout the world. Another way of discussing what happened to "The Frog King" in the hands of the Grimms would be to focus on how it "latched" on to them and their readers and kept insisting that it be replicated in some form or another, always adapting to cultural conditions and revealing something about mating customs in a particular society. By "latching," I do not mean to imply that the tale can actively grab hold of and attach itself to a listener or reader. Rather, I am seeking to explain how a tale as a cultural artifact may become so attractive in form and relevant in meaning that it captivates and draws the attention of readers and listeners who are already or may become predisposed to retaining the tale in their minds. Humans have "innate expectations about objects in their environment and the nature of relationships among them."[9] The power of the tale depends on the human agent's receptivity and use of it in understanding the environment, that is, the socio-cultural context, and in translating it in other situations. The dissemination of the tale is prompted by the cultural significance, a striking quality, that a tale has achieved in a given population or culture, and thus it may become embedded in the brains of humans as a meme and propel them to spread it. This memetic force, however, cannot drive the spread of the tale unless it benefits humans and their need to adapt to their environment and to select mates in accordance with the evolution of their culture. Though there are many ways to interpret "The Frog Prince"—and every narrative opens up a space for contested meanings and ideologies—the "essential" paradigmatic, ostensive, and attractive aspect of the tale from an evolutionary perspective, in my opinion, concerns mating strategies and practices, and I want to concentrate on these aspects to understand its persistent appeal to readers and listeners throughout the world up to the present.

If we examine the different texts that the Grimms produced, they all deal with how a young girl, who has probably reached puberty, is ready to marry, that is, to mate with a desirable partner. The carrying of the golden ball, her most precious possession, symbolic of her virginity and her own physical appeal, into the woods, and her temporary loss of it indicate that she is testing the waters, so to speak, looking for the appropriate mate. She is also being tested. When the frog appears, it is apparent from his looks that he is not the right mate for her, while he recognizes that she is what he desires because of her youth, beauty, and wealth. Though the princess is repulsed by him, she feigns acceptance of his proposal and uses him to regain her ball. Abandoned, if not betrayed, the frog knows that the only way to court and bed the princess is through her father, the authority figure, and therefore, he pursues the princess by appealing to the courtly "moral" principles that the father enforces. As we know, during the period in which the Grimms lived and during most of the previous centuries in Europe, mating and marriage were not based on love, and women, particularly from the upper classes, were often forced to marry men for whom they did not care. The ultimate authority was generally the father representing patriarchal law and custom. In the case of "The Frog Prince," it is apparent that the frog, perhaps symbolical of an ugly old aristocrat, has the father's implicit approval and wants his daughter to mate with him, or at least, to treat him with respect. The resistance of the daughter is clear and is in great part due to the natural inclination of women to select attractive men with good genes and qualities as their partners who will guarantee that she will be protected and that her offspring will have good genes and a bright future. Hence, it is only when she makes her will known clearly by smashing the frog against the wall that he can fulfill her expectations and their mating can be consummated. Her natural inclination to choose what's best for her leads her to rebel against the moral strictures of her father, a strange rebellion, because it engenders the appropriate mate that her father would have chosen for her. As for the frog, he had to transform himself and conform in status and appearance, otherwise he would not have gained royal approval for a wedding. Ugly beasts must show that they know how to groom themselves, or at the very least they must devise a strategy to deceive their brides and influence their brides' fathers if they want to obtain the object of their desire.

Women's and Men's Mating Strategies and Some Scholarly Strategies

As anyone familiar with folklore and fairy-tale scholarship also knows, each and every fairy tale can be approached and analyzed from many different perspectives. The more classical and canonical a fairy tale becomes, such as "The Frog Prince," and the more it is mediated through oral traditions and cultural institutions, the more it will be dissected and interpreted in different ways. For instance, not only are there numerous references and essays written about this famous fairy tale throughout the world, there are also three scholarly books in German: *Wage es, den Frosch zu küssen! Das Grimmsche Märchen Nummer Eins in seinen Wandlungen* (1987) by Lutz Röhrich, *Der Froschkönig . . . und andere Erlösungsbedürftige* (2000) edited by Helga Volkmann and Ulrich Freund, and *Der Froschkönig: Grimms Märchen tiefenpsychologisch gedeutet* (2003) by Eugen Drewermann as well as an American M.A. thesis *The Fairy Tale as the Tree of Knowledge: Freudian, Jungian, and Feminist Approaches to "The Frog Prince"* (1984) by Trudy Luebke Cox, not to mention numerous self-help books published in the UK and America. Many of the interpretations deal with the theme of sexual maturation. For instance, Bruno Bettelheim uses a neo-orthodox Freudian approach to explain that

> the awakening to sex is not free of disgust or anxiety, even anger. Anxiety turns into anger and hatred as the princess hurls the frog against the wall. By thus asserting herself and taking risks in doing so—as opposed to her previous trying to weasel out and then simply obeying her father's commands—the princess transcends her anxiety, and hatred changes into love.
>
> In this way the story tells that to be able to love, a person first has to become able to feel; even if the feelings are negative, that is better than not feeling.[10]

Aside from being overly simplistic and implying that the princess is anxious when she is more cunning and furious than anything else and simply wants to destroy the frog, because he is inadequate and repulsive as a mate, Bettelheim makes it seem that the princess is unaware of the sexual implications of the frog's proposal and why she wants nothing to do with him, whereas her actions prove otherwise. In contrast to Bettelheim's faulty interpretations, the Jungians dismiss the sexual aspects of the tale to celebrate spiritual wholeness, although not all agree. J. C. Cooper, however, represents a common position when he argues that

> in *The Frog Prince* the Princess encounters the Frog rising from the watery element, symbolic of the chaotic and unmanifest, but she tries to ignore this dark side by first forgetting, then rejecting it. The King, the masculine solar aspect, makes her keep her rash promise, face and accept the dark side and convert it into the light in the handsome Prince.[11]

It is clear that the frog prince may be a symbolic representative of sexual repulsion (although he is often pictured as cute by numerous illustrators) and may also represent the dark side of the princess's life, but it is doubtful that Freudians and Jungians can help us grasp why this tale has such a powerful grip on our minds, especially when they want to stabilize its meaning and impose categories that are nebulous and misleading so that the tale becomes paradigmatic for their theories and detached from its historical and cultural context. This is not to say that psychological theory cannot shed light on fairy tales. But it seems to me that psychological critics of fairy tales, especially Jungians and Freudians, have neglected the evolutionary aspect of psychology as well as history for too long a time to offer a valid approach to folk and fairy tales. Therefore, I would like to suggest that an evolutionary psychological approach might be able to provide a method for interpreting "The Frog Prince" (and other classical tales) that not only sheds greater light on the conflicts within the Grimms' text but also enables us to comprehend why and how the tale has retained its relevance throughout the world, has become a meme, and continues to exercise its memetic force today.

In *The Evolution of Desire: Strategies of Human Mating*, David Buss, a professor of psychology at the University of Texas, explains that

> strategies are methods for accomplishing goals, the means for solving problems. It may seem odd to view human mating, romance, sex, and love as inherently strategic. But we never choose mates at random. We do not attract mates indiscriminately. We do not derogate our competitors out of boredom. Our mating is strategic, and our strategies are designed to solve particular problems for successful mating. Understanding how people solve those problems requires an analysis of sexual strategies. Strategies are essential for survival on the mating battlefield. Adaptations are evolved solutions to the problems posed by survival and reproduction.[12]

Tales of all kinds enable us to comprehend our strategies and to learn how to court and mate. They also help us adapt, especially as cultural and environmental conditions change. This is why fairy tales are in part so significant. If we examine the numerous diverse tale types that concern mating, especially those that involve an ugly male desiring a beautiful young woman, or an ugly female desiring a handsome young man—and there are literally hundreds of these tale types—we can see how closely their narrative plots are predicated on the actual strategies used by women and men to win their mates. The fairy tales that stick in our brains as memes serve to guide us and provide information about our attractions and help us resolve problems that we may encounter as we proceed to choose a mate under the conditions of a particular civilizing process.

In her provocative and significant book, *What's Love Got to Do with It? The Evolution of Human Mating*, the anthropologist Meredith Small states:

> The evolutionists argue that each sex should be expected to look for partners of high reproductive value. By the value of the partner they mean what he or she has to offer to help advance our genes. Men, for example, should want fertile women. And women should be attracted to men who can help them bring up any children they produce. This is the bottom line advanced by evolutionary psychologists, based . . . on how much each sex invests in gametes and offspring, with men investing little and women investing a great deal. A more elaborate version of this paradigm suggests that women should be concerned with a man's wealth, his status, and his earning potential, because these are the resources that she wants for her children. And men should be interested in finding a young woman who is more likely to have a long reproductive life before her.[13]

Although Small believes that evolutionary psychologists and anthropologists exaggerate the differences between men and women with regard to their desire and expectations, most (including Small) would tend to agree with Elizabeth Cashdan, who argues that women not only have sharp conflicts of interest with men but also with women. As she argues,

> Because males and females can best enhance their fitness in different ways, conflicts of interest between women and men are, unfortunately, an intrinsic part of the mating game. A man can enhance his fitness by investing in his children and maximizing his number of mates, but time and resources devoted to one interfere with the other. These trade-offs lead to variation in male strategies, with the polar types . . . being "cads" (low investment males seeking to maximize mating opportunities) and "dads" (high investment males committed to one sexual partner). The trade-offs facing men define the choices facing women. Should a woman try to secure an investing mate, who may have lower mate value in other respects, or should she content herself with getting good genes and immediate resources from a non-investing cad? She will have trouble doing both at the same time, because flaunting her sexuality, the behavior that attracts a cad, will put off a dad, who wants evidence of fidelity, and vice versa.[14]

Both women and men have their mating strategies, and though there are basic dispositions in women and men that have existed for thousands of years, they have changed and been modified as different societies and cultures have been organized and established formal and informal rules for mating and set the conditions in which women and men play out their sexual urges and replicate the species. As numerous anthropologists, historians, ethnologists, and psychologists have demonstrated (not to mention biologists), the formation of polygamous, monogamous, matrilineal, matrilocal, patrilineal, and patriarchal societies throughout the world have created diverse conditions under which women and men mate. The choices a woman makes to seek a mate in one society will not necessarily be accepted or tolerated in another. The same applies to men. The first question, however, that men and women have posed consciously and unconsciously throughout the centuries and in all parts of the world is how to devise a strategy for copulation and reproduction, that is, how to mate most effectively, to enjoy the sex, and get the most out of the union, whether it is brief or long-lasting. Since women have always had to consider the possibility that they might get pregnant and have a child, and since they produce less eggs than men do sperm and need a long time to give birth and nurture their children, their thinking and mating strategies have tended to be different and more selective than those of men. Love, as Small so bluntly asserts, has had very little to do with it. And as Buss explains,

> Women are judicious, prudent, and discerning about the men they consent to mate with because they have so many reproductive resources to offer. Those with valuable resources rarely give them away indiscriminately. The costs in reproductive currency of failing to exercise choice were too great for ancestral women, who would have risked beatings, food

deprivation, disease, abuse of children and abandonment. The benefits of choice in nourishment, protection, and paternal investment for children were abundant.[15]

As early Indian, Greek, Roman, Egyptian, Arab, and African tales and myths as well as early medieval European stories and documents demonstrate, mating and mating strategies were the subjects of many conversations and stories and were ritualized in tribes and societies thousands of years ago. We have all kinds of artifacts that reveal how mating practices were cultivated, and in western society, there are numerous artifacts, records, documents, poems, anecdotes, romances, and different types of folk tales that deal with mating. There is some evidence that "The Frog Prince" was an ancient tale and may not have always been related to mating at first. For instance, in many stories frogs kept popping their heads out of wells, springs, rivers, woods, and so on to announce a forthcoming pregnancy. That is, they were often symbols of fertility. The situation is different in ancient Greece and Rome. In *Fairytale in the Ancient World*, Graham Anderson remarks that there is a reference to "the man who was (once) a frog is now a king" in Petronius' *Satyrica*, and he also points to another possible source in the myth about the forty-nine obedient daughters of Danaus of Argos.[16] The focus of the classical myths appears to be more on the power of the gods and seduction and rape than on strategies of mating. However, courting and mating are important themes as are transformations into and out of animal shapes by both men and women. Often human beings are changed into a lowly animal such as a donkey as is the case in Apuleius' second-century work, *The Golden Ass*, which contains the famous tale of "Eros and Psyche," which, in turn, served as a model for many of the French literary versions of "Beauty and the Beast" during the seventeenth and eighteenth centuries.

It is obvious that "The Frog Prince" is related to all the ancient and modern tales of the beast/bridegroom variety. In an article titled "The Story of 'The Frog Prince': Breton Variant, and Some Analogues" (1890), the erudite British folklorist William Alexander Clouston refers to numerous medieval versions of "The Knight and the Loathly Lady," oral and literary, that may have contributed to the ultimate formation of the Grimms' "Frog Prince" such as an Icelandic version from the Latin of Torfœus, another Icelandic version from Grim's Saga, Turkish Sanskrit, Kaffir analogues, Arabic variants, Chaucer's "The Wife of Bath's Tale" in *The Canterbury Tales*, and Gower's "Tale of Florent" in the first book of the *Confessio Amantis*.[17]

What is significant about Clouston's article is the way he associates "The Frog Prince" with numerous tales that involve a young *man* or knight who must *kiss* a frog to attain money or to save his life. He translates M. F. M. Luzel's Breton variant,

"Jannac aux Deux Sous" as "Penny Jack," which involves a poor orphan, who is confronted by an enormous frog at a fountain. Though horrified, Penny Jack agrees to kiss the frog when she promises him a great deal of money. The third time that he kisses her, she is transformed into a beautiful princess, who had been held under a charm until "a virgin young man should kiss her thrice."[18] However, he must prove that he is worthy of her before she takes him to her father, a powerful king of the East. Therefore, "he was to return to town, and after a year and a day he must come to the fountain at eight in the morning, alone and fasting. She would be there, and would take him to her father. He must kiss no other woman, and take care to come fasting, else he should not see her."[19] Of course, he fails to do this three times. The princess disappears and returns to her Castle of Gold held by four chains over the Red Sea. Jack must endure many trials and hardships until he can see her and marry her. As Clouston points out, this Breton oral tale has much in common with a variety of beast/bridegroom tales and also tales that do not even involve animal transformation such as Gower's "Tale of Florent," in which a young knight must solve a riddle—"What do women most desire?"—or be killed. He encounters a loathly woman, who promises to help him only if he weds her. After pondering his situation, he agrees and learns that women would be sovereign of man's love and have their own will. Once he is pardoned by the grandmother of Branchus, who has sought his death, he returns to the loathly woman because he is a true knight who keeps his word, and he must kiss her and bed her only to discover that she is the beautiful daughter of the King of Sicily who had been transformed into an ugly woman by her stepmother until a good knight would give her his love and allow her mastery over him.

As we can see from see from Clouston's study, there were numerous oral and literary tales, which were either variants of a frog/animal transformation or analogues of "the loathly lady," that were circulating in Europe during the late medieval period and Renaissance. At one point, the Grimms' informant, a young woman in the Wild family in Kassel, perhaps Dortchen Wild, who later married Wilhelm, heard some version pertaining to "The Frog Prince" and changed it to suit her "desires." Interestingly, the Wild family was a French Huguenot family that had settled in Germany. The frog had symbolically come to represent a male, a phallic figure, who, under pressure through enchantment or a curse, had to mate to be liberated and to regain his human form. Or perhaps the frog had represented a female, who needed a kiss and power over a man to regain her human form and to be wedded. Clearly, the Grimms' informant used tales that stemmed from other European traditions, and it is striking that the storyteller appears to have been familiar with Celtic and Scottish variants.

As I have already indicated, Lutz Röhrich, one of the most dependable and insightful German folklorists, maintains that motifs of the tale are ancient. In the West there are clear signs throughout the early and late Middle Ages that a tale about a male frog circulated in the oral tradition and also in Latin about an enchanted prince transformed into a frog. The earliest text can be found in *The Complaynt of Scotland* (c. 1550), a political and literary work by Robert Wedder-burn, in which a young lady is sent by her stepmother to the well at the world's end to fetch some water. A frog appears at the well and allows her to draw water only if she will marry him. If she doesn't, he threatens to tear her to pieces. Of course, she accepts, and later the frog appears at the door and demands:

> Open the door, my hinny, my hart,
> Open the door, mine ain wee thing:
> And mind the words that you and I spak
> Down in the meadow, at the well-spring![20]

This tale was still well-known and widely disseminated in Scotland and Eng-land until the end of the nineteenth century, as the works of James Orchard Halliwell-Phillipps, J. F. Campbell, and Joseph Jacobs reveal.[21] Toward the end of Jacobs' popular version, the frog says,

> Go with me to bed, my hinny, my heart,
>   Go with me to bed, my own darling;
> Mind you the words you spake to me,
>   Down by the cold well, so weary.

And the narrator continues: "But that the girl wouldn't do, till her stepmother said: 'Do what you promised, girl; girls must keep their promises. Do what you're bid, or out you go, you and your froggie.'"[22] The girl lets the frog sleep in her bed, but keeps her distance, and in the morning, the frog asks her to chop off his head. She hesitates, but since he is so persistent, she complies, and of course, he turns into a prince who carries her off to his castle and marries her.

What is significant about the Scottish and English versions and the Grimms' later version is that the Brothers Grimm evidently brought together all the char-acters, motifs, and the topic of mating in such an efficient and aesthetically pleasing manner that the tale stuck in the minds of many people and spread in many different versions in Europe and elsewhere throughout the nineteenth century and well into the twentieth century. The plot did not always remain the same, and the Grimms' text may not have served as the basis for the rewriting or re-telling of each new variant. For instance, in the very first English translation of the Grimms' version in 1823, Edgar Taylor changed the title to "The Frog Prince," and the princess allows the frog to sleep in her bed three times. On the third occasion, he becomes a prince and weds the princess. The motif of the frog that must sleep in the princess's bed three times was common in European and American literature throughout the nineteenth century and can even be found in the American writer/ illustrator Wanda Gág's 1936 adaptation *Tales from Grimm.* In other European and Asian tales the frog asks to have his skin cut off and burned so that he can become a prince. Sometimes his head must be chopped off, as was common in the Scottish versions. In almost all the tales, he must somehow be transformed either by the princess's act of throwing him against a wall or by gaining permission to sleep in the princess's bed before the enchantment can be broken. Very rarely does a kiss change the prince in the nineteenth century, if ever. In *Handbuch zu den "Kinder- und Hausmärchen" der Brüder Grimm*, Hans-Jörg Uther maintains that the kiss began appearing at the end of the nineteenth century, but he does not provide documentation. There is plenty of evidence, however, in the tales in which a princess is the frog that the male must often kiss and bed the frog (loathly woman) to transform her. Significantly, no matter whether the frog is a male or female, the male must change or pass trials to suit the taste and to meet the mating standards of a young woman. Often the young woman goes to a well to draw water and loses a ring in the water. She is not a princess, nor is the frog an enchanted prince. But both are brought together in a mating game and must devise strategies to obtain what they want or do not want. Whatever the variant or outcome may be, "The Frog Prince" has become relevant as a communication and is disseminated widely because it enables people to reflect upon the possibilities and hazards of mating and to draw their own conclusions. Though the Grimms sought to moralize mating, especially with the addition of the faithful servant at the end, their tale, which is not *their* tale *per se*, undercut their intentions, for love, fidelity, and morality have little to do with mating. Even their protagonist, the young princess, makes it clear by rejecting her father's final command and the advances of the frog. Sexual choice, governed in large part by desire and fitness for adaptation, is key to understanding how and why we mate, and for the evolutionary psychologist Geoffrey Miller, sexual choice is also a driving force in the mind's evolution.

Miller's thought-provoking book, *The Mating Mind*, argues

> that we were neither created by an omniscient deity, nor did we evolve by blind, dumb natural selection. Rather, our evolution was shaped by beings intermediate in intelligence: our own ancestors, choosing their sexual partners as sensibly as they could. We have

inherited both their sexual tastes for warm, witty, creative, intelligent, generous companions, and some of these traits that they preferred. We are the outcome of their million-year-long genetic engineering experiment in which their sexual choices did the genetic engineering.[23]

Miller's comprehensive study traces historically and scientifically how the growth of the brain size of the human species and the origination of language opened the way for humans to devise strategies of sexual choice in mating that have effected the evolution of the mind.

> Talking about themselves gave our ancestors a unique window into one another's thoughts and feelings, their past experiences and future plans. Any particular courtship conversation may look trivial, but consider the cumulative effects of millions of such conversations over thousands of generations. Genes for better conversational ability, more interesting thoughts, and more attractive feelings would spread because they were favored by sexual choice. Evolution found a way to act directly on the mental sophistication of this primate species, not through some unique combination of survival challenges, but through the species setting itself a strange new game of reproduction. They started selecting one another for their brains. . . . The intellectual and technical achievements of our species in the last few thousand years depend on mental capacities and motivations originally shaped by sexual selection.[24]

What becomes evident in Miller's analysis is that the manner in which men compete for women, and women compete for men has fostered great and diverse innovations in the arts, sciences, and technology that account for a variety of cultural transformations, and in turn, these cultural transformations may have contributed to biological adaptations and affected the way we transmit cultural artifacts with our brains.

Relevance Theory, Memetics, Evolutionary Psychology

But what does the brain and evolutionary psychology have to do with "The Frog Prince" and the thousands of variants connected to mating? In my recent book *Why Fairy Tales Stick* (2006), I endeavored to demonstrate how relevance theory, memetics, and evolutionary psychology may help us understand why *certain* fairy tales become so deeply embedded in our minds and culture that we tend to spread them almost as if they were viruses. Particular tales seem to become so "contagious" that they catch and spread themselves randomly. Some scientists and social scientists liken them to genes and call them memes, following a notion first proposed by Richard Dawkins in his 1976 book, *The Selfish Gene*.[25] Though many critics have attacked and mocked the notion of meme and memetics—some have even urged

Figure 2 Italian nineteenth-century picturebook of "The Frog Prince." The illustrator is unknown.

Dawkins to abandon the term[26]—meme has spread memetically throughout the world and is now recorded in the *Oxford English Dictionary* and others as well. The term meme itself has become memetic and has replicated itself in hundreds if not hundreds of thousands of ways. The thought-provoking philosopher Daniel Dennett has used memetics as a basis to explain religion as a natural phenomenon in his recent book, *Breaking the Spell: Religion as a Natural Phenomenon* (2006), and in an article in *The Encyclopedia of Evolution*, written four years earlier, he argues that that memes must be understood as coded messages of information formed by neurons that are passed from person to person in different shapes. "Memes, cultural recipes, similarly depend on one physical medium or another for their continued existence (they aren't magic), but they can leap around from medium to medium, being translated from language to language, from language to diagram, from diagram to rehearsed practice, and so forth."[27]

Dawkins proposed that almost any cultural artifact can become a meme and implied that it would be scientifically impossible to describe a meme and its functions. Dennett asks the rhetorical question "Just how big or small can a meme be?" He then answers his own question by stating:

> A single musical tone is not a meme, but a memorable melody is. Is a symphony a single meme or is it a system of memes? A parallel question can be asked about genes, of course. No single nucleotide or codon is a gene. How many notes or letters or codons does it take? The answer in both cases tolerates blurred boundaries: a meme, or a gene, must be large enough to carry information worth copying.[28]

What is worth copying, that is, what is valuable, will depend in each case on individual transmitters and cultural conditions, even if the meme is persistent and acts selfishly to replicate itself no matter what information it is carrying. What many theoreticians and critics of memetics sometimes forget is that a meme is *not* eternal and that it cannot endure outside systems of cultural evolution. As we shall also see, a meme does not replicate itself with fidelity or determine the form and contents of its variant or the version produced by its individual carrier. It will not be perpetuated unless it enables adaptation to a changing environment, and its changes in replication are reflective of relative transformation in the environment. Memes change, shape shift, and have their own specific evolutionary history, as can be seen clearly in the evolution of certain folk and fairy tales. But there are core qualities in style, plot, and content that are retained and distinguish it from other memes. It is through distinction and selection that people as agents activate a particular meme as story to enable them to relate to a particular situation.

In a recent insightful essay, "The Gene Meme," the biologist David Haig clarifies Dawkins' notion of gene and meme and demonstrates precisely why Dawkins' analogy between gene and meme can help us to grasp certain principles of cultural evolution.

> There are two principal kinds of things we observe that provide evidence about the nature of memetic transmissions. The first are communication acts including sounds, texts, actions, and artefacts. The second are insights from introspection when we register a communication act, when we integrate the content of a communication act into our private set of concepts, and when we emit communication acts. Introspection may be an unreliable guide because unconscious aspects of our motivations are hidden and our conscious perceptions may be partial, inaccurate, and misleading. Communication acts appear closer to the concept of genotype (things transmitted) whereas the conscious and unconscious effects of these acts on our internal state appear closer to phenotype (effects that influence what is transmitted). In the history of genetics, the phenotype was apparent and the genotype hidden. But this relation seems to be reversed for memetics. Memes are observed, rather than inferred from their effects, whereas their efforts are in large part hidden.[29]

In the case of folk and fairy tales, memes are easily observed in the communicative act between storyteller and listener. Moreover, they assume material form in the shape of texts in printed books, plays, operas, toys, songs, music, clothes, paintings, films, hypertexts on Internet sites, advertisements, greeting cards, and so on. "The Frog Prince," for instance, has been replicated in all these material forms and others, implying different meanings and causing diverse effects that make the tale memorable, while opening a discourse on modes of mating and perhaps other topics connected to mating. Here the analogy with the gene is significant. As Haig notes,

> The gene has a material definition in terms of a DNA sequence that maintains an uninterrupted physical integrity in its transmission from generation to generation. Memes also have a physical form in their transmission from one individual to another, sometimes as sound vibrations, or text on paper, or electronic signals relayed through a modem. When these "outward" forms of a meme are perceived, they elicit changes in a nervous system that constitutes the meme's "cryptic" form. The material basis of the cryptic form is probably unique to each nervous system colonized by the meme. Memetic replication, then, has nothing like the elegant simplicity of the double helix.[30]

Since it is not entirely clear how a fairy tale as meme functions within the brain and nervous system, that is, whether there is a special module or groups of modules that register the communication and facilitate its replication, it is difficult to postulate how a specific fairy tale maintains its integrity and guarantees that it will be transmitted from one person to another person within the conditions of cultural evolution. Hence, its cryptic nature. However, other theories can be brought to bear on this problem, and I should like to discuss some of the more significant theories to illustrate how we might appreciate the possible advantages that an evolutionary approach to folk and fairy tales may offer in helping us understand how tales are disseminated and why certain, and only certain, tales become memes.

For the past thirty to forty years, biologists, geneticists, ethnologists, evolutionary anthropologists and psychologists, and other scientists have increasingly turned their attention to culture and have made important scientific contributions to our comprehension of how culture evolves. For instance, the eminent Italian biologist Luigi Cavalli Sforza began publishing studies with Marcus Feldman on cultural transmission in the 1970s on the joint transmission of what he called cultural characters (his term for memes) in populations in relation to genetic evolution, and in his most recent book, *L'evoluzione della cultura* (2004), he explained:

> With regard to cultural transmission, the first phase is mutation, or transformation that brings about the creation of a new idea. This phase is the phase of creation or invention. If new ideas are not created, there is also the possibility of another kind of mutation—the loss of an idea, or a custom.
>
> The innovation won't be transmitted unless there is a desire to teach it, that is, to disseminate it and learn it. One could say that the transmission passes through two phases: the communication of information, of an idea, by a teacher (transmitter) to a student (transmittee), and the comprehension and acquisition of the idea. This is the act of reproduction of the idea that happens when the idea passes from one brain to another. Assuming that we consider such an act analogical to the generation of a child, we can speak about the self-reproduction (*autoriproduzione*) of the idea. It is clear that the mechanisms are profoundly different in biology and in culture, but the result is essentially the same. A DNA can generate many copies of itself that lodge among bodies of different individuals, and the idea can generate many copies of itself in other brains. Without a doubt we are dealing with self-reproduction also in the case of the idea, and it is just as clear that ideas have the possibility of mutation. It is necessary to understand the mutation in a more general sense in so far as there is the possibility for completely new ideas to emerge like a generation from nothing, a true creation. Ideas (even if we do not know exactly what they are) are material objects inasmuch as they require material bodies and brains in which they are produced for the first time and reproduced in the process of transmission: like the DNA they are material objects, even if they are profoundly different from the DNA.[31]

Another renowned biologist, Edward Wilson, published an important book, *Consilience Theory: The Unity of Knowledge* (1998), in which he demonstrated how seemingly disparate phenomena in the world are connected. The French ethnologist Dan Sperber coined the terms mental representation and public representation to explain how ideas were fostered and disseminated in material culture in his book *Explaining Culture: A Naturalistic Approach* (1996). In short, there have been a host of studies, books, and essays, that have endeavored to clarify the relationship between genetic and cultural evolution, including the work by Dawkins and Dennett that I have already mentioned.

One of the more recent and most stimulating books to explore this relationship is *Not by Genes Alone: How Culture Transformed Human Evolution* (2005) by Peter Richerson and Robert Boyd, who previously published a significant study, *Culture and Evolutionary Process*, in 1985. In their latest work they define culture as "information capable of affecting individuals' behavior that they acquire from other members of their species through teaching, imitation, and other forms of social transmission. By information we mean any kind of mental state, conscious or not, that is acquired or modified by social learning and affects behavior."[32] Instead of using the term "meme," cultural character, or "mental representation" to define the "bits" of information disseminated by humans to form culture,[33] they use the term "cultural variant," which is learned and spread in distinct population groups.

> Our definition is rooted in the conviction that most cultural variation is caused by information stored in human brains—information that got into those brains by learning from others. People in culturally distinct groups behave differently, mostly because they have acquired different skills, beliefs, and values, and these differences persist because the people of one generation acquire their beliefs and attitudes from those around them.[34]

Interestingly, Richerson and Boyd do not dismiss the notion of "meme"; instead, they have a very strict definition of the term:

> population thinking that does not require cultural information takes the form of *memes*, discrete, faithfully replicating genelike bits of information. A range of models are consistent with the facts of cultural variation as they are presently understood, including models in which cultural information is not discrete and is never replicated. The same goes for the processes that give rise to cultural change. Natural selection—like processes—are sometimes important, but processes that have no analog in genetic evolution also play important roles. Culture is interesting and important because its evolutionary behavior is distinctly different from that of genes. For example, we will argue that the human cultural system arose as an adaptation because it can evolve fancy adaptations to changing environments rather more swiftly than is possible by genes alone. Culture would never have evolved unless it could do things that genes can't![35]

Richerson and Boyd develop a theory of co-evolution of cultural variants and genes to explain how human behavior is determined by a historically evolved biological process and a historical social process of dissemination of cultural variants. Most of their examples are convincing, and their claims are modest. They freely admit that there is still much that we do not know about how cultural variants operate. Toward the end of their study, they state:

We really know very little about how cultural evolution works. Some of you may have concluded that this is because cultural evolution is beyond scientific understanding, at least of the sort we advocate. But we believe that thinking about culture using Darwinian tools opens many new avenues for investigation. . . . Some studies based on qualitative data are rather sophisticated, but many opportunities to do better work exist. We need to characterize cultural variation in the same quantitative detail as genetic variation. Recent work in cross-cultural psychology and in the use of economic games to investigate the norms of fairness cross-culturally will open a new era of quantitative ethnography that will revolutionize our understanding of human behavioral variation.[36]

In fact, the problem that confronts any theory of cultural evolution related to genetic evolution or based on a co-evolution of culture and genetics is that we know very little about how the brain and language operate precisely to dispose us toward particular behaviors. In addition, we must take into consideration technologically advanced inventions in mass media and globalization processes that have transformed particular cultural variants into trans-cultural variants, and we must be able to explain why cultural variants stick in diverse cultures, especially if they are fomented and reinforced by culture industries and political and religious institutions. We must also decide whether such a term as meme should be defined in such narrow terms as do Richerson and Boyd, for nothing can ever be copied or replicated with complete fidelity or always remain discrete. In fact, Dawkins maintained that replication does not entail fidelity. Memes can be and are culturally varied and transformed by human carriers precisely because they enable adaptation to the social and natural environment. But it is too early to determine scientifically just how a meme operates until we learn much more about how the brain functions.

What we can continue to do, as Richerson and Boyd and other scientists suggest, is to bring together the research in the humanities and natural sciences so that we have a clearer picture of how culture evolves and how folklore and fairy tales play a role in this evolution. Here I believe the work of Deirdre Wilson and Dan Sperber can help us further understand how mental representations or cultural variants might function in language and how particular mental representations (cultural variants) might successfully be replicated as memes or in some kind of memetic process. Wilson and Sperber have demonstrated through cognitive linguistics that when people speak and want to communicate, our brains function as efficiently as possible to maximize the relevance of an utterance and to convey a presumption of its own optimal relevance. The brain takes inputs from internal and external sources to form a communication that becomes ostensive, that is, draws attention to whatever the transmitter wants to communicate. The inferred meaning, its intention, must be grasped on some level in order for the communication to be successful. This is true of any folk or fairy tale. Despite the possible ambivalence of meaning, there is something implied in any folk or fairy tale. In my opinion, it is only because the tale makes itself relevant as meme or has been made relevant by human speakers to enable them to adapt to their environments and to cultural communities and for sexual selection that it sticks in brains and is replicated in manifold ways. Without relevance, that is, without being made relevant, a meme cannot successfully propagate itself over long periods of time, and like a gene, it may cooperate with other memes to be successful to maintain itself and to be passed on. For example, "The Frog Prince" is a specific kind of "Beast-Bridegroom tale type" and cooperates with similar type tales (cultural variants) to form a memeplex. Within this memeplex, it is often chosen over others to be disseminated as a meme in a particular socio-cultural context.

If the actions of individuals depend to a great extent on their selfish genes, as Dawkins has demonstrated, human beings are bound to produce and to be attracted to memes that will assist them in reproducing their genes and particular aspects of their culture. Tales have evolved out of the basic needs of human beings as forms of communication that contain vital information for the reproduction and adaptation of the human species, and the tales have been generated out of the experiences that people have gathered over hundreds of thousands of years—experiences that have led to the gradual transformation of genes and genotypes and phenotypes and the formation of culture. Since information about how we mate, why we mate, and what makes us attractive so that we can select a mate of our choice is vital for both genders, it is not by chance that hundreds of thousands if not millions of tales as communications about mating have been produced ever since language came into being. What is interesting in the development of folklore and storytelling is that specific types of tales that address specific areas of human behavior began to develop and to evolve at a certain point in history as a discourse, and these tales were passed on in many different forms. In the modern era, that is, in the period since the revolutionary invention of the printing press in the fifteenth century, certain tales that had already circulated widely became stabilized *and* flexible in print and facilitated their replication in ways that had been impossible before the emergence of the printing press. Thus, the printed text became a reference point that, to be sure, was not always copied with true fidelity, but the continued reprinting of more or less the same text along with oral replication of variants and later other technological means of replication enabled tales, relevant for the adaptation and propagation of the species, to be spread. In the process mating tales evolved and continue to evolve with "The Frog Prince" as meme playing a significant role in the evolution of culture—specific cultures and globalized culture. "The Frog Prince" has never remained the same but evokes a similar response and associations in people disposed to react to its communication about mating. The communication will never be blandly or passively accepted and may be a debatable communication, but it does reveal and say something important about the human adaptation of mating strategies in a socio-cultural context.

The Frog Prince in Contemporary Culture

Those folk and fairy tales about mating that become memetic open and constitute a discourse on bodies over bodies about a particular behavior in a setting that provides information about how women and men go about choosing their mates. The "Frog Prince" discourse that is conveyed memetically will not draw a response from listeners/readers/spectators unless its relative cultural meaning about sexual selection is made relevant in a socio-historical context. Interestingly, "The Frog Prince" as meme acts on two levels to guarantee its preservation and replication: 1. its most generic text, "The Frog Prince" by the Brothers Grimm, continues to be retold, reprinted, and re-presented in images so that it is not forgotten, emphasizing a basic genetic disposition of men and women to choose mates who will best further the propagation of their own genes; 2. the thousands of variants of the generic text have been generated and continue to be generated within specific cultural discourses involving many different genres because human dispositions and expectations have been altered in diverse cultures, and as cultural artifacts the folk and fairy tales about the strange courtship between the repulsive frog prince and the reluctant princess communicate information about these alternations (and also alternatives) while recalling the generic text that is very much connected to the historical evolution of psychology and culture. It is possible to argue that the memetic significance of particular fairy tales such as "The Frog Prince" is so germane to the historical evolution of the human species in every culture in which it exists that, as meme, it has employed and has been employed in every possible means of mass communication to disseminate information about mating. Furthermore, it is possible to argue that people themselves, sensing that their ancestors were the originators of this mental representation thousands of years ago, have responded by using every possible means of mass communication to elaborate, embellish, critique, parody, and expand the information.

To show how "The Frog Prince" continues to be preserved and disseminated in contemporary culture, I want to discuss several diverse examples in literature

Figure 3 "The Frog King" in Walter Crane, *The Story Book I*, 1874–1876.

and film. These examples will be taken largely from cultural artifacts in the Anglo-American tradition, primarily books and stories, but also some films disseminated in America and the UK during the last thirty years. It should be noted that "The Frog Prince" as meme *cannot* be found in every culture in the world, and thus is culturally bound in distinct populations. However, I suspect that every culture that has an oral and literary tradition of tales possesses a particular narrative discourse that concerns courtship, sexual preference, and mating. For instance, most of the major cultures in the world have beast-bridegroom tale types. With regard to "The Frog Prince," we shall see that the implicit sexual connotations of the tale in the Grimms' version that was de-eroticized and sanitized for family reading has been altered to meet certain socially coded expectations of readers/listeners/viewers.

Though there is no clear demarcation to indicate when major shifts occurred in the discursive tradition of "The Frog Prince"—for instance, it is not clear when and why the kiss replaced the slam against the wall or the sleeping together in bed motifs—certain transformations in the variants suggest that how we select our mates has significantly changed since the rise of the feminist movement in the late 1960s if not before. For example, there has recently been an extraordinary proliferation of self-help books that reflect how "The Frog Prince" has played and continues to play a central role in the thinking about mating strategies in the past thirty or forty years. Just the titles of the works indicate the memetic significance of "The Frog Prince": Joanne Vickers and Barbara Thomas, *No More Frogs, No More Princes: Women Making Choices at Midlife* (1993), Nailah Shami, *Do Not Talk to, Touch, Marry, or Otherwise Fiddle with Frogs: How to Find Prince Charming by Finding Yourself* (2001), Michael McGahey, *Why Kiss a Frog? Your Prince is Out There! Every Woman's Complete Guide to Friends, Lovers, and the Search for a Perfect Partner!* (2002), Kathleen Hardaway, *I Kissed a Lot of Frogs: But the Prince Hasn't Come* (2002), and Lydia Lambert, *Kissing Frogs: The Path to a Prince* (2005). Most of these books are written from a feminist viewpoint and concern how women have been deceived by men who seem to be charming princes and how they must become more independent, that is, not dependent on men and a system of patriarchy. There is a clear indication that the "The Frog Prince" meme is invoked in these works in order to comment on the inadequacy of the approved mating standards. There are, however, some self-help books such as Geoff Dench's *The Frog the Prince and the Problem of Men* (1994), which, using the fairy tale of "The Frog Prince," argues that the shortcomings of feminism have led to the marginalization of men:

Over-emphasis on female independence, and rejection of sacrifice, has spawned a frog culture in which the sexes are polarising, and men are becoming increasingly marginal as they revert to a wild state. Their objective inferiority is potentially much greater than any secondary public status assigned to women under patriarchy, and lacks the compensation of a countervailing domain to sustain them. Is that what women really want? Not many, I think. Women want men to be responsible people like themselves. But few will be if women deny them reasonable opportunity to acquire what most people need in order to become civilised beings, and that is personal dependants—other people for whom to be responsible.[37]

Whether or not one agrees with Dench, it is clear that feminism has brought about major changes in the relations between the sexes. In the last forty years most poems, stories, novels, and films have either eliminated or minimized the role played by the father as an authority figure in sexual selection. The young woman, who is no longer a princess but every woman, is responsible for her choice, and not every frog is a prince. Nor are good looks the most important attributes that compel a woman to choose a mate. And in the case of enchanted frogs, they are not always satisfied with alluring princesses.

In those books manufactured and distributed for young readers between the ages of five and fourteen—and sometimes these books are primers to teach children the alphabet and how to read—the sexual elements in the mating of the frog and princess are generally eliminated or dealt with in a comic fashion. Nevertheless, the interaction of frog and princess indicates that significant rules and customs of courting and mating have either been totally reformed or are being questioned. For instance, several picture books depict a frog who refuses to become a prince or prefers to remain a frog than court a princess. In *The Strange Story of the Frog Who Became a Prince* (1971) by Elinor Lander Horowitz, a wicked witch transforms a handsome frog into a prince, and when he wishes to be the frog he was, she forgets the spell necessary to re-convert him and transforms him into many different comical creatures until she finally undoes the harm she has caused. In A. Vesey's *The Princess and the Frog* (1985), after the princess returns home and tells her mother that a frog, who retrieved her golden ball from a pond, has followed her, the queen tells her not to worry, for he will turn into a prince. The frog, who is obnoxious and bossy and leads a life of luxury in the castle, keeps annoying the princess, who complains to her mother. Once again the queen tells her not to worry and to kiss the frog. When the princess does this, he does not turn into a prince. More angry than ever, the princess demands an explanation, and the frog replies that he never pretended to be a prince. In fact, he is married with children and intends to bring his entire frog family to the palace to enjoy the luxuries of life. In *A Frog Prince* (1989) by Alix Berenzy the frog realizes that he is no match for the princess when she throws him into a corner and tells him to look at his ugly face in the mirror. When he does this, he sees nothing wrong and the moon tells him:

> Little green Frog alone at night,
> Beauty is in the Beholder's sight.
> Follow the Sun, then follow me,
> To lands beyond, across the sea.
> In another kingdom you shall find
> A true princess of a different kind.[38]

Indeed, in a mock version of a knight's voyage, he travels to another kingdom to find a sleeping frog princess, whom he wakens with a kiss and marries. In *The Frog Prince Continued* (1991), Jon Scieszka portrays the prince and princess after the marriage and describes their unhappiness because the princess cannot tolerate the fact that the prince continues to behave like a frog. Consequently, he runs away and tries to find happiness as a frog in the woods. After he has three encounters with three different witches and none of their magic helps him, he returns home because he misses his wife. Ironically, when he kisses her, they both turn into frogs and hop off happily ever after. In *The Horned Toad Prince* (2000) by Jackie Mims Hopkins, a feisty cowgirl named Reba Jo strikes a bargain with a horned toad when she loses her sombrero in a well. She tries to break the bargain, but her father compels her to live up to it. So, when she kisses the toad, he changes into Prince Maxmillian José Diego López de España, who leaves her in the lurch, for he wants his freedom more than he wants a wife.

In each of these picture books, there are clever twists, indicating that the male frog, as the major protagonist of the tale, is more interested in finding his identity and living autonomously than he is in pleasing a princess. Her wealth, status, and beauty are not sufficient reasons for him to want to bed or marry the princess. In other longer novellas for young readers, there is often a gender shift. For instance, in Ellen Conford's *The Frog Princess of Pelham* (1997), a lonely rich girl named Chandler, living in a suburb of New York, is transformed into a frog when Danny, the most popular boy in her school, kisses her to win a bet. Feeling responsible, Danny tries to take care of her until the army learns about the talking frog. When it appears that Danny will be arrested for not revealing the secret of the talking frog, Chandler intercedes, and this brave gesture brings about the re-transformation of the frog princess into a young girl. Chandler and Danny remain friends and sort out their personal difficulties. In E. D. Baker's *The Frog Princess* (2002), the princess Emeralda runs off into the forest to avoid spending time with Prince Jorge, whom her mother hopes she will marry. There, in the woods, she encounters a frog named Prince Eadric, and when she kisses him, she herself is turned into a frog. Together princess and prince have all sorts of adventures trying to survive as frogs until they learn how they have both been cursed. Fortunately, a fairy enables both of them to return to their human forms, and Emeralda decides that the struggles she and Eadric have gone through have brought them together. So, she will marry him instead of Prince Jorge. Finally, in Patricia Harrison Easton's *Davey's Blue-Eyed Frog* (2003), a young boy discovers a talking frog named Amelia in a pond, and she tries to convince him that she needs a kiss before two cycles of the moon pass to turn her back into her human form. However, he wants to show her off to his friends and refuses to kiss her. After taking her home, he must protect her from his little brother Kevin and other people as well. In the end he resolves her dilemma.

In each one of these novels for young readers, the father, who generally sets the standard for morality, is absent, and the focus is less on mating than it is on establishing one's identity and finding the confidence to accept oneself. What was once a mating tale in the Grimms' version of "The Frog King" becomes an extended adventure story in which a young girl must demonstrate that she has the virtues necessary to make her own decisions. The emphasis on adventure and tests is most clear in the three humorous novels for young readers published by Donna Jo Napoli: *The Prince of the Pond Otherwise Known as De Fawg Pin* (1992), *Jimmy, the Pickpocket of the Palace* (1995), and *Gracie, The Pixie of the Puddle* (2004). This trilogy records the vicissitudes of two generations of frog/humans. The first novel lays the groundwork for all the others. Told from the perspective of Jade, a female frog, this adventure involves a natural mating between Jade and the fawg pin (frog prince), who was once a human prince and had been transformed into a frog by a hag. Most of the novel concerns how Pin must accustom himself to becoming a frog and how he and Jade fall in love and have fifty froglets. Their favorite son, Jimmy, is threatened by the hag, and Pin must save him. In the course of the action, Pin is accidentally kissed by a princess and turns back into a naked prince. Jade is confused and takes her froglets back to the pond, while the prince waits for the princess to bring him clothes. The second novel is told from the perspective of the son Jimmy, who discovers that his father is now a human prince. He travels to the palace, and after he, too, becomes human and helps defeat the hag again, he returns to the pond as a frog. In the last novel, the narrative is told from the perspective of the frog Gracie, who is in love with Jimmy and does not believe that he is the human prince's son. When Jimmy learns that the evil hag is about to destroy all the frogs in the pond, he travels to retrieve the magic ring that his father has kept, for it will help Jimmy and the other frogs defeat the hag. Gracie follows him because she wants to win his love. After many strange encounters that involve the hag becoming a crocodile, Jimmy turns human again and manages to retrieve the ring. But he must decide whether he will return to the pond as a frog with Gracie or stay human and live with his father. In the end, he wishes to be with Gracie and, at the same time, causes the hag to be turned into a toad.

While Napoli's novels focus on the comic adventures of Pin and his son Jimmy and how they discover their true identities, they are also about mating and fidelity. Pin, though his nature is different from Jade's, looks after her and their family, just as Jimmy promises to do the same with Gracie. The difference is that Jimmy, born a frog, will stay in a pond with Gracie. Jade comes to realize that Pin will never return and moves on in her life with another mate. Whether frog or human, it is through common experiences and mutual support that the couples learn to love one another and choose each other as mates. Once again, fathers are absent, and there is no pressure placed on either the male or female to marry according to class or prestige.

In the novels and stories published for an adult reading audience, the central focus tends to be on the mating process, the false promises generated by the classical story of the frog prince by the Brothers Grimm, and on marriage. Stephen Mitchell's *The Frog Prince: A Fairy Tale for Consenting Adults* (1999) is more an ironical philosophical meditation on mating than a novel. The frog employs his great rhetorical skills and intellect to convince a proud princess that beauty is in the eyes of the beholder, while she begs him to trust her as she throws him against the wall so that he can become human. At the end, Mitchell writes,

> Researchers recently studied a number of ex-frogs who are now handsome, happily married princes (a necessarily small number since, as the philosopher says, all things excellent are as difficult as they are rare). These ex-frogs were unanimous in their accounts. The great transformation they said, had three requirements: a sustained not-knowing, the willingness to be thrown against a wall, and, always the love of a visionary woman. And a fourth requirement: patience. Yes, an enormous patience, since the interval between the being-thrown and the actual impact may last for a decade or more.[39]

The tone is much different in Nancy Springer's *Fair Peril* (1996), a mock comic feminist novel, which concerns Buffy Murphy, a 40-year-old storyteller, who has been scorned and divorced by her husband and has let herself go to pieces. When she finds a frog in a forest, she refuses to kiss it even when he declares that he is a prince named Adamus d'Aurca. Buffy explodes.

> "What the hell do I need a prince for?" Men. They all seemed to assume they were God's gift. "I just got rid of one dickheaded male. I don't need another one." Especially as she'd reached

a point in her life where celibacy was far preferable to the terror of getting pregnant. "Anyway, what on earth do you think you're prince of? England? Monaco? Those slots are taken."[40]

Buffy tries to keep the talking frog as a pet to help her with her storytelling and does not trust the manner in which the frog tries to court her. However, her 16-year-old daughter, Emily, does fall for the frog and kisses him. Once this occurs, and the frog becomes a gorgeous young man, Buffy's main task then involves saving her daughter, who has escaped with the prince to a shopping mall, from being seduced. The mall turns at times into the realm of Fair Peril. In the end, Buffy manages to save both the prince and Emily from being cursed. Ironically, when she finally develops compassion for the prince, she kisses him, and he turns into a teenager named Adam, who heads west to find himself. At the same time, Buffy appears to be calm and content, for she apparently has learned to overcome her distaste for frogs and deal with her illusions and delusions. Springer's focus is more on a dowdy divorced woman, who discovers that the happily ever after story of "The Frog Prince" is an illusion, and a divorce, which smashes that illusion, will demand that she learns to stand on her own two feet and tell her own story.

Recently, Jane Porter has written a similar but much more trite novel, *The Frog Prince* (2005), about a young woman named Holly Bishop, who, at twenty-five, is about to get divorced after one year of marriage and moves from Fresno to San Francisco to become an event planner. Brought up on fairy tales, Holly tries to get over their deceptive messages about successful mating and begins the dating game. After a succession of dates and difficulties at her office, she gains confidence at her work place and sorts out her relationships so that she can declare at the end of this predictable poorly written work:

> Getting married and divorced in a year was pretty damn awful, but I have to say, kissing that toad two years ago probably saved my life. I wouldn't be where I am today if I hadn't discovered that all the magic I ever wanted is right inside me.
> I *am* a princess. I'm the Frog Princess.[41]

Many of the contemporary stories and cartoons for adults about the frog prince concern a false expectation based on the fact that the classical tale by the Brothers Grimm has become memetic: the frog does not change into a charming prince but changes into an ugly toad; he is simply not the right choice for the princess. Marriage is a disaster. The woman is generally conned into believing that the fairy tale is a true story, and her happiness depends on kissing the frog. This feminist critique of "The Frog Prince" is developed in a more nuanced way in some of the films adapted from the Grimms' text or memories of the text. For instance,

Jim Henson's *Tales from Muppetland: The Frog Prince* (1972) and Eric Idle's *The Tale of the Frog Prince* (1982) produced by Shelley Duvall's Faerie Tale Theatre, mock the king and queen who want to arrange a marriage for their daughter. In contrast, one of the first films made by Tom Davenport, who has produced numerous Appalachian versions of the Grimms' tales, follows the traditional plot of the tale and essentially reinforces its patriarchal tendencies. The sexual drives of prince and frog are downplayed in his traditional version. However, sexuality is at the heart of David Kaplan's *The Frog King* (1994), a short black and white experimental film. In this version, the teenage princess is obviously disgusted by the phallic appearance of the frog, and her decrepit old parents, a peasant couple, old enough to be her grandparents, compel her to comply with the frog's desires. Kaplan ends his film with an ironic shot of the parents, who are content that their daughter is mating with the frog turned prince.

Perhaps the most interesting cinematic depiction of "The Frog Prince," which explores different kinds of courting and mating is the made-for-television film, *Prince Charming* (2001), directed by Allan Arkush. The setting is England in 1500, and young Prince John of Arkan is obliged to marry a princess from another realm to end years of the Tulip Wars. However, Prince John cannot keep his sword in his pants, and he is constantly rescuing damsels in distress only to seduce them. In fact, he runs off and copulates in a church tower with a luscious peasant woman on the day of his wedding. For this mistake he and his squire are transformed into frogs for eternity unless the prince can find a princess who will kiss him. Once he is transformed into a prince, however, he has five days to marry the princess and must remain true to her. Five hundred years pass, and Sir John and his squire are accidentally picked up as frogs by an American in England and transported to New York City. By chance, they make their home in Central Park, which they consider a forest, and Prince John is accidentally kissed by a vain actress playing different aristocratic roles in Shakespeare in the Park. He and the squire reassume their natural forms, and John soon falls in love with a young woman named Kate, who drives a horse and buggy in Central Park. It is only by demonstrating that he can keep his sword in his pants and be true to Kate that John, despite the curse, can retain his human shape.

There are all kinds of contemporary courting and mating practices portrayed in this sentimental film that is enlivened by the comic situations. The squire mates with a woman named Serena, the actress's assistant, because of her interest in magic. The actress, married three times, wants the director of Shakespeare in the Park to marry her, while she competes for him with a younger actress. Kate must be convinced that Prince John is not a con man because she has recently been dumped by a cad. None of the characters follow rules. Instead, their natural inclinations and mental deliberations determine their love interests and strategies, though it is clear that the men, especially Prince John and the director, are more apt to spread their sperm indiscriminately and perhaps have other relationships than with the "princesses" they choose to fulfill their lives. Apparently, their genes will sway their actions.

What is interesting about all these films and other cultural artifacts (books, stories, plays, cartoons, and so on) is that their "messages" or their reception are dependent on the reading and some knowledge of "The Frog Prince," whether it be through the text by the Brothers Grimm that is constantly republished in some form or another, through word of mouth, hearsay, advertisement, illustration, cartoon, poster, or some other kind of reference. Whatever the case may be, in most western societies, "The Frog Prince" exists as meme in millions of brains. Whether it will always remain there is difficult to say, but as long as men and women, whether heterosexual or homosexual, develop mating strategies that stem from their natural dispositions and mental capacities to make sexual choices influenced by changing social codes, "The Frog Prince" will play a role in the discourse about mating as a social symbolic act that will enable us to understand the ramifications of decisions we seem to make freely and decisions that are made for us.

And Nobody Lived Happily Ever After: The Feminist Fairy Tale after Forty Years of Fighting for Survival*   6

It is impossible today for anyone, male or female, whether heterosexual, transvestite, androgynous, homosexual, lesbian, sadist, masochist, straight, black, yellow, white, tan, or rainbow, to write a serious artful fairy tale, even comical or farcical, without taking into account the vast changes wrought by feminism in the last forty years. I am speaking now primarily about writers and the fairy tale in the USA and the UK. As a genre, the fairy tale has benefited greatly from a feminist re-vision and re-writing of the canonical tales generally represented by the works of Charles Perrault, Jacob and Wilhelm Grimm, and Hans Christian Andersen. In my opinion, the two most significant books that brought about a thoughtful, sensitive, and radical approach to the long entrenched tradition of patriarchal classical fairy tales were Anne Sexton's *Transformations* (1971) and Angela Carter's *The Bloody Chamber and Other Tales* (1979). These two seminal works in poetry and prose—and there were others, including feminist criticism—changed and expanded the genre in the 1970s so that it soon flourished in unimaginable ways in the next three decades and continues to flourish, despite a harsh backlash against feminist causes and the rise of insidious religious fundamentalism of all kinds throughout the world.

Ever since 1980 there has been an inextricable, dialectical development of

* Special thanks to Cristina Bacchilega and Carol Dines for their helpful suggestions and critical observations.

mutual influence among *all* writers of fairy tales and fairy-tale criticism that has led to innovative fairy-tale experiments in all cultural fields: the theater, the opera, the musical, film, art, ballet, television, publicity, cartoons, illustration, the Internet, and so on. Pierre Bourdieu has remarked that

> the literary or artistic field is a *field of forces*, but it is also a *field of struggles* tending to transform or conserve this field of forces. The network of objective relations between positions subtends and orients the strategies which the occupants of the different positions implement in their struggles to defend or improve their positions (i.e. their position-takings), strategies which depend for their force and form on the position each agent occupies in the power relations (*rapports de force*). . . . The meaning of a work (artistic, literary, philosophical, etc.) changes automatically with each change in the field within which it is situated for the spectator or reader.[1]

If we accept Bourdieu's notion that a cultural field of production is a force field of conflicts in which various writers, artists, and groups of people contend for power, then it is easy to see how the fairy tale has certainly been used in almost all cultural fields to articulate positions and to criticize societal contradictions that reveal disparities among the sexes, ethnic groups, and social classes. Gender issues and conflicts, in particular, are central to the positions taken by writers, artists, musicians, and filmmakers. Talented writers such as A. S. Byatt, Marina Warner, Margaret Atwood, Jane Yolen, Robert Coover, Francesca Lia Block, Emma Donoghue, Donna Jo Napoli, and numerous others have pried open the confines of the fairy tale in their novels and short stories to reveal gender stereotypes and to explore alternatives to prescribed societal modes of behavior. Kiki Smith has exhibited unusual sculptures and etchings of fairy-tale figures in her installations that provoke onlookers to question their assumptions about fairy tales and gender. Claire Prussian, Sharon Singer, Jo Ellen Rock, and Vanessa Jane Phaff have refigured fairy tales in their paintings and drawings that reveal some repulsive features of the tales that are not unrelated to the unfinished business of feminism. Pina Bausch has created a modern ballet about Bluebeard that turns the tale on its head. The musical *Into the Woods* (1991) written by Steven Sondheim and James Lapine has transformed several fairy tales into a tragic-comic operetta that does not end happily and makes us wonder whether we can ever rid the world of evil. In the anthology, *The Poets' Grimm* (2003), Jean Marie Beaumont and Claudia Carlson have produced the most comprehensive selection of fairy-tale poems of the twentieth century that indicate significant cross connections and major debates about the meanings of the canonical tales and how fairy tales are enmeshed in our lives. In the UK, Shahrukh Husain, who edited Angela Carter's last volume of *Virago Fairy Tales for Women* in 1990 as Carter was dying, went on to produce some important anthologies about strong vibrant women such as *Women Who Wear Breeches: Delicious and Dangerous Tales* (1995) and *Temptresses: The Virago Book of Evil Women* (1998). In America Ellen Datlow and Teri Windling have been responsible for a series of remarkable collections of tales, *Black Thorn, White Rose* (1993), *Snow White, Blood Red* (1994), *Ruby Slippers, GoldenTears* (1995), *Silver Birch, Blood Moon* (1999), *Black Heart, Ivory Bones* (2000), *A Wolf at the Door and Other Retold Fairy Tales* (2000), all of which include a large variety of fairy tales that take different positions regarding the sexes. Kathleen Ragan's *Fearless Girls, Wise Women and Beloved Sisters: Heroines in Folktales from Around the World* (1998) and Jane Yolen and Heidi Stemple's *Mirror, Mirror: Forty Folktales for Mothers and Daughters to Share* (2000) are explicitly dedicated to a feminist tradition of fairy and folk tales. There are now hundreds of fascinating fairy-tale websites or hits with hypertexts of varying quality including interactive programs that concern political and sexual struggle. Among the most interesting are "The Endicott Studio of Mythic Arts," "Sur-la-Lune," "Fair e-Tales," and Atomfilms.com, which has produced one of the most controversial cinematic renditions of "Little Red Riding Hood," called *Black XXX-mas*, that I have ever seen. It was also produced as a DVD and does not have a major distributor, nor do the important feminist films *Red Riding Hood* (1996) directed by David Kaplan and *The Red Shoes* (1999) and *The Little Match Girl* (1999) directed by Michael Sporn. But there are feature fairy-tale films produced for a larger international market such as *Freeway* (1996) and *Ever After* (1998) as well as *Shrek* (2001), *Shrek Two* (2003), and *Shrek Three* (2007), which portray intrepid female protagonists who manage to survive one disaster after another despite the fact that their societies offer little support as they seek to overcome prejudices, not just against women but against anyone who deviates from the social norm.

Of course, the myriad production of fairy tales in all the different cultural fields of production since the 1970s has not occurred without critics and scholars taking notice. In 2000, the American journal *Marvels & Tales* published a special issue focusing on "fairy tale liberation—thirty years later," and the essays in this issue were gathered into a book expanded by five new articles and published under the title *Fairy Tales and Feminism: New Approaches* (2004), edited by Donald Haase. In his preface, Haase stresses the importance of interdisciplinary work, and he provides a thorough and thoughtful analysis of feminist scholarship on fairy tales in an introductory essay. His focus is primarily on the important work produced in the last thirty years. However, he voices some dissatisfaction with a good deal of feminist criticism by citing Susan Gubar's essay "What Ails Feminist Criticism?" and by asserting:

Some feminist fairy-tale analyses remain stuck in a mode of interpretation able to do no more than reconfirm stereotypical generalizations about the fairy-tale's sexist stereotypes. Such studies are oblivious to the complexities of fairy-tale production and reception, socio-historical contexts, cultural traditions, the historical development of the genre, and the challenges of fairy-tale textuality.

Then he claims that

The essays in this volume demonstrate the possibilities of feminist-inspired fairy-tale studies and their potential to advance our understanding of the fairy tale. They eschew a monolithic view of the woman-centered fairy tale; allow for ambiguity within female-authored tales and for ambivalence in their reception; explore new texts and contexts; and reconsider the national, cultural, and generic boundaries that have shaped the fairy tale and often limited our understanding of it.[2]

Now I am not convinced that all the essays in Haase's book accomplish successfully what he believes they set out to do. However, he does raise some key questions that pertain to rewriting the canon in English-speaking women's literature by arguing for a more interdisciplinary and comparative approach to the study of fairy tales while retaining a more discriminating feminist perspective. Although I agree with Haase's general position, there are, of course, still some problems that need to be clarified when we talk about an interdisciplinary and sophisticated critique of fairy tales, otherwise the politics of the critique may become lost.

The problems concern largely our ideological understanding of rewriting fairy tales, the misconceptions about the development of the genre and the canon, and the present situation of feminism and whether women have ever really broken with the canon of fairy tales. In reconsidering where women's writing of fairy tales stands today, or, rather, feminist writing, I want to suggest that women have never broken with the past. Rather, they have seized it, made the past their own, and, in the case of fairy tales, have greatly influenced and inspired male writing. In this regard, I think it is a mistake to separate women's writing of fairy tales from men's writing, or to consider just women's literature alone. If writing, whether by women or men, is a political act, as Adrienne Rich, Fredric Jameson, Toril Moi, and others have argued, then it is important to appraise the present situation of fairy-tale writing by women and men in relation to the canon with regard not only to the production of new alternative texts but also to the reception and the position of fairy-tale writing in the fields of cultural production. To do justice to the accomplishments and difficulties of fairy-tale writing and especially feminist contributions to the genre of the fairy tale, I would have to write a book or several books. Therefore, I want to present several succinct theoretical premises and to examine some recent fairy-tale writing by women in America and the ramifications of this writing. For the most part, though I prefer not to do this, I shall be separating women's and men's writing of fairy tales because I think it is important for a critic to understand how non-hegemonic groups look within themselves for history, recognition, and affirmation, especially when the backlash against feminism is great, and how, in this particular historical period, women's writings and concerns continue to change the genre of the fairy tale as a whole, while contending with reactionary forces in American society.

First some theoretical premises:

1. It is misleading to think that the canon of fairy tales excluded women's writing or that it was totally constituted by men and totally served patriarchal interests. Nothing in the fairy-tale canon has ever been totally male or totally patriarchal, even though women's voices have constantly been obfuscated, discarded, and submerged. As Marina Warner and other feminist scholars of the fairy tale have demonstrated, women *and* men have always told tales for many thousands of years, and women played a crucial role in the European formation and cultivation of the fairy tale, especially as the oral tales interacted with and engendered literary tales. For instance, the inclusion of "Beauty and the Beast" in the canon of fairy tales was primarily due to the efforts of French women writers Mme d'Aulnoy, Mme de Villeneuve, and Mme Leprince de Beaumont, who were familiar with the tale of "Cupid and Psyche" and other oral beast/bridegroom stories; their versions of "Beauty and the Beast" reflect the dilemma of women writers, who extolled so-called female virtues that actually tended to reinforce the roles that men appreciated and cultivated for them. Still, women's concerns forged the canonization of this tale and others as well, and there is a good deal of sublimated outrage in early women's writing of fairy tales. The rage can easily be detected in the works of the French salon writers of the seventeenth century and also in the Victorian women's writing of the nineteenth century.[3]

2. Despite the continual efforts of women to make their voices heard in the formation and diffusion of the western fairy tale, the canon of fairy tales was, indeed, largely determined by men and played (and continues to play) a key role in the civilizing process of Europe and North America, as I have argued in my book, *Fairy Tales and the Art of Subversion*.[4] This civilizing process, though constituted by conflicting force fields of production, was and is still largely predicated on male values, social codes, literary standards, and needs, consistent with the development of capitalism and its processes and

operations. An analysis of fairy tales and the impact of feminism cannot be incisive and accomplish much today, I believe, without a critique of global capitalism. As Toril Moi has argued,

> feminist theory is critical theory; feminist critique is therefore necessarily political. In making this claim I draw on the Marxist concept of critique, succinctly summarized by Kate Soper as a theoretical exercise which, by "explaining the source in reality of the cognitive shortcomings of the theory under attack, calls for changes in the reality itself."[5]

3. As the fairy tale became instituted as a genre in the eighteenth century and as certain tales became canonized, women played an active role in disseminating, challenging, and appropriating the tales. They were never passive even if they accepted the sexist stereotypes in the canonical tales. Historically, it is largely through the rise of the suffragette movement at the end of the nineteenth century that women writers became more aware of the patriarchal implications and prejudices of the canon and thus began a more conscious revision of the classical tales, especially in the UK. But the classical tales were never discarded by women writers. They never broke with the past.

4. If there was something "revolutionary" about the Anne Sexton's *Transformations*, Angela Carter's *The Bloody Chamber and Other Tales*, and other feminist rewritings of the 1970s, it had nothing to do with a break with the past. Rather it had more to do with what Jürgen Habermas and other writers of the Frankfurt School have called "Aufarbeiten der Vegangenheit" or working through, absorbing, and elaborating the past. Both Sexton and Carter had a profound knowledge of the tales written by the Brothers Grimm and Perrault. In fact, Carter was actually translating Perrault's fairy tales while she wrote some of the tales for *The Bloody Chamber*. If one analyzes Sexton's poems and Carter's tales carefully, it becomes readily apparent that they had fully incorporated the canonical tales into their minds and bodies, and I mean this in a literal sense. They took these tales and made them part of their lives, felt them, sensed them, digested them, and re-generated them to comment politically on the situation of women in their times and on the struggles between the sexes. They appropriated and transformed the canonical tales for themselves and their times. It is only because they did *not* reject the canonical tales but *worked through* them to grasp how many of the problems in these tales, raised by these tales, were still with us that they were able to articulate their very particular positions as very different women who critically wrote about social and political norms in the American and British societies of their times.

5. We are living in very much different times than the 1970s. Some people call our time the era of globalization. Others call it a period dominated by the ideology of consumerism. Both of these labels have merit, but I prefer to try to grasp social and political relations in light of Guy Debord's notions elaborated in *Society of the Spectacle* (1995) and in light of the critical notions presented by Giorgio Agamben in his recent book, *Il Regno e la Gloria: Per una genealogica teologica dell'economia e del governo* (*The Realm and the Glory: Towards a Theological Geneology of Economy and Government*, 2007). Debord pointed out, we live in a world of the spectacle that causes our lives to be mediated and determined by illusory images. He explained that "the spectacle is not a collection of images; rather it is a social relationship between people that is mediated by images."[6] In particular, he examined the totalitarian or totalizing tendencies of the spectacle or what he called the specular, because the spectacle is constituted by signs of the dominant organization of production and reinforces behaviors and attitudes of passivity that allow for the justification of hierarchical rule, the monopolization of the realm of appearances, and the acceptance of the status quo. Only by grasping how the spectacle occludes our vision of social relations will we be able to overcome the alienation and separation that pervades our lives. Debord insisted that

> by means of the spectacle the ruling order discourses endlessly upon itself in an uninterrupted monologue of self-praise. The spectacle is the self-portrait of power in the age of power's totalitarian rule over the conditions of existence. . . . If the spectacle—understood in the limited sense of those "mass media" that are its most stultifying superficial manifestation—seems at times to be invading society in the shape of a mere *apparatus*, it should be remembered that this apparatus has nothing neutral about it, and that it answers precisely to the needs of the spectacle's internal dynamics. If the social requirements of the age which develops such techniques can be met only through their mediation, if the administration of society and all contact between people now depends on the intervention of such "instant" communication, it is because this "communication" is essentially *one-way*; the concentration of the media thus amounts to the monopolization by the administrators of the existing system of the means to pursue their particular form of administration.[7]

Agamben bases part of his study on Debord and Michel Foucault to build critically on their work; he explains how glory and acclamation have substantially become hegemonic modes of representation used by governments and corporations through the mass media to maintain their power.

> If we join the analyses of Debord with the theses of Carl Schmitt about public opinion as a modern form of acclamation, the whole problem of the contemporary domination of the spectacle by the media over every aspect of social life appears in a new

> dimension. . . . Contemporary democracy is a democracy fully based on glory, that is,
> on the efficacy of acclamation, multiplied and disseminated by the media beyond
> anyone's imagination.[8]

In short, from a highly critical if not pessimistic perspective, the voice of the
people in modern democracy is mainly manipulated to acclaim celebrities and
people of power rather than to evaluate them and grasp what functions they
are playing to reinforce the status quo.

6. If we have virtually no political voice except to acclaim (and perhaps to com-
    plain), what use is the fairy tale? What use is the woman's voice or a feminist
    position articulated through a fairy tale? Here I want to return to the sober
    position of Bourdieu, who believed that, even in politics and the economy,
    there were conflicting voices and images among those who reigned, and that it
    was possible to penetrate the spectacle of society through resistance. (And by
    the way, both Debord and Agamben clearly wrote their works to provoke
    readers to see what they don't see or don't want to see, i.e. to counter passivity
    and complacence.) Fundamentally, then, I want to ask, to what extent does
    women's writing of fairy tales in America today enable us to see what is
    happening before our eyes that glorifies and acclaims the present reign of
    power? Where is the resistance? How is it expressed through the fairy tale? Is
    there any hope provided by the fairy tale?

About fifty years ago the great German philosopher of hope, Ernst Bloch,
insisted that the fairy tale would always address what is lacking in society and
would illuminate a better future. Strange to say, the "utopian" fairy tale is more
alive in hopeless America than in any other country of the West. Libraries,
bookstores, and Internet sites such as Amazon are filled with fairy tales for
children, adolescents, and adults. The Disney corporation continues to spew out
fairy-tale films in all kinds of formats: DVDs, CDs, live-action films, animated
films, and it also makes millions of dollars each year through various kinds of
toys, games, clothes, products, and theme parks. Hundreds of canonical fairy-tale
operas, musicals, and plays are performed each year throughout America. Commercials and television programs thrive on fairy-tale motifs. Publishers produce
special fairy-tale series, while universities offer numerous courses that deal with
the fairy tale. Most recently, in 2005, another one of many self-help books that
use fairy tales to explain the world has appeared with the title, *Spinning Straw into
Gold: What Fairy Tales Reveal about the Transformations in a Woman's Life*. Its
author, Joan Gould, following in the footsteps of neo-Jungians and popular psychologists, de-historicizes fairy tales and their reception and blissfully explains

how fairy tales record the three primary transformations of maiden, matron, and crone that women must learn to recognize and accept. Her key theme is that females are the vehicles for transformations in this world, that they are not passive. Yet, she makes claims for fairy-tale heroines that are misinformed if not completely false. In a reader's guide to her book, she maintains that feminists have misunderstood fairy tales, as though women were really the source of the canonical tales that represent the natural cycles that bring about wholeness.[9] Gould's book is not alone in preaching the beneficial aspects of the classical fairy tales in contemporary America. It is, indeed, somewhat of a paradox that one of the most violent, stressful, and religious cultures in the world thrives on the happy-ever-after of false endings of the fairy tale in almost all cultural fields. Or is it a paradox?

One of the important political purposes of women's writing of fairy tales was to demonstrate that nobody lived happily ever after the fairy tale seemingly ended, whether in fantasy or reality, and nobody will ever live happily ever after unless we change not only fairy-tale writing but social and economic conditions that further exploitative and oppressive relations among the sexes, races, and social classes. This general purpose is still at the root of the best and most serious writing of fairy tales by women, but it has become more and more difficult to make this message heard because feminism and the fairy tale have both been co-opted by the mass media and the society of the spectacle.

For the most part, the fairy tale has become commercialized in America, and the majority of the fairy tales produced for children and adults pay lip service to feminism by showing how necessary it is for young and old women alike to become independent without challenging the structural embodiment of women in all the institutions that support the present socio-economic system. Some good examples of commercialized fairy tales are the series of fairy-tale books for young readers by Gail Carson Levine (*Ella Enchanted*, 1997; *The Princess Test*, 1999; *The Fairy's Test*, 1999; *Cinderellis and the Glass Hill*, 2000) and the numerous DAW Books anthologies such as *Little Red Riding Hood in the Big Bad City* (2004), edited by Martin Greenberg and John Helfers, *Rotten Relations* (2004), and *Hags, Sirens, and Other Bad Girls of Fantasy* (2006), edited by Denise Little. Yet, despite the predictability of the plot and stereotypical characters, Levine's stories have the virtue of supporting strong female protagonists, and some of the many stories in American fairy-tale anthologies edited by Greenberg and Little are serious, inventive narratives that do not cater to the lowest common denominator of reader comprehension. However, it is striking how most of the authors try to service the market interests of publishers and coyly play with language and plot to awaken interest in how cleverly they can manipulate fairy-tale motifs. The depth of these fairy tales, even when they may be feminist, is low.

Yet, not every writer of fairy tales in the twenty-first century writes for the market. The implied readership of serious writers, in my opinion, is constituted by dissidents, or readers willing to listen to and read dissident voices that speak to people troubled by the degeneration of American culture. The works of three young authors, Aimee Bender, Lauren Slater, and Kelly Link, along with some writers of stories and poems in two of the recent issues of the *Fairy Tale Review*, edited by Kate Bernheimer, will serve as examples of the adversarial approach to socio-political developments taken by women. Instead of focusing directly on gender issues and radicalizing the canon, women writers nowadays tend to depict baffled and distressed women and men caught in a maize of absurd situations. In doing this, they are endeavoring to unravel the causes of their predicaments and use narrative strategies that both reflect the degeneration of communication and are somewhat degenerate themselves. The result is dissent that seeks to disassociate writer and reader from the brutalization and banalization of American life, but it is also a dissent that is worrisome, for it reflects how estranged Americans are from one another.

Indeed, something uncanny has been happening to America and to the fairy tale that seems related to our postmodern psychotic times. The fairy tale has become more charged with neurotic intensity and more layered. It is also able to evoke a startling feeling of reality even with bizarre characters and events. Yet, Sigmund Freud asserted the contrary in his famous essay on E. T. A. Hoffmann's "The Sandman" and the uncanny,[10] declaring that the fairy tale was too predictable and anticipated the expectations of readers. Only unpredictable fantasy literature, he claimed, could awe readers, make them hesitate and question the fine line between imaginative and real worlds. To say the least, Freud was completely wrong. Hoffmann, the very subject of his essay, not only wrote dark and lurid stories in the nineteenth century but also disturbing fairy tales that we might today designate as tales of magic realism that celebrated the utopian potential of art and the artist. His unique style and approach to fairy tales has been carried on well into the twenty-first century as can be seen in Aimee Bender's two collections of startling short stories, *The Girl in the Flammable Skirt* and *Willful Creatures*. Bender has managed to transform the short story into an exquisite and terse narrative form that combines elements of the folk tale, magic realism, the grotesque, and the macabre and that ruptures readers' expectations. It is difficult to categorize her stories because they are so bizarre and so realistic at the same time. Obviously, she is following in the footsteps of other writers of magic realism and postmodernism such as Angela Carter, Salman Rushdie, A. S. Byatt, Isabel Allende, Donald Bartheleme, and Robert Coover. Bender's perspective reminds me also of Kafka's; however, she is at times more preposterous than Kafka. The first sentences of her tales begin with such phrases as "God put a gun to the writer's head," "the boy was born with fingers shaped like keys," "the pumpkin-head couple got married," or "the man went to the pet store to buy himself a little man to keep him company," and the reader must accept the preposterous proposal of the narrative unconditionally until he or she becomes caught in a web of incredible but comprehensible circumstances. The paratactic sentences build upon one another and assert themselves as truths that cannot be denied. Nothing is strange or unreal in Bender's stories because everything is so concrete. The unreal condition is an immediate given and takes over the characters and the reader at the same time so that all unimaginable inferences and possibilities appear to be realistic and viable. Time after time, Bender tells tales that assume the form of contemporary marvelous folk tales because the strange types that inhabit her worlds become recognizable and familiar through their weird behavior. For instance, in "Meeting" she reverses the traditional role-playing of the fairy tale and the stereotypical notion of love at first sight. The story begins this way:

> The woman he met. He met a woman. This woman was the woman he met. She was not the woman he expected to meet or planned to meet or had carved into his head in full dress with a particular nose and eyes and lips and a particular brain. No, this was a different woman, the one he met. When he met her he could hardly stand her because she did not fit the shape in his brain of the woman he had planned so vigorously and extensively to meet. And the non-fit was uncomfortable and made his brain hurt. Go away, woman, he said, and the woman laughed, which helped for a second.[11]

We never discover the name of either the man or the woman, but what we discover is that she resists his expectations and does what she desires, only to find that the man continues to return to her, upset, and yet wanting to marry her. In the end, they come together, and we never know what will happen to their relationship, except that he will become different. Clearly, the man has no idea why he wants to be with her. Their relationship is based entirely on estrangement, not on the happy fulfillment of a fairy tale.

In another tale, "Debbieland," told in the first person plural by a troubled and blunt-speaking lesbian, the question of change and difference is treated with more irony. The narrator, totally unaware of how offensive and narrow-minded she is, seemingly speaks for what she believes to be all women through her use of "we". She maligns and beats up a teenage classmate named Debbie, who is like a straight innocent fairy-tale princess, while they are in high school. She does this, she thinks, in the name of all women. Many years later, after various experiences including an unrequited love affair, the narrator meets Debbie, who is married and a contented mother, while the narrator still appears to be very discontent and disturbed. Debbie wants to know why the narrator treated her so cruelly and informs the narrator that her real name is Anne. When the narrator is helpless to explain her behavior, Anne leaves her in disgust. Nevertheless, the narrator rationalizes the situation, and by deceiving herself, she feels somewhat liberated. Bender's narrative, though not a fairy tale per se, comments on the self-hate and self-denial of a gay woman, who envies the typical fairy-tale girl.

Though Bender does not offer penetrating psychological explanations to explain the actions of her characters, she has a remarkable capacity to make us wonder about and probe the minds of the protagonists. They generally act out of desperation or unusual situations that reveal a great deal about their mind-sets, helplessness, and the absurdities of life that exclude closure. This is because Bender is an ironical and skeptical writer who opens up different horizons that have no endings and awaken us to the relative conditions of a world that lacks foundation and legitimacy. If the relations in the world are indeed more specular than anything else, that is, dependent on the spectacle, Bender's narratives tend to invert fairy-tale and fantastic motifs to puncture the charades of the artifice of social life and to reveal its absurd aspects.

In Lauren Slater's book, *Blue Beyond Blue: Extraordinary Tales for Ordinary Dilemmas* (2005), she, too, has given a Kafkaesque twist to the sixteen stories in her collection. They all begin on familiar terrain and appear to be traditional fairy tales or stories with fairy-tale motifs, but within seconds they quickly baffle and unsettle us so that we must dispense with conventional cues and motifs that usually help us navigate through fairy-tale plots. Slater deftly turns fairy tales into traumatic dream worlds in which her protagonists are compelled to deal with weird predicaments that resemble Alice's horrendous experiences once she falls down the rabbit hole, or Gregor Samsa's plight when he is turned into a huge insect. Take, for instance, Slater's title tale, "Blue Beyond Blue," in which a childless woman finds an egg that grows until she slits it open with a surgical knife. Out pops a three-year-old girl, who eventually sprouts wings as a teenager. To keep her from flying away, the woman cuts off her wings while the girl sleeps. Later, when the "daughter," now a young woman, falls in love with an acrobat, her mother must explain her past to her, and her wings sprout again. Then the daughter marries, gets pregnant, and hatches an egg. Out pops a boy with a note requesting that he be returned to the blue beyond the blue when he grows up.

The weird incidents in each one of Slater's tales threaten the psychological stability of the protagonist. Although the world seems or turns absurd, Slater indicates that psychological crises may enable people to grow and become stronger. Time and again she compels her protagonists to grapple with the reality of absurd situations. In "My Girlfriend's Arm," Seamus, the first-person narrator, who is afraid of marriage, informs us that on the day he broke with his lover, she left behind one of her arms. As time passed, other body parts of women mysteriously joined the arm until a mulatto woman was formed. Only after he is blindfolded is he able to accept a new woman into his life. In "The Mermaid," the narrator is a teenage girl, who falls in love with a new classmate, an odd mermaid. After a brief fling, the mermaid jilts her for a boy and sends the narrator into a depression—unreciprocated love as in Andersen's "The Little Mermaid" brings about torment. Yet, as the roles are reversed, so is the message, and the young girl learns to breathe and swim under water and inhale her grief.

Slater has a unique style. It is almost matter-of-fact and has a terse staccato rhythm. The lines between real and imaginary fuse, but rarely is there a smooth ending. Unlike Bender's stories, her plots tend to have cathartic endings that prompt the reader to reflect on the hazardous journey of the protagonist. At times her stories turn into psychological parables intended to assist her "patient" readers to live with contradictions and to grasp their strange dreams, or at least, to stir them to think about separation, death, unfulfilled wishes, disappointment, and so on.

While Slater, a professional psychologist, believes that her tales may provide therapeutic release for her readers, there is rarely any release or relief in any of Kelly Link's tales in *Magic for Beginners* (2005). Like Bender's stories, they all begin enigmatically or preposterously: "Fox is a television character, and she isn't dead yet," "Cats went in and out of the witch's house all day long," or "Q: And who will be fired out of the cannon? A: My brother will be fired out of the canon." However, unlike Bender's tales that have an unsettling logic to them, the nonsense in Link's tales do not always make sense. The stories are unnerving and sometimes boring because of the constant repetition of non sequiturs, and plots that lead nowhere while seemingly following some kind of traditional narrative structure. The motto of her tales is announced in her introductory story, "The Fairy Handbag": "Promise me that you won't believe a word." In almost every tale there are aside remarks to the reader that function like estrangement effects; they continually compel the reader to step back and reflect on the veracity of the narrator. It is, of course,

obvious that the narrator can never be trusted, and it is even questionable sometimes whether it is worthwhile reading further into the labyrinths that Link creates.
Yet, many of the opaque stories are compelling and often raise questions that
pertain to dissolution of identity through words that provide very little meaning
and validation of identity. In "Catskin," for instance, one of the few tales that recalls
some traditional fairy-tale motifs, a bizarre mother witch steals, buys, and creates
children because she wants heirs. And in the course of the years, the narrator
explains,

> Some of the children had run away and others had died. Some of them she had simply
> misplaced, or accidentally left behind on buses. It is to be hoped that these children were
> later adopted into good homes, or reunited with their natural parents. If you are looking for
> a happy ending in this story, then perhaps you should stop reading here and picture these
> children, these parents, their reunions.

Then there is a pause, and the narrator continues in another typical aside remark to
the reader. "Are you still reading? The witch, up in her bedroom, was dying. She
had been poisoned by an enemy, a witch, a man named Lack."[12]

What follows is similar to the plot of a traditional fairy tale like "Puss in Boots,"
but much more bizarre. The dying mother gives three gifts to three of her children
Flora, Jack, and Small. The two eldest depart to explore the world, and Small takes
a brush and is guided to take revenge on Lack by a large white cat named "The
Witch's Revenge," who enables Small to change back and forth into a cat. Together
they wreak revenge on the male witch Lack, and after numerous adventures that
involve manifold transformations with Small growing bigger, he finally learns that
his mother is dead and is reunited with her mother through The Witch's Revenge.
In the end, the narrator tells us: "There is no such thing as witches, and there is no
such thing as cats, either, only people dreamed up in catskin suits. They have their
reasons, and who is to say that they might not live that way, happily ever after, until
the ants have carried away all of the time that there is, to build something new and
better out of it?"[13]

Link spoofs the fairy-tale stereotypical gender types in all her tales that the
Internet encyclopedia Wikipedia has described as "slipstream," a combination of
science fiction, fantasy, horror, mystery, and realism. In one of her best fairy tales,
"Travels with the Snow Queen," published in her first collection of "slipstream"
stories, *Stranger Things Happen* (2000), she articulates a position that indicates the
direction that most feminists and women writers have been taking for the last
twenty years or more. It begins in media res: "Part of you is always traveling faster,
always traveling ahead. Even when you are moving, it is never fast enough to

satisfy that part of you."[14] The brief introductory passage clues the reader into realizing that this narrative, told entirely and brilliantly in the second person singular, will revise Andersen's "The Snow Queen," and she ends the introduction by asking: "Ladies, has it ever occurred to you that fairy tales aren't easy on the feet?"[15]

This is a tale told to women, for women, about women. (Of course, male readers can read it and learn a lesson or two.) Link expunges all the pathetic Christian sentimentalism and mysticism from Andersen's tale to recount the story of a young woman who has an argument with her lover Kay, and the next morning, when he goes out to buy some cigarettes, he disappears, supposedly carried away by a beautiful woman in a long white sleigh pulled by thirty white geese. At first, the young woman, whose name is Gerda, hesitates about pursuing him. Then we learn from the narrator that finally after two months,

> you left and locked the door behind you. You were going to travel for love, without shoes, or cloak, or common sense. This is one of the things a woman can do when her lover leaves her. It's hard on the feet perhaps, but staying at home is hard on the heart, and you weren't quite ready to give him up yet. You told yourself that the woman in the sleigh must have put a spell on him, and he was probably already missing you. Besides, there are some questions you want to ask him, some true things you want to tell him. This is what you told yourself.[16]

What follows can be regarded as a mock journey that follows Andersen's plot of "The Snow Queen." Gerda encounters the princess, the robber's daughter, the reindeer's mother, the wise woman of Lapland along her journey that tears up her bare feet. Each encounter, however, questions Andersen's tale and compels Gerda to question whether it is worth pursuing Kay, because all the women she meets tell her that he doesn't love her anymore. Still, she must discover this for herself, and she does. What she learns is that Kay is not worth the trouble to liberate, that the Snow Queen is not an oppressor, and that her feet are perfectly good for traveling and exploring alternatives in the world. Ironically, Link has Gerda accept a proposition by the Snow Queen to set up a travel agency, and the story that had been told is actually a record of how Gerda came to open a travel agency called "Snow Queen" to lead other women on trips of self-discovery.

All of the tales written by Link, Bender, and Slater begin with the assumption that women are indefinable and must define themselves in a world that pretends to have stable and homogenized norms of gender while in actuality these arbitrary and prescribed norms, set for the most part by male-dominated "specular" relations in a society of spectacle, are being exposed and critiqued not only by feminist writers but by numerous concerned social organizations and writers consisting of people from all walks of life. The emphasis on resistance to male engendered norms in women's writing of fairy tales is also notable in the two issues of the *Fairy Tale Review* founded by Kate Bernheimer in 2005. Bernheimer has also edited an important anthology titled *Mirror, Mirror on the Wall: Women Writers Explore their Favorite Fairy Tales* (2002), which is self-explanatory, and two novels, *The Complete Tales of Ketzia Gold* (2001) and *The Complete Tales of Merry Gold* (2006), parts of a trilogy that employs folk-tale motifs to describe the survival strategies of three unusual sisters. In the *Fairy Tale Review* Bernheimer has not set a feminist agenda of any kind. She wants to publish diverse types of fairy-tale experiments that reveal the profound nature of the fairy tale as a genre. It is not by chance, however, that gender issues play a significant role in the stories, poems, and excerpts from novels published in the journal. For example Ayse Papatya Bucak's very brief tale, "Once There Was, Once There Wasn't" concerns a sultan's daughter and the son of a fishmonger who fall in love. The narrator tells us:

> When the girl loved the boy he knew what it was to be a fish set free into the rushing straits of the Bosporus after being caught in the crowded net of a fishmonger. And when the boy loved the girl, she knew what it was to be five flowers lifted on a single breath. And as for the rest of the story, well, it was not as good, and it is not happy, and it is not love. But once it was.[17]

Social class continues to destroy and limit love relationships that appear possible in a traditional fairy tale which often recounts incidents of a peasant marrying a princess. Bucak's narrative is a sober reflection of the false impressions left by the canonical tale. Differences are not so easily bridged, and there is a sense of longing for difference and alternatives that haunt the tales and poems written by women in this issue of the *Fairy Tale Review*. In one of the fairy-tale poems, "Finding the Lark," Carmen Giminez Smith depicts the dilemma of young women bound by the strictures of a well-to-do provincial village or suburbia. The poem begins:

Once there was a milkman
Who wore a lark on her shoulder

Good God Gave her a Lark.
Good God broke His Shoulder
on the Slippery Walk.

Because the houses of Quiet Restraint
had so few gifts in them. Because mothers
lived quiet as a ring in a velvet box.

One spoke into the other
they spoke of our longing.
In this way they decided what
to offer us: salves, furs,
cigarettes wrapped in linden leaves.[18]

The female milkman and her lark are liberating forces for the young women and urge the daughters to burn down their modest houses. But one day the lark disappears, and the narrator's mother, whom she thought she knew but did not, goes in search of the lark. In the last part of the poem, we read:

Because our pencils became dull. Because
the ink ran dry. Because the smoke cleared.
Because the wind was cold at our shoulders.
Because our fathers were ghosts of industry.
Because our mothers wrapped themselves in cloaks
at night. Every night, they looked in the trees.
Su-weet, they called out, searching for the source of smoke.
Sweet Girl. They became strangers with sticks in their hair.
Lark, come home. Lark, find the milkman, she needs
you. When the milkman kisses me, she tastes like soot.[19]

What has apparently gone missing in the lives of the young women is the Lark's song, *Arson is Invention*. But the poem indicates that much more has gone missing from the lives of the young women that have gone dry. The lark as a symbol of inspiration, truth, innovation, and love points to the lack and gaps not only in the lives of women but in those of most people, young and old. In other stories in this issue such as Rikki Ducornet's "Blue Funk" and such poems as Jean Marie Beaumont's "Is Rain My Bearskin?" and "Ma Belle," and Kate Meads' "On the Palace Steps, She Pauses" the obtuse meanings, disjointed language, and unsettled moods are characteristic of a disturbing feature of postmodern writing.

In her significant groundbreaking study, *Postmodern Fairy Tales: Gender and Narrative Strategies* (1997), Cristina Bacchilega argued that the postmodern rewriting of fairy tales

involves substantive though diverse questioning of both narrative construction and assumptions about gender. Nor is such a narrative and ideological critique necessarily one-sided or negative. Postmodern revision is often two-fold, seeking to expose, make visible, the fairy tale's complicity with "exhausted" narrative and gender ideologies, and, by working from the fairy tales' multiple versions, seeking to expose, bring out, what the institutionalization of such tales for children has forgotten or left unexploited. This kind of rereading does more than interpret anew or shake the genre's ground rules. It listens for the many "voices" of fairy tales as well.[20]

Following Bacchilega, Cathy Lynn Preston has studied recent cartoons, films, and television programs and maintains that, "although no performance has displaced the authority associated with the older fairy-tale genre, contemporary texts have cumulatively achieved a competitive authority, one that is fragmented, multivocal, fraught with contestation, and continually emergent."[21]

Bacchilega and Preston clearly demonstrate that, whether fairy tales are written by women or men, postmodernism has led to a blurring of genres and genders within the fairy-tale experimentation, and the experimentation and innovation have diminished the authority of the cannon. Yet, along with the subversion of the genre, it appears to me that there are recent disconcerting textual and visual signs in women's writing of fairy tales that need to be distinguished within the glow of "positive" postmodern writing.

Women's writing of all kinds, whether modern or postmodern, has not always been resistant to the standard and acceptable modes of writing because of the way many women have positioned themselves complicitly within capitalist organizations and because of a habitus of collusion within their respective societies. If some American women writers have used the fairy tale to refract images of gender and to communicate discontent and rebellion, they have always asked whether it is possible to survive in a society filled with collusion, complicity, violence, mutilation, prejudice, lies, deceit, and illusions. More recently, mutilation and survival are directly connected to their language, for the images and metaphors employed by women writers are often reflective of general conditions in America. Whereas early feminist fairy tales in the 1970s and 1980s tended, I believe, to try stridently to establish a position of authority within the genre and exuded hope that once this authority was established and women possessed the equality that they sought legally and socially, the fairy tales of the 1990s and early twenty-first century show the crippling effects of bitter struggles for survival in American society that grants women the rights they have sought, only as long as they contribute to the continual exploitation of human and natural resources demanded by the present socio-economic and political system. Communication in American cultural fields often becomes muted and mutilated because of the manner in which relations are mediated to become specular and only allow for a monologue of praise and glory among the ruling classes. In explaining how Bourdieu can enable us to grasp how relations function within cultural fields, Toril Moi remarks,

If the field as a whole, however, functions as a form of censorship, every discourse within the field becomes at once an enactment and an effect of *symbolic violence*. This is so because a field is a particular structure of distribution of a specific kind of capital. The right to speak, *legitimacy*, is invested in those agents recognized by the field as powerful possessors of capital. Such individuals become spokespersons for the *doxa* and struggle to relegate challengers to their position as *heterdox*, as lacking capital, as individuals whom one cannot *credit* with the right to speak. The powerful possessors of symbolic capital become the wielders of symbolic power, and thus of symbolic violence. But given the fact that all agents in the field to some extent share the same habitus, such richly endowed agents' right to power is implicitly *recognized* by all, and not least by those who aspire one day to oust them from their thrones. That different factions within the (battle)field fight to the bitter end over politics, aesthetics, or theory does not mean that they do not to some extent share the same habitus; in the very act of engaging in battle, they mutually and silently demonstrate their recognition of the rules of the game. It does not follow, as far as I can see, that they will all play the game *in the same way*. The different positions of different players in the field require different strategies.[22]

Women have staked out different positions in different cultural fields as declared feminists or as women non-involved in or even opposed to feminist causes, depending on their habitus. In almost all cultural fields, the fairy tale as genre has been employed to articulate a position with regard to identity, gender, and many other different social and political issues. As the battles for dominance within cultural, social, and political fields has, to my mind, become more vicious, the writing, performing, and producing of fairy tales has become more intense, and the fairy tale's characteristics are marked by the attitudes of the contenders for legitimacy and power. Thus far, the canon of fairy tales within different fields of cultural production has not been effaced, but it is frayed and torn at its edges. The dissent and dissonance expressed by women writers of fairy tales have left powerful tell-tale marks that urge a reconsideration of how we form gender, class, and race relations. Whether the fairy-tale canon will ever be transformed by women's writing to allow for clearer, more joyful and hopeful artistic expression will not depend on magic and wishful thinking, but on fostering illumination of alternatives and strong resistance to playing by the rules of the game as they exist and on writing with the purpose of enabling readers to recognize how the games are tilted to blind us to the realities of political struggle.

Storytelling as Spectacle in the Globalized World 7

Once upon a time, many years ago. . . . No, let's change this story. I'm not going to tell a fairy tale.

Once upon Our time, Truth suddenly vanished from the globe.

When people soon realized what had happened, they were greatly distressed, and they immediately sent five wise men in search of Truth. One went in this direction and the other in that. All of them were fully equipped with traveling expenses and good intentions. For ten long years they searched all over the globe. When they finally began returning to the people and saw each other from a distance, they waved their hats. Each one shouted that he had found Truth.

The first stepped forward and declared Truth to be Science. He was not able to finish his report, however, because one of the other wise men pushed him aside and accused him of lying. Instead, he proclaimed Truth to be Religion and that he had found it. The man of Science became furious, and while he began arguing with the man of Religion, a third wise man announced in beautiful words that Love was clearly Truth. But he was contradicted by the fourth man, who stated, quite curtly, that he had Truth in his pocket, that it was Gold, and that all the rest was childish nonsense. Finally the fifth wise man arrived. Yet, he had trouble standing on his legs. With a gurgling laugh, he confessed that Truth was Wine. He had found Truth in Wine, after looking everywhere.

Since the five wise men couldn't come to an agreement, they began fighting mercilessly and battered each other so brutally that it was horrible to see. The man of Science had his head broken, while the man of Love was covered with so much dirt that he had to change his clothes before he could show himself in respectable society. The man of Gold was so thoroughly stripped of all his glitter and coating that people realized he was worthless. When the man of Wine's bottle broke, the wine flowed into the ground and became muddy. But the man of Religion came off worst of all: everybody took a whack at him and belittled him so that he became the laughingstock of all the spectators and almost lost his faith.

Soon the people took sides, some with this one and some with that, and they shouted so loudly and began pushing each other so violently that they could neither see nor hear because of the noise. Meanwhile, some of the people sat down and mourned because they thought that Truth had been torn to pieces and would never be made whole again.

Now, as they sat there, a little girl came running up and said that she had found Truth. It was not far from where they were sitting, she said, and she asked them to come with her. Truth was sitting in the midst of the world, in a green meadow.

Slowly the people stopped fighting, for the little girl looked so very sweet, and they wanted to believe her. First one person went with her, then another, and ever more. . . . At last, when they were all in the meadow, they discovered a figure the likes of which they had never seen before. It was impossible to determine whether it was a man or a woman, an adult or a child. Its forehead was pure as that of one who knows no sin; its eyes deep and serious as those of one who has read into the hearts of all human beings. Its mouth opened with the brightest smile and then quivered with a great sadness impossible to describe. Its hand was soft as a mother's and strong as the hand of a worker; its foot trod the earth firmly, yet crushed not a flower. Most fascinating of all, the figure had large, soft wings, like the birds that fly at night.

Now as the people stood there and stared, the figure drew itself erect and cried, in a voice that sounded like bells ringing:

"I am Truth!"

"It's a Fairy Tale!" said the man of Science.

"Just a Fairy Tale!" cried the men of Religion, Love, Gold and Wine.

Convinced in their opinions, the five wise men and their followers stormed away. They resumed their fighting until the world was shaken to its core. But a few old and weary men and women and a few young men and women with ardent and eager souls and thousands of children with great wide eyes—all these people remained in the meadow where the Fairy Tale has continued to exist even up to our very day.[1]

I have begun this essay about storytelling in a globalized world with the nineteenth-century Danish writer Carl Ewald's wonderfully provocative tale because it is impossible to discuss the nature of storytelling today without talking about the global neglect of truth and authenticity. It is also frustrating and exasperating to talk about storytelling in our contemporary world in any kind of general way because of the immense diversity and complexity of storytelling, and because the truth claims about where the heart of storytelling lies and what storytelling is are often fallacious, deceitful, nefarious, and ignorant. Even those sincere and inspired endeavors to extol and explore the profound spiritual and ontological essence of storytelling often gush with so much religious reverence that the practical nature of storytelling as vital and practical communication is grossly obfuscated. As we all know, we live in a world of lies in which states, business conglomerates, the mass media, educational institutions, and organized religions use story to cloud truths and to devastate the lives of millions of human beings. We live in a world in which truth has been abandoned for the spectacle of cruel and imperious deceit.

But this does not mean that we should abandon storytelling to the deceivers, nor should we hark back to and long for the simple days when storytelling was more communal and perhaps more beneficial to people. Nostalgic longing for authentic storytelling and truth, even when such storytelling is utopian and can push us forward, cannot help us make our way through the barbed-wire network of multi-functional storytelling and spectacle in our globalized world. What might help us, I believe, is a clear, critical, sociological analysis of what has happened to storytelling with the advent of globalization and of where each one of us concretely stands, given the immense social and political changes that have occurred in the world in which we seemingly live side by side with people in distant areas of the globe where their wars, conflicts, and diseases are virtually ours. Sometimes even their joys. So I want to ask: What role does storytelling play in a globalized world that appears to bring us closer together while tearing us apart? And to try to answer my own question, I shall first say a few words about what I personally mean by the term globalization and then talk about storytelling as a cultural field of production and the problems faced by storytellers in a global society of spectacle and consumerism. Finally, I want to make some observations about the dilemma of sincere professional storytellers, who seek to celebrate story with integrity when the rights to storytelling are being contested and monopolized by celebrities, corporate voices, and media moguls.

Globalization

Globalization is both a euphemistic and a very precise term referring to the process of advanced capitalism that began to flourish in the 1980s and created greater free trade and economic, social, and cultural interdependence among states, especially since the dissolution of the Soviet Union in the 1990s. It has brought about the adaptation of capitalist market and production practices in China and other so-called communist countries and has played a significant role in the rapid modernization of developing countries such as India, South Korea, and Indonesia. Economically and technologically globalization has fostered the rise of multi-national corporations, the centralization of worldwide banking and financing, the increase of cultural and social contacts between people and groups of different classes and ethnic groups, the domination and homogenization of cultural values of the West, and increased divisions of social classes and contested areas of conflict in belief systems. Globalization is a term that has been defined positively and negatively in hundreds of ways so that it appears as though it were self-explicable; it seems entirely natural that we use the term even though we may not really understand what it means. Indeed, it has already reached mythic proportions, for almost everyone accepts that we are living in an age of globalization almost as if it were fate and ordained by the gods. We sense that the globe is getting smaller and are told that it is wonderful that the world is getting smaller, and aside from being obliged to affirm our loyalty to and membership in our particular nation-states, we are encouraged to become and feel that we should become good global citizens. Yet, like any mythic age, the age of globalization is filled with contradictions, for as many of us know and sense, the more we are globally in touch with one another, the further apart we grow, not only from other people in our local communities but from ourselves.

In *Globalization: The Human Consequences* (1998), Zygmunt Bauman focused on what I consider the major contradiction of globalization by analyzing how time and space are now organized so that there are greater differentiation and differences in our lives.

> *Rather than homogenizing the human condition, the technological annulment of temporal/ spatial distances tends to polarize it.* It emancipates certain humans from territorial constraints and renders certain community-generating meanings extraterritorial—while denuding the territory, to which other people go on being confined, of its meaning and its identity-endowing capacity. For some people it augurs an unprecedented freedom from obstacles and unheard-of ability to move and act from a distance. For others, it portends the impossibility of appropriating and domesticating the locality from which they have little chance of cutting themselves free in order to move elsewhere. With "distances no longer meaning anything," localities separated by distances, also lose their meanings. This, however, augurs freedom of meaning-creation for some, but portends ascription to meaninglessness for others. Some can now move out of the locality—any locality—at will. Others watch helplessly the sole locality they inhabit moving away from under their feet.[2]

Following in the footsteps of Max Weber, who lamented the dissolution or transformation of *Gemeinschaft* (community) into *Gesellschaft* (society) at the beginning of the twentieth century, Bauman goes one step further at the onset of the twenty-first century to demonstrate that space and time have been reorganized by state powers and multinational corporate forces so that the majority of people can be more tightly administered, regulated, and controlled, thereby limiting autonomy and self-definition. At the same time certain people are given privileges so that they can transcend space and time really or virtually to profit from the reorganization of capitalism that pervades and determines the lives of people all over the globe. The hyper rapidity of technological and social changes brings about a clear non-synchronicity in the majority of people's lives that have brought us precipitously to the brink of global disaster. The term non-synchronicity (*Ungleichzeitigkeit*) was conceived by Ernst Bloch, the great German philosopher of hope, in 1935 when he sought to analyze in his book *Heritage of Our Times* (*Erbschaft unserer Zeit*) why and how the Nazis came to power. Simply put, Bloch maintained that modernity and industrial capitalism and all the momentous changes that they engendered made most people feel out-of-step with the times. They felt passed over, trampled, and discarded and thus longed for security and solid traditions that endowed their lives with deep-rooted meaning. The Great Depression of 1929 and the immense political and religious battles during the Weimar period widened the non-synchronicity and engendered greater disparities and extreme proposals for creating harmony and security—to bring people in step with the times and/or to harness the times to respond to the deep needs of the people. The Nazis offered a mythic system of beliefs and practices that appeared to be grounded in German tradition and history, while the social democrats and communists argued among themselves and overlooked how technology and urbanization were fostering rapid transformations that bewildered people. Not only did the Nazis attract floundering and under-nourished people, they developed close-knit and tightly controlled communities and bonds while retelling the so-called betrayal of the German people by alien forces as a messianic triumph of the German people led by a chosen leader named Hitler, who resembled the sleeping King Barbarossa.

Mythic storytelling was the key to the success of the Nazis, and it took the form of what Walter Benjamin called the aestheticization of politics. Numerous storytellers of all kinds rose to the occasion to aestheticize political realities, not only in Germany but in fascist and non-fascist countries throughout the world, and voices of authority and the growing mass media celebrated patriotic forces and imagined nation-states in mass spectacles as providers of security. Nationalistic storytelling, born during the period of colonialism and imperialism in the nine-teenth century, grew and sought to camouflage and harmonize social and political conflicts; it was continually re-invented from the 1920s onward to co-exist with and dwarf regional and local legends, myths, rumors, and anecdotes. This celebra-tion of nationalism could not be totally accomplished, but certainly the tendency was totalitarian; it tended to conceal loss of community and identity and to set fixed standards of racial, ethnic, sexual, and religious identity that complied with the dominant interests of the nation-state. Today, however, despite vanguard movements of fundamentalist patriotism, the nation-state no longer exercises control over social and cultural integration. Rather it acts as a policing agency that supervises deregulation in the service of multinational corporations that set their own laws that curb the autonomy of individuals and communities. Whatever identity a community or individual seeks to establish can only be accomplished within the socio-cultural fields of production constructed by economic and political forces.

It is not by chance that Bauman's very next book in 2001, after writing *Globalization*, was given the title *Community: Seeking Safety in an Insecure World* and sought to provide a more nuanced critique of the devastating effects of globalization on community and individual identity formation, while suggesting alternatives to these effects. Bauman asserted that

> Nations, once securely ensconced in the armoury of the multidimensional sovereignty of the nation-state, have found themselves in an institutional void. Existential security has been shattered; the old stories reiterated to replenish the confidence of belonging are losing growing amounts of their credibility, and as Jeffrey Weeks has indicated in another context, when the old stories of group (communal) belonging no longer ring true, demand grows for the "identity stories in which we tell ourselves about where we came from, what we are now and where we are going; such stories are urgently needed to restore security, build trust and make meaningful interaction with others possible. As the old certainties and loyalties are swept away people seek new belongings. The trouble with new identity stories, in sharp distinction from the old stories of naturally belonging verified daily by the seemingly invulnerable solidity of deeply entrenched institutions, is that trust and commitment have to be worked at in relationships that no one dictates should last unless individuals choose to make them last."[3]

The result is, as Bauman succinctly claims, a normative void. On the one hand, the majority of people, who are non-synchronic, that is, out of step with the rapid pace of hyper-globalization, become defensive, fundamentalist, exclusive, and susceptible to ideologies and notions of imagined communities that promise salvation and security. They seek solid norms when their existence is threatened by social and political forces that they cannot grasp, and when all they hold sacred is vanishing into thin air. Community becomes more like a ghetto that is either imposed or chosen out of necessity. At the same time, educated and privileged people, whom Bauman refers to as the knowledge classes, are freed through the process of globalization to enjoy the excess of life and propose an indifferent ideology of multiculturalism that enables this class of people to detach from community and have the space to tolerate without commitment or care. As Bauman bitterly remarks,

> in the absence of norm, excess is life's only hope. In a society of producers, excess was

equivalent to waste and for that reason resented and preached against; but it was born as a disease of life-towards-norm (a terminal disease, as it transpired). In a world devoid of norms, excess had turned from poison into medicine for life illnesses; perhaps the sole life support available. Excess, that sworn enemy of the norm, has itself become the norm; perhaps the only norm there is. A curious norm to be sure, one escaping all definition. Having broken normative fetters, excess lost its meaning. Nothing is excessive once excess is the norm.[4]

And nothing has really changed since Bauman published his book on the lack of community and the necessity to develop "a community woven together from sharing and mutual care; a community of concern and responsibility for the equal right to be human and the equal ability to act on that right."[5] Globalization continues to terrorize and minimize the lives of most people on this globe while providing excessive forms of movement and consumption for privileged groups of people who set ever-changing norms that rationalize their choices and life styles.

The Role of the Storyteller in the Force Field of Cultural Production

Given the conflicting norms, growing class divisions, and the transformation of nation-states in our globalized world, we must ask where does the field of storytelling and where do storytellers stand? Can those people, who declare ourselves to be professional storytellers, even bother to tell stories? Should they? Can they provide some sense of hope or truth in our stories that can help people find their own way to contend with the high voltage changes of globalization? These are enormous questions, and it would be presumptuous of me to pretend that I can answer them. As an American, who does a fair amount of work in the field of storytelling and spends many months each year in Europe as a member of what Bauman calls the knowledge class of intellectuals, I can at best address as critically as possible and self-critically some of the conditions of professional storytelling in America and also comment on some experiences that I have had on the Continent and in the UK.

So much has been written about the value of story and storytelling in the last forty years as a means of spiritual communication, educational growth, and community formation that it would seem impossible to add anything of relevance to the discussion. However, I want to start with the premise that the great success of storytelling since the 1970s, the increase in the number of professional and amateur storytellers and storytelling events, the large production of scholarly studies and handbooks dealing with storytelling, and the enormous value placed on it are indications of its lack, its illusive eclecticism, its excessive commodification, and our alienation. Put more positively, the more value we place on storytelling as affording some kind of solution to our social problems or political salvation in our globalized world, the more we realize that it is not providing and cannot provide what is missing in our lives. The value of storytelling is a sign of lack and failure. We demand from storytelling the impossible—a sense of true community and authentic norms that can help us create deep human bonds. Yet, until we relate to one another differently by overcoming the socio-economic forces that foster non-synchronicity, relentless violence, and estrangement, and until our relations are *not* mediated by spectacles that prevent cognition and self-reflection, storytelling will not nourish us but merely entertain us, help us pass our time on the globe with less suffering, and minimize our struggles to determine our fates. At its very best, it will counter the lies that invade our lives and puncture the delusions and illusions that interfere with communication.

We are, of course, all storytellers, and we use story constantly every day to navigate and narrate ourselves through our prescribed existential situations. Many people learn to unravel the woven stories that bind them to particular confining destinies with the result that they find ways to liberate themselves and weave their own identities, while many others are stitched through closely woven stories to repeat and act out words that are not their own. In either case, the stories we tell, imagine, invent, hold to be true, and disseminate are conditioned by a force field of cultural production in a specific historical period. Within the force field, there are positions that we, as storytellers, choose or positions that are given to us that will determine the stories we need, prefer, and communicate. There will always be limitations to what we choose, tell, and want to become. And if we don't realize what they are, we shall end up like "The Cock Who Wanted to Become Pope." This is a wonderful Sicilian folk tale with many Italian variants about a cock who, once upon a time, wanted to go to Rome and have himself anointed Pope. So he sets out on his way, and during his journey, he finds a letter which he takes with him. At one point he meets Mrs. Hen, who asks him, "Mr. Cock, where are you going?"

"I'm going to Rome and want to become Pope."

"Will you take me with you?" she asks.

"First I must check my letter to see if you can come," the cock says and looks at the letter. "All right, you can come. When I become Pope, you can become Mrs. Pope."

So Mr. Cock and Mrs. Hen continue on their way together, and they meet a cat and a weasel, who decide to tag along and assist the future Pope.

When it becomes dark, they come upon a little cottage inhabited by a witch. Since she had just gone out to do some mischief, each one of the animals chooses a comfortable place to sleep. The weasel lies down in the closet, the cat on the warm ashes in the hearth, while the cock and the hen fly to the top of the beams to roost above the door. When the witch comes home, she wants to fetch a candle from the closet, but the weasel whacks her in her face with his tail. In spite of this she manages to grab the candle and rushes to the fireplace to light it. However, she mistakes the shining eyes of the cat for glowing coals and tries to light the candle with them. As she sticks the candle into the eyes of the cat, the cat springs at her face and gives her terrible scratches all over. The witch screams, fearful that her house is filled with ghosts. When the cock hears all the noise, he begins to crow very loudly. All at once the witch realizes that there are no ghosts in her house but simple dumb animals. So she takes a club and chases all four of them out of the house.

Now the cat and the weasel, almost beaten to death, no longer have any desire whatsoever to continue the journey, but the cock and the hen keep on their way. When they finally reach Rome, they enter the church, and the cock says to the sacristan, "Let the bells ring. I'm here to be anointed Pope."

"Yes, indeed," said the sacristan. "We certainly can do this. Just come with me."

So he leads Mr. Cock and Mrs. Hen into the sacristy, where he closes the door, grabs hold of them, twists their necks off, and puts them into a cooking pot. Then he invites some portly priests and friends to a sumptuous dinner, and they take great pleasure in eating the delicious Mrs. Hen and Mr. Cock, who wanted to go to Rome to be anointed Pope.

Now, far be it from me to suggest that all storytellers are cocks, but there is a lesson to be learned from the cock's presumption and fate. I tell this story because I think it helps explain how we common people, and not so common people, seek to anoint ourselves professional storytellers without taking into consideration the conditions and dangers confronting storytellers. It seems to me that, though we are all born storytellers, we are not really storytellers per se until we profess to be storytellers and are then anointed or self-anointed. This is the simple but important distinction I make when I allude to the difference between everyday traditional storytellers and professional storytellers and their trade: a professional storyteller is he or she who professes to be a special, gifted, talented, superb, fascinating, wondrous, unique storyteller of some kind, deserving of a distinctive title and ready to serve those institutions that hire, make use of, and recognize storytellers who profess to be professional storytellers. When people declare that they are ready to be anointed, paid, and recognized as members of the select group, if not the best of the elect in the church of storytellers, they are, however, not aware of the dangers that this declaration or anointment involves, especially if they forget who they really are—simply, people with very particular dispositions and talents. Put bluntly, we may indeed decide for ourselves that we are professional storytellers and act as though we are autonomous and talented and have something to say that other people want to hear, but the only way we can survive and prevent ourselves from being stewed in a pot like the cock is by not forgetting our origins, whatever they may be, and by realizing that, by declaring to be a storyteller, we are not autonomous and must comply as professionals with the rules, regulations, demands, and needs of institutions within the field of storytelling or institutions outside the field that storytellers serve. Complying with institutions does not necessarily mean conforming to the institutions; it means that we must be aware that we are not free, that we are not going to lead the Church as Pope, that the social role of the professional storyteller demands assuming a certain habitus or comportment that I shall define later. First I want briefly, perhaps a bit superficially, to describe the field of storytelling and its institutions in America because they shape the habitus.

Although it is possible to obtain a master's degree and in some rare cases a Ph.D. in storytelling in America, or to take storytelling workshops and study at private schools, most professionals who have had some kind of formal and informal training become storytellers through declaration, that is, hanging a shingle on their door or website and advertising their services as storyteller. Many storytellers now offer themselves on the market in glossy magazines and on the Internet with sparkling websites. Confirmation of professionalism can only come through a loose network of institutions that constitute the field of storytelling: schools, libraries, theaters, youth centers, prisons, businesses, hospitals, old age homes, established storytelling festivals, societies such as the National Storytelling Network in America and the Society for Storytelling in the UK, bars, pubs, storytelling experiments, coffee houses, and the entertainment industry including television and film. No one storyteller can service all these institutions, but one storyteller can adapt and serve two or three if not more at the same time. A successful professional storyteller is generally a free-floating chameleon, ready to change colors, shape, and attitude at the drop of a hat, and ready to perform in a functional space of a given institution. Very few professional storytellers have or owe an allegiance to a community. That is, they do not make it their purpose to cultivate strong human bonds and values within the community in which they live. They are "extraterritorial," so to speak, ready to go beyond the territory of their communities at all times. Some storytellers even teach and advertise their wares and talents as digital storytellers on the Internet. This does not mean that they neglect their communities, or that they play a negligible role within their communities. It means that the institutions of the field do not enable or require them to enhance and articulate the values of a specific community. Let me give some examples by focusing on how professional storytellers work within American elementary and high schools and what limits and conditions the schools set. Bear in mind that I shall be making generalizations and that there are many exceptions to the rule.

1. Schools have strong censors that limit the scope of a storyteller. A storyteller may not use curse language, be overtly political, question the authority of the school, religion, or patriotism, spend more time than is allotted in a classroom or auditorium, or tell stories explicitly related to problems within the community that need attention. Schools are also responsive to complaints by parents who may object to particular kinds of storytelling that they find offensive or inappropriate for children, as though they knew what is appropriate.

2. Schools hire and welcome storytellers as entertainers who can come and spend a few hours once a year and amuse large groups of children. They also believe in ethnic storytelling and multicultural values and think that children can learn about others just by listening to "foreign" tales told by a storyteller in the persona of a foreigner.

3. The climate and conditions within a school vary immensely from jungle and prison to idyllic paradise of learning. There are often guards and monitors who are hired to protect the students and the building. A storyteller can never know what to expect unless he or she has a long-standing connection with the school and commitment to develop a storytelling program within the school.

4. Schools are controlled by bureaucratic superintendents and boards of education that deprive schools of autonomy and the necessary funding to create innovative programs that will further the interests of local communities. There has been a great trend toward the privatization of the public school system and teaching only the fundamentals of writing, reading, and arithmetic to meet the standards of positivist testing. Storytelling is not regarded highly as an art form that can enhance the education of young people.

5. Even when there are programs that encourage storytelling in the high schools, generally in speech or drama courses, the young people are taught that there are certain prescribed ways and techniques of delivering stories. Local competitions between schools and national competitions have been established with so-called experts who judge whether the young storytellers meet arbitrary standards of storytelling. The result is more than often copy-cat imitation of television and nightclub comics and performers who tell tales in theaters and other theatrical venues. Very rarely are professional storytellers hired to teach courses at high schools.

If we consider the great disparities and differences in American schools, even in a single city, it is apparent that the professional storyteller must learn how to adapt to the conditions in those schools and to their requirements; otherwise he or she will be turned away or cooked. The storyteller cannot simply arrive and be anointed Pope or even be recognized as a sacristan. It is the other way around. The school designates the title of storyteller by recognizing that the talents or wares that a person brings are beneficial to and respect the functional goals of the school. In other words, the school system determines the proper habitus of the storyteller. And this is generally the case throughout America: it is the institution within the cultural field of production that defines the habitus of the storyteller.

Habitus, as I have already discussed in this book, is a loaded term. Conceived originally by the great French sociologist Pierre Bourdieu, he maintained that we all distinguish ourselves and seek distinction by assuming a particular habitus that can be regarded as a set of predispositions and dispositions that generate practices and perceptions within a field. The dispositions are formed first by the social conditions of birth and become inculcated into the personality of each individual so that he or she will act as though the predispositions and dispositions consisting of attitudes and values were second nature. The habitus is durable and also flexible so that a person can imbibe and learn to assume the habitus that distinguishes a position or profession in a particular field. Therefore, a person with a working-class habitus can eventually become a priest, policeman, banker, or social worker if he or she learns to acquire the beliefs, gestures, attitudes, clothes, and power of a particular profession that serve as recognizable markers of the profession. A habitus is not fixed, but the preferences and dispositions that were first developed in childhood will play a role in the manner in which a person cultivates a habitus later in life whatever job, role, or profession one occupies. To occupy a position and distinguish oneself as belonging to that position, a person must demonstrate through behavior, material possessions, and manifest beliefs that he or she deserves to be recognized as an authority or legitimate occupier of a position. Without recognition, the individual is nothing, a non-entity, which is also a form of the habitus so that it is virtually impossible not to have a habitus. Even a homeless person has a habitus.

Given the fact that the cultural field of production to which the professional storyteller belongs is so immense and amorphous, it is difficult to recognize the professional storyteller by his or her habitus. In some societies such as India or Morocco, or in small villages in the Americas and Europe, where traditional storytelling still exists, it is possible to know and determine who a professional or communal storyteller is by his or her dispositions, clothes, gestures, and preferences. Yet, for the most part, in the globalized West, the most distinctive feature of the storyteller's habitus is his or her chameleon-like quality. It is impossible to define the features, ideologies, comportment, clothes, mannerisms, religious beliefs, or social class of a "typical" professional storyteller, though we might intuit a basic underlying habitus after a long acquaintance. Certainly, some storytellers become celebrities and are known by their special kind of storytelling, such as family stories or ethnic stories. They have a trademark and negotiate their perform-ances and appearances commercially as a brand of storyteller. Patrick Ryan has made some very pertinent critical comments about these storytellers, whom he calls revivalists:

> Means used thus far to revive storytelling, motivated by desires to preserve or promote an important, loved art form, have precariously and without challenge been derived mostly from homogenizing mass market approaches, because such methods appear to serve us well in other areas of life. With emphasis on acquiring and disseminating knowledge, and tight-ening definitions to control access to the profession and protect limited chances for income, instead of a free exchange of knowledge, as in traditional societies, storytelling knowledge becomes a commodity as easily marketed as Walt Disney films or new computer social networks.[6]

Indeed, most professional storytellers are like AC/DC adapters: they will func-tion according to the cultural institution's needs or requirements and will act and dress according to the situation, even if they have a persona. They are definable mainly in a particular context, and once they step out of that context, they will probably assume the habitus of another role, job, or occupation while maintaining some distinct dispositions that characterize their social occupation. Very few pro-fessional storytellers make a living simply by selling their wares and talents. Per-haps this is another quality of the habitus: most professional storytellers are not rich and cannot make a living through storytelling. Unless one becomes a notable stand-up comic, celebrity storyteller, pure entertainer, garrulous media journalist, or puppet politician, it is difficult to earn a great deal of money by telling stories. Put another way, professional storytellers tend to be altruistic and egotistical at the same time. They have a great desire to share their favorite tales with others with the hope that they might cheer their audiences or even change their lives. They also love to hear themselves talk and want to be on center stage. Many will do this for very little money or nothing. There is a deep private satisfaction to deliver a well-told tale, to communicate efficaciously, to identify oneself through story before a large crowd or even small group of people who recognize you as a storyteller.

The Purpose of Storytelling in a Globalized World

Can one really gain personal and social satisfaction as a professional storyteller in a world that dissolves identity as soon as it creates it and disconnects us from each other as soon as it connects us? Is it possible to be authentic as a storyteller? Is authentic storytelling possible? Since authenticity depends on community, I want to explore whether it is still possible to be authentic when the forms of community have changed and been changed rapidly by globalization in the last twenty-five years so that the very nature and structure of communities have become artificial and amorphous. Globalization has not only brought with it the dissolution of ties to the nation-state but also threatened religion and ethnicity, one of the reasons fundamentalism has become stronger as a reaction to multinationalism, multiculturalism, and secularization. In defense of their threatened values, many communities have tightened the bonds and defined values more strictly than ever before so that the debates and conflicts over authentic values and qualities have intensified. In the long run, I believe, the results will show that there is no such thing as an essential or authentic value. Rather, to use a term that has become overused and abused, our values are socially constructed and determined. What may be viable and valid in one society in a certain historical period may not be the case twenty years later. Yet, within a given historical period there are relative values based on truth claims that are more viable and beneficial to the majority of people than others and foster greater universal humanistic understanding of what makes for democratic self-determination, justice, fairness, and compassion.

Whether conscious or unconscious, millions of people on this globe are endeavoring to form communities based on truth claims. They voice their claims through storytelling, and some of these people become storytellers, not always the best, but certainly well-trained, tutored, and manicured; they decide to become professional and receive payment for their stories which they often copyright and stake out property claims as the authentic creators of their tales. This is very much in keeping with capitalist market practices. In this case, not only do their stories and methods become wares, but they, too, reify themselves and become objects; their values and function are determined by the market and the institutions in which they choose to work. For instance, if a storyteller works for a Fortune 500 company, he or she, given the chameleon-like quality of professional storytellers, will shape-shift into a member of that community and furnish the needs of a corporation that seeks profit, cost efficiency, obedience, fair practices, and conformity to a corporate culture. If a storyteller works for a theater company like Roadside Theatre in Virginia or the Children's Theatre Company of Minneapolis, he or she will collaborate with social and political groups to encourage critical thinking, social involvement, positive racial identity, and make an effort to share and disseminate stories free of charge. It is even possible in some cases that a storyteller will work for both a corporation and a community theater at the same time. In a recent special issue of the American journal *Storytelling, Self, Society* (2006) on "Storytelling and Organizations," Jo A. Tyler, who edited the issue and is both an executive and professional storyteller, remarks,

> I became smartest about organizations when I could really hear the stories of those who did the work and saw what that work meant, close up. It is because of the stories I heard, because of what they taught me, that I was able to make "good" decisions—those that balanced the interest of profits and people. It was because of the stories that I could "trust my gut" in complex situations where no single straightforward solution was forthcoming. And it was by sculpting and sharing authentic stories—and by keeping my relationship to those stories clear—that I was able to help people ask questions that were reflective and important. The stories were thresholds opening up to different ways of thinking about the world—ways that were at the same time exciting and scary. When people crossed over those thresholds, they found rooms of shadow and light, filled with challenges to their assumptions, tables on which to unpack them, and, yes, more stories.[7]

If there is something as an "authentic" storyteller or "authentic" story in our globalized world, Tyler puts her finger on it, but does not fully elaborate its significance. She suggests that stories emerge spontaneously from the interaction of people, their experiences, in particular contexts, and that the stories communicate relevant information that can help people make decisions in complex situations. Tyler also states that she as storyteller took possession of the stories, "sculpted" them as an artist, and gave them back to the people, recognizing that she did not own them, so that they could question their environment, become innovative and inventive. This process that she describes reveals some clear qualities about storytellers and stories today:

1. Once a story is told and taken out of its context, it can no longer be authentic.
2. If a storyteller wants to preserve and perpetuate a particular story, for whatever reason, it will be artfully "sculpted" to make it more memorable, appealing, and important so that other people will want to tell and disseminate it.
3. Once a storyteller tells a story freely, it is no longer his or hers. Another person or group of people may appropriate the tale and tell it in a totally different context and change its meaning. If a professional storyteller hears a story and likes it, he or she will mold it and shape it carefully so that it becomes his or her own.

4. The story can become authentic again if in the brief retelling, the story-teller believes in it, believes that the story can open up new vistas for a listener, believes that the story might be serviceable in a specific community, and believes that it provides meaning for his or her life.

Authenticity depends on the integrity of the storyteller, and the integrity of the storyteller depends on his or her critical recognition that dedication to the art of storytelling and the truth claims of story and experience are more important than the requirements of institutions that determine the conditions of storytelling and that "legitimize" the storyteller as professional. But the storyteller with integrity does not need such legitimization and is not a chameleon or a cock, but a sub-versive who understands that the globalized world mediated by spectacle is an illusion and foments lies, that service to institutions is not service to community, and that new forms of fleeting political and ethnic communities demand thought-ful storytellers, who want to intervene in all the institutions in which they work to question skeptically how the institutions and communities function and to help change them so that more people can take charge of their own stories. In a recent article in *Storylines*, Neil Lanham pointed out that people of an oral background such as the Inuit possess something that we in our urban-techno-literate society have lost, namely metaphorical thinking. He concludes his open letter to Ben Haggarty by arguing,

> The most important thing, I believe, is for all of us to try to bring back the naturally metamorphic mind and this must surely be by helping young people all we can to develop metaphor by telling us their stories from their experiences. I do not believe that it will come by reading "book" stories at them. Stories from experience pass truth. They teach one to associate, to relate, to correlate and to reason (see Darwin). I believe that the ability to correlate information into principle of understanding is an essential of life.[8]

What we lack is an indication of what we value most, and the more success that globalization has had in commodifying and exploiting storytelling as spec-tacle, the more storytelling with integrity assumes value by pointing to this lack. This is why Lanham would like us to bring back metaphoric thinking connected to truth and integrity. Though I am somewhat skeptical as to whether dedicated professional storytellers can preserve and convey their truths and integrity in a globalized world that fosters estrangement and brief encounters with fluctuating communities, I am not without hope, for we cannot live without the passionate truths of story and storytellers passionate to tell these truths and to vie with the lies of spectacles.

Notes

Preface

i   Bauman, *Liquid Society* (London: Polity, 2005): 146.
ii *Ibid.*, 143.

1 The Reconfiguration of Children and Children's Literature in the Culture Industry

1 Paula Fass, *Children of a New World: Society, Culture, and Globalization* (New York: New York University Press, 2007): 255.
2 In *Consuming Kids: Protecting Our Children from the Onslaught of Marketing and Advertising* (New York: Anchor, 2004), Susan Linn comments: "The Lines between publishing children's books and marketing to kids are so blurred that Scholastic, Inc., publisher of *Harry Potter* and the *Miss Spider* series, and which for years has had a stellar reputation in children's publishing, was the focus of a national letter-writing protest when the company co-sponsored the Advertising and Promoting to Kids conference in 2001" (66).
3 See also Stephen Kline, *Out of the Garden: Toys and Children's Culture in the Age of TV Marketing* (London: Verso, 1993); Ellen Seiter, *Sold Separately: Parents & Children in Consumer Culture* (New Brunswick: Rutgers University Press, 1995); Gary Cross, *Kids' Stuff: Toys and the Changing World of American Childhood* (Cambridge, MA: Harvard University Press, 1997); Beverly Lyon Clark and Margaret R. Higonnet, eds., *Girls, Boys, Books, Toys: Gender in Children's Literature and Culture* (Baltimore: Johns Hopkins University Press, 1999); Jyotsna Kapur, *Coining Capital: Movies, Marketing, and the Transformation of Childhood* (New Brunswick: Rutgers University Press, 2005); Kay S. Hymowitz, *Liberation's Children: Parents and Kids in a Postmodern Age* (Chicago: Ivan R. Dee, 2003); Linn, *Consuming Kids*; Juliet Schor, *Born to Buy* (New York: Scribner, 2004); and Ellen Seiter, *The Internet Playground: Children's Access, Entertainment, and Mis-Education* (New York: Peter Lang, 2005). Some of these works will be discussed in more detail later in the essay.
4 Some of these groups are: Campaign for a Commercial-Free Childhood (CCFC), Action Coalition for Media Education (ACME), Alliance for Childhood, American Academy of Child and Adolescent Psychiatry: The Television and Media Committee, Canadians Concerned About Violence in Entertainment (C-CAVE), Center for the New American Dream, Children Now: Children and the Media Program, Commercial Alert, Dads and Daughters, Free Press,

Kids Can Make a Difference, Motherhood Project, New Mexico Media Literacy Project, Slow Food USA, and Teachers Resisting Unhealthy Children's Entertainment. For a more complete listing, see Linn, *Consuming Kids*, 221–232 and Schor, *Born to Buy*, 225–226.

5 Paula Fass, *Children of a New World*, 254.

6 Daniel Thomas Cook, "Beyond Either/or," *Journal of Consumer Culture* 4.2 (2004): 151.

7 Schor, *Born to Buy*, 13.

8 Robert W. McChesney, *Rich Media, Poor Democracy: Communication in Dubious Times* (Urbana: University of Illinois Press, 1999): 37–38.

9 See Viviana Zelizer, "Kids and Commerce," *Childhood* 9.4 (2002): 375–396 and Lydia Martens, Dale Southerton, and Sue Scott, "Bringing Children (and Parents) into the Sociology of Consumption," *Journal of Consumer Culture* 4.2 (2004): 155–182. Zelizer argues that children are actively engaged in all aspects of production, distribution, and consumption that have not been sufficiently studied. Martens, Southerton, and Scott argue that too much attention has been spent on the production of consumption. They focus more on how children learn to consume and form identities in objective and subjective relations with their parents and modes of consumption.

10 Pierre Bourdieu, *The Field of Cultural Production: Essays on Art and Literature*, ed. Randal Johnson (New York: Columbia University Press, 1993): 30.

11 See Harvey Graff, *The Legacies of Literacy: Continuities and Contradictions in Western Culture and Society* (Bloomington: Indiana University Press, 1987), and R. A. Houston, *Literacy in Early Modern Europe: Culture and Education 1500–1800* (London: Longman, 2002).

12 Judith Rosen, "Where the Sales Are: The Changing Landscape of Children's Book Outlets," *Publishers Weekly* 247 (February 14, 2000): 95.

13 Schor, *Born to Buy*, 111.

14 Shelby Anne Wolf and Shirley Brice Heath, *The Braid of Literature: Children's Worlds of Reading* (Cambridge, MA: Harvard University Press, 1992): 180–181.

15 Manuel Castells, *The Rise of the Network Society* (Malden, MA: Blackwell, 1996): 13.

16 *Ibid.*, 19.

17 Cook, "Beyond Either/or," 147.

18 Karen Klugman, "A Bad Hair Day for G. I. Joe," in *Girls, Boys, Books, Toys*, 174.

19 *Ibid.*, 180.

20 Stephen Kline, *Out of the Garden*, 17.

21 *Ibid.*, 212.

22 *Ibid.*, 280.

23 *Ibid.*, 349.

24 Seiter, *Sold Separately*, 4.

25 *Ibid.*, 6.

26 *Ibid.*, 50.

27 Cf. Louis Marin's incisive analysis of degenerate utopias in his chapter "Utopic Degeneration: Disneyland" in *Utopics: Spatial Play*, trans. Robert A. Vollrath (Atlantic Highlands, NJ: Humanities Press, 1984): 239–258. Marin explains the fantasyland of Disneyland is formed by the banal routine images of Disney's films that reflect the bankrupt signs of an imagination homogenized by the mass media. Marin remarks that "one of the essential functions of the utopic image is to make apparent a wish in a *free* image of itself, in an image that can play in opposition to the fantasy, which is an inert, blocked, and recurrent image. Disneyland is on the side of the fantasy and not on that of a free or utopic representation" (246).

28 Anne Haas Dyson, *Writing Superheroes: Contemporary Childhood, Popular Culture, and Classroom Literacy* (New York: Teachers College Press, 1997): 7.

29 *Ibid.*, 178.

30 Zelizer, "Kids and Commerce," 379.

31 Daniel Thomas Cook, *The Commodification of Childhood: The Children's Clothing Industry and the Rise of the Child Consumer* (Durham, NC: Duke University Press, 2004): 11–12.

32 Lang is referring to George Ritzer's book, *Enchanting a Disenchanted World: Revolutionizing*

the Means of Consumption (Thousand Oaks, CA: Pine Forge Press, 1999).

33 Beryl Langer, "The Business of Branded Enchantment: Ambivalence and Disjuncture in the Global Children's Culture Industry," *Journal of Consumer Culture* 4.2 (2004): 255–256.

34 Martens, Southerton, and Scott, "Bringing Children (and Parents) into the Sociology of Consumption: Towards a Theoretical and Empirical Agenda," 163.

35 *Ibid.*, 165.

36 Gunther Kress, *Literacy in the New Media Age* (London: Routledge, 2003): 9–10.

2 Misreading Children and the Fate of the Book

1 Michael Morpurgo, "On Teaching Children to Read," *The Royal Society of Literature Review* (2008): 3.

2 Ralph Lombreglia, "Humanity's Humanity in the Digital Twenty-First," Sven Birkerts, ed., *Tolstoy's Dictaphone: Technology and the Muse* (St. Paul, MN: Graywolf Press, 1996): 240.

3 For example, on January 21, 2008, the London newspaper, the *Telegraph*, published an excerpt from Michael Morpurgo's essay "On Teaching Children to Read," which appeared in *The Royal Society of Literature Review* (2008) with a simplistic solution that idealizes books. As in most countries and the media, the *Telegraph* proposed that children must learn to love stories (Morpurgo's point) if they are to become readers for life. Then the newspaper published a list of 300 books that infants, children, and adolescents should read. Morpurgo's article was picked up in Italy by the newspaper *La Repubblica*, which reported also on January 21, 2008 that there was a drop in literacy and the quantity of reading in Italy among young people. The article included graphs that showed how minimal reading had become throughout the world in different nations. This article was later followed by a long report, "Dottor analfabeta" ("Doctor Illiterate") on February 6, 2008, which discussed the growing illiteracy in Italy and the students who graduated from high schools without being able to read or write.

4 Tom Bradshaw and Bonnie Nichols, eds., *Reading at Risk: A Survey of Literary Reading in America* (Washington, DC: National Endowment for the Arts, 2004): ix–xii.

5 Sunil Iyengar, ed., *To Read or Not to Read: A Question of National Consequences* (Washington, DC: National Endowment for the Arts, 2007): 5.

6 Sven Birkerts, "The Fate of the Book," Sven Birkerts, ed., *Tolstoy's Dictaphone: Technology and the Muse* (St. Paul, MN: Graywolf Press, 1996): 189.

7 Maryanne Wolf, *Proust and the Squid: The Story and Science of the Reading Brain* (New York: HarperCollins, 2007): 16–17.

8 *Ibid.*, 3.

9 Janet Adam Smith, *Children's Illustrated Books* (London: Collins, 1948): 38.

10 Miller is referring to John Kasson, *Amusing the Million: Coney Island at the Turn of the Century* (New York: Hill & Wang, 1978).

11 Laura Miller, *Reluctant Capitalists: Bookselling and the Culture of Consumption* (Chicago: University of Chicago Press, 2007), 131–132.

12 Ursula K. Le Guin, "Staying Awake: Notes on the Alleged Decline of Reading," *Harper's Magazine* 316.1893 (February 2008): 35.

13 See Miller, *Reluctant Capitalists*, 77. "The practice of publishers' running titles by chain buyers in the early stages of acquisition has continued into the present. Rumors circulate of books cancelled after chain buyers inform publishers that their stories will pass on a title. From a publisher's perspective, sales that could be made outside chain avenues may not be worth the trouble, cost, and risk of publishing a book."

14 See "Fairies From Never Land Arrive At Disneyland," http://www.prnewswire.co.uk/cgi/news/release?id=152299.

15 Wolf, *Proust and the Squid*, 135.

16 The reference is to Carol Gilligan's *In a Different Voice: Psychological Theory and Women's*

Development (Cambridge, MA: Harvard University Press, 1982). Gilligan maintained that girls uttered their needs and desires in distinctly different ways than boys.

17 *Ibid.*

18 Le Guin, "Staying Awake," 37.

19 Bess Altwerger, "Reading for Profit: A Corporate Coup in Context," in Bess Altwerger, ed., *Reading for Profit: How the Bottom Line Leaves Kids Behind* (Portsmouth, NH: Heinemann, 2005): 3.

20 Wolf, *Proust and the Squid*, 135.

21 Patrick Shannon, *Reading against Democracy: The Broken Promises of Reading Instruction* (Portsmouth, NH: Heinemann, 2007): xiv–xvi.

22 Allan Luke and Peter Freebody, "A Map of Possible Practices: Further Notes on the Four Resources Model," *Practically Primary* 4 (1999): 5.

23 Miller, *Reluctant Capitalists*, 57.

24 See Normimitsui Onishi, "Thumbs Race as Japan's Best Sellers Go Cellular," *The New York Times* (January 20, 2008), http://www.nytimes.com/2008/01/20/world/asia/20japan.html and Ashley Phillips, "Will Cell Phone Novels Come Stateside?" ABC News (January 23, 2008): http//abcnews.go.com/Technology/GadgetGuide/story?id=417182

25 See the important article by Cynthia Lewis and Bettina Fabos, "Instant Messaging, Literacies, and Social Identities," *Reading Research Quarterly* 40.4 (2005): 470–501.

26 Wolf, *Proust and the Squid*, 226.

27 Allan Luke and Carmen Luke, "Adolescence Lost/Childhood Regained: On Early Intervention and the Emergence of the Techno-Subject," *Journal of Early Childhood Literacy* 1.1 (2001): 96.

28 Gunther Kress, *Literacy in the New Media Age* (London: Routledge, 2003): 35.

29 Stuart McNaughton, "On Making Early Interventions Problematic: A Comment on Luke and Luke (2001)," *Journal of Early Childhood Literacy* 2.1 (2002): 99.

3 Why Fantasy Matters Too Much

1 Sandro Cappelletto, "Esercizi di memoria," interview with Maurizio Pollini, *Classic Voice* 107 (April 2008): 20.

2 See Tzvetan Todorov, *The Fantastic: A Structural Approach to a Literary Genre*, trans. Richard Howard (Ithaca, NY: Cornell University Press, 1975) and Rosemary Jackson, *Fantasy: The Literature of Subversion* (London: Methuen, 1981). Todorov's book first appeared in French in 1971.

3 William Little, H. W. Fowler, and J. Couldson, eds., *The Oxford Universal Dictionary* 3rd ed. (Oxford: Clarendon Press, 1955): 675.

4 Theodor Adorno, *Aesthetic Theory*, trans. Robert Hullot-Kentor (Minneapolis: University of Minnesota, 1997): 173.

5 *Ibid.*, 173–174.

6 *Ibid.*, 174.

7 *Ibid.*, 175.

8 *Ibid.*, 175–176.

9 Lucy Armitt, *Theorising the Fantastic* (London: Arnold, 1996): 2–3.

10 Maria Nikolajeva and Carole Scott, *How Picturebooks Work* (New York: Routledge, 2001): 17.

11 Peter Sís, *The Wall: Growing Up Behind the Iron Curtain* (New York: Farrar, Straus and Giroux, 2007): unpaginated.

12 *Ibid.*, unpaginated.

13 Vladimir Radunsky, *Le grand Bazar* (Paris: Éditions du Panama, 2006): cover page.

14 Neil Gaiman, *The Wolves in the Walls*, illustr. David McKean (New York: HarperCollins, 2003): unpaginated.

15 Joel Shoemaker, "Hungry . . . for M. T. Anderson: An Interview with M. T. Anderson," VOYA 27.2 (June 2004): 99.
16 Julia Caniglia, "The All-Seeing Eye: Questions for Steven Heller—Writer, Teacher, Art Director," *The Rake* 6.69 (November 2007): 21.

4 The Multicultural Contradictions of International Children's Literature: Three Complaints and Three Wishes

1 Philip Pullman, "Introduction," in *Outside In: Children's Books in Translation*, eds. Deborah Hallford and Edgardo Zaghini (Chicago: Milet, 2005): 6–7.
2 See *Sticks and Stones: The Troublesome Success of Children's Literature from Slovenly Peter to Harry Potter* (New York: Routledge, 2000).
3 Zygmunt Bauman, *Globalization: The Human Consequences* (New York: Columbia University Press, 1998): 2, 3.
4 See Joseph Stiglitz, *Globalization and Its Discontents* (New York: Norton, 2002) and *Making Globalization Work* (New York: Norton, 2008).
5 Carl Tomlinson, ed., *Children's Books from Other Countries* (Lanham, MD: Scarecrow Press, 1998): 12–13.
6 Mitsumasa Anno, *All in a Day*, with illustrations by Raymond Briggs, Ron Brooks, Gian Calvi, Eric Carle, Zhu Chenglian, Leo and Diane Dillon, Akiko Hayashi, and Nicolai Ye. Popov (London: Hamish Hamilton, 1986): unpaginated.
7 Michael Rosen, ed., *The Oxfam Book of Children's Stories: South and North, East and West* (Cambridge, MA: Candlewick, 1992): 94.
8 See the important work by Carl M. Tomlinson, ed., *Children's Books from Other Countries* (Lanham, MD: Scarecrow Press, 1998): especially 12–17.
9 Peter Hunt, ed., *International Companion Encyclopedia of Children's Literature* (Routledge: London, 1996).
10 Gundel Mattenklott, *Zauberkreide: Kinderliteratur seit 1945* (Frankfurt am Main: Fischer, 1994).
11 Hans-Heino Ewers, *Literatur für Kinder und Jugendliche: Eine Einführung* (Munich: Fink, 2000).
12 Annie Renonciat, ed., *The Changing Face of Children's Literature in France/Livres d'enfance, livres de France* (Paris: Hachette, 1998).
13 Jean Perrot, *Jeux et enjeux du livre d'enfance et de jeunesse* (Paris: Éditions du Cercle de la Librairie, 1999).
14 Pino Boero and Carmine De Luca, *La letteratura per l'infanzia* (Rome-Bari: Laterza, 1995).
15 Emer O'Sullivan, *Comparative Children's Literature* (London: Routledge, 2005).
16 Deborah Hallford and Edgardo Zaghini, *Outside In: Children's Books in Translation* (Chicago: Milet, 2005).
17 Maria Nikolajeva, *Beyond Babar: The European Tradition in Children's Literature* (Lanham, MD: The Scarecrow Press, 2006).
18 *Märchen der Brüder Grimm*, illustr. Nikolaus Heidelbach (Weinheim: Beltz & Gelberg, 1995).
19 See *The Crow Who Stood on his Beak*, trans. Anthea Bell, illustr. Els Coob (New York: North-South Books, 1996). This book is based on the picture book, *Der Schnabelsteher* (Zurich: Nord-Süd, 1995).
20 Kirsten Boie, *Erwachsene reden. Marco hat was getan* (Hamburg: Friedrich Oetinger, 1994): 95.
21 See *Tales of the Rue Broca*, trans. Emily Arnold McCully (Indianapolis: Bobbs-Merrill, 1969).
22 Gianni Rodari, *Tante Storie per giocare*, illustr. Paola Rodari (Rome: Riuniti, 1971): 7.
23 See Marcello Argilli, *Rodari: Una biografia* (Turin: Einaudi, 1990): 102–03.

5 What Makes a Repulsive Frog So Appealing: Applying Memetics to Folk and Fairy Tales

1 For a thorough account of the different ways that the tale has been disseminated, including many different scholarly interpretations, see Gail de Vos and Anna E. Altmann, 'The Frog King or Iron Henry," *New Tales for Old: Folktales as Literary Fictions for Young Adults* (Englewood, CO: Libraries Unlimited, 1999): 77–107.

2 There are now a few hundred or more scholarly endeavors to explain what a meme is. Two of the more stimulating and "orthodox" approaches are: Susan Blackmore, *The Meme Machine* (Oxford: Oxford University Press, 1999) and Robert Aunger, *The Electric Meme: A New Theory of How We Think* (New York: Free Press, 2002). Dawkins has recently elaborated his original definition in *The God Delusion* (Boston: Houghton Mifflin, 2006): 191–201. He makes some interesting points that may have some bearing on how and why certain folk tales are retained in human minds. "For didactic purposes, I treated genes as though they were isolated units acting independently of one another. But of course they are not independent of one another, ... Genes, then, cooperate in cartels to build bodies, and that is one of the important principles of embryology. It is tempting to say that natural selection favours cartels of genes in a kind of group selection between alternative cartels. That is confusion. What really happens is that the other genes of the gene pool constitute a major part of the *environment* in which each gene is selected versus its alleles. Because each is selected to be successful in the presence of the others—which are also being selected in a similar way—cartels of cooperating genes *emerge*" (197). Then Dawkins goes on to say: "Although meme pools are less regimented and structured than gene pools, we can still speak of a meme pool as an important part of the 'environment' of each meme in the memeplex. A memeplex is a set of memes which, while not necessarily being good survivors on their own, are good survivors in the presence of other members of the memeplex" (198).

3 See Hans-Jörg Uther, *The Types of International Folktales: A Classification and Bibliography*, vol. 1 (Helsinki: Suomalainen Tiedeakatemia, 2004): 262–263. This catalogue is based on the system of Antti Aarne and Stith Thompson.

4 For the most exhaustive history and analysis of this tale, see Lutz Röhrich, *Wage es, den Frosch zu küssen! Das Grimmsche Märchen Nummer Eins in seinen Wandlungen* (Cologne: Diederichs, 1987) and "Froschkönig (AaTh 440)," *Enzyklopädie des Märchens*, vol. 5, ed. Rolf Wilhelm Brednich (Berlin: de Gruyter, 1999): 410–422.

5 Heinz Rölleke, ed., *Die älteste Märchensammlung der Brüder Grimm* (Cologny-Genève: Fondation Martin Bodmer, 1975): 144. My translation.

6 Friedrich Panzer, ed., *Kinder- und Hausmärchen der Brüder Grimm: Vollständige Ausgabe in der Urfassung* (Wiesbaden: Emil Vollmer Verlag, n.d.): 63.

7 *Ibid.*, 398–399.

8 Jack Zipes, ed. and trans., *The Complete Fairy Tales of the Brothers Grimm*, 3rd ed. (New York: Bantam, 2003): 2.

9 Joseph Henrich and Robert Boyd, "On Modeling Cognition and Culture: Why Replicators Are Not Necessary for Cultural Evolution," *Culture and Cognition* 2.67 (2002): 112.

10 Bruno Bettelheim, *The Uses of Enchantment: The Meaning and Importance of Fairy Tales* (New York: Knopf, 1976): 288.

11 J. C. Cooper, *Fairy Tales: Allegories of the Inner Life* (Wellingborough, UK: Aquarian Press, 1983): 116.

12 David Buss, *The Evolution of Desire: Strategies of Human Mating*, rev. and expanded ed. (New York: Basic Books, 2003): 5.

13 Meredith Small, *What's Love Got to Do with It? The Evolution of Human Mating* (New York: Doubleday, 1995): 140.

14 Elizabeth Cashdan, "Women's Mating Strategies," *Evolutionary Anthropology* 5 (1996): 139.

15 Buss, *The Evolution of Desire*, 47.

16 Graham Anderson, *Fairytale in the Ancient World* (London: Routledge, 2000), 176–177.

17 W. A. Clouston, "The Story of 'The Frog Prince': Breton Variant, and Some Analogues," *Folk-Lore Quarterly Review 3* (September 1890): 493–506.

18 *Ibid.*, 494.

19 *Ibid.*, 494.

20 In Lutz Röhrich, *Wage es, den Frosch zu küssen!*, 23.

21 See James Orchard Halliwell, *Popular Rhymes and Nursery Tales* (London: John Russell Smith, 1849); J. F. Campbell, *Popular Tales of the West Highlands* (London: Alexander Gardner, 1890); and Joseph Jacobs, *English Fairy Tales* (London: David Nutt, 1890).

22 Joseph Jacobs, *English Fairy Tales and More English Fairy Tales*, ed. Donald Haase (Santa Barbara, CA: ABC-CLIO, 2002), 153.

23 Geoffrey Miller, *The Mating Mind: How Sexual Choice Shaped the Evolution of Human Nature* (New York: Doubleday, 2000): 10.

24 *Ibid.*, 21.

25 See the most recent, revised, thirtieth anniversary edition, Richard Dawkins, *The Selfish Gene* (Oxford: Oxford University Press, 2006).

26 See Jerry A. Coyne, "His Tale Is True," *Times Literary Supplement* (June 16, 2006): 7–9, a review of Dawkins' thirtieth anniversary edition of *The Selfish Gene* and Alan Grafen and Mark Ridley's book, *Richard Dawkins: How a Scientist Changed the Way We Think*: "Dawkins' ambivalence toward memes is not hard to understand. It is difficult to disown an idea, however problematic, if it has helped to make you a celebrity. But intellectual courage demands that you admit when your ideas do not add up—and might be expected in someone like Dawkins, who has shown immense courage in standing up before the world as a vocal opponent of religion. It is time for him to detach himself from the herd of people who have taken memes far more seriously than he intended, and to reprove these advocates for their excesses" (9).

27 Daniel Dennett, *Breaking the Spell: Religion as a Natural Phenomenon* (New York: Viking, 2006): 350.

28 *Ibid.*, 353.

29 David Haig, "The Gene Meme" in Alan Grafen and Mark Ridley, eds., *Richard Dawkins, 61–2*.

30 *Ibid.*, 61.

31 Cavalli Sforza, Luigi Luca, *L'evoluzione della cultura* (Turin: Codice, 2004): 68.

32 Peter Richerson and Robert Boyd, *Not by Genes Alone: How Culture Transformed Human Evolution* (Chicago: University of Chicago Press, 2005): 5.

33 Of course, culture can be defined in much different ways. See Stephen Greenblatt, "Culture," in *Critical Terms for Literary Study*, eds. Frank Lentricchia and Thomas McLaughlin, 2nd ed. (Chicago: University of Chicago, 1995), 225–232. He begins by citing the famous British anthropologist, Edward Tylor: "Culture of civilization, taken in its wide ethnographic sense, is that complex whole which includes knowledge, belief, art, morals, law custom, and many other capabilities and habits acquired by man as a member of society" (225). For an excellent summary of how culture has been viewed by sociologists and Marxist thinkers, see William Outhwaite, "Culture," in Tom Bottomore, ed., *A Dictionary of Marxist Thought* (Cambridge, MA: Harvard University Press, 1983), 109–112. Outhwaite cites Herbert Marcuse's important definition in "On the Affirmative Concept of Culture": "There is a general concept of culture . . . that expresses the historical process of society. It signifies the totality of social life in a given situation, in so far as both the areas of ideational reproduction (culture in the narrower sense, the 'spiritual world') and of material reproduction ('civilisation') form a historically distinguishable and comprehensible unity" (111). There is an apparent lack of sociological categories in Richerson and Boyd's book, and many important studies such as Norbert Elias's *The Civilizing Process* are not taken into account. In a review of the Richerson and Boyd book, Dan Sperber and Nicolas Cladière maintain that, "when anthropologists and others talk of culture—independently of the way they might define it—, they refer to this widely distributed information and to the mental representations, behaviors, artifacts and institutions that, one way or another, implement this information. Richerson and Boyd's definition of culture

. . . does not mention the scale of this distribution and would be satisfied, for instance, by the micro-local information that John acquires from Helen when she says, 'Careful, the coffee is hot!'. Still, it is clear that they mean by 'culture' widely distributed beliefs, norms, and skills, and not such ephemeral trivia. What we want to stress, however, is that there is a continuum of cases between these and widely distributed information. Throughout this continuum, most mental representations and behaviors are shaped by a mix of individual and social inputs, so that there is no way of prying apart cultural information from all the information found in a human population." "Defining and Explaining Culture (Comments on Richerson and Boyd, *Not by Genes Alone*)" to appear in *Biology and Culture* (forthcoming), http://www.dan.sperber.com/on%20Richerson%20&20Boyd.htm.

34 *Not by Genes Alone*, 5–6.

35 *Ibid.*, 6–7.

36 *Ibid.*, 250–251.

37 Geoff Dench, *The Frog the Prince and the Problem of Men* (London: Neanderthal Books, 1994): 251.

38 Alix Berenzy, *A Frog Prince* (New York: Henry Holt, 1989): unpaginated, c. 6.

39 Stephen Mitchell, *The Frog Prince: A Fairy Tale for Consenting Adults* (New York: Harmony Books, 199): 184–185.

40 Nancy Springer, *The Fair Peril* (New York: Avon, 1996): 6.

41 Jane Porter, *The Frog Prince* (New York: Warner, 2005): 371.

6 And Nobody Lived Happily Ever After: The Feminist Fairy Tale after Forty Years of Fighting for Survival

1 *The Field of Cultural Production: Essays on Art and Literature*, trans. Randal Johnson (New York: Columbia University Press, 1993): 30.

2 Donald Haase, ed., *Fairy Tales and Feminism: New Approaches* (Detroit: Wayne State University Press, 2004): ix–x.

3 See Laurence Talairach-Vielmas, *Moulding the Female Body in Victorian Fairy Tales and Sensation Novels* (Aldershot, UK: Ashgate, 2007).

4 See Jack Zipes, *Fairy Tales and the Art of Subversion: The Classical Genre for Children and the Process of Civilization*, 2nd exp. ed. (New York: Routledge, 2006).

5 Toril Moi, "Appropriating Bourdieu: Feminist Theory and Pierre Bourdieu's Sociology of Culture," *New Literary History* 22 (1991): 1017.

6 Guy Debord, *The Society of the Spectacle*, trans. Donald Nicholson-Smith (New York: Zone Books, 1995): 12.

7 *Ibid.*, 19–20.

8 Giorgio Agamben, *Il Regno e la Gloria: Per una genealogia teologica dell'economia e del governo* (Venice: Neri Pozza, 2007): 280.

9 See Joan Gould, *Spinning Straw into Gold: What Fairy Tales Reveal about the Transformations in a Woman's Life* (New York: Random House, 2005): 409–410. Here is the phony question and answer set up by the publishers (Random House) in which Gould characteristically misrepresents the contents and incidents of fairy tales.
   RH: We've all heard charges from feminists that the old fairy tales are demeaning to girls because the heroines seem to do nothing but lie around and mope until a Prince comes along to save them? What do you think about this?
   JG: The idea that fairy-tale heroines are passive creatures who wait for a deliverer is a twentieth-century notion that's out-and-out wrong. Sisters rescue brothers in fairy tales far more often than brothers rescue sisters. Daughters rescue fathers or lovers rather than the reverse. Beauty goes into the beast's castle prepared to die in order to save her father. Hansel scatters bread crumbs to mark the way out of the woods (men like to serve as pathfinders), but it's Gretel who pushes the witch into her own oven. Cinderella is supposed to be the most

passive heroine of all, waiting to be rescued from the ashes. Then why does she run away from the Prince three times in the German version, after dancing with him at the ball?

No, it's not the fairy-tale heroines who are passive victims. It's the heroines of the Walt Disney movies, especially the earlier ones, who warble and weep on the sidelines and then accept rescue by a Prince instead of transformation.

10 See Sigmund Freud, *The 'Uncanny'*, trans. James Strachey (London: Penguin, 1985).
11 Aimee Bender, *Willful Creatures* (New York: Doubleday, 2005): 51.
12 Kelly Link, *Magic for Beginners* (New York: Harcourt, 2005): 126.
13 *Ibid,*, 155.
14 Kelly Link, "Travels with the Snow Queen," *Stranger Things Happen* (Booklyn, NY: Small Beer Press, 2001), 99.
15 *Ibid.*, 100.
16 *Ibid,* 102.
17 Ayse Papatya Bucak, "Once There Was, Once There Wasn't," *Fairy Tale Review* (2006): 53.
18 Carmen Giminez Smith, "Finding the Lark," *Fairy Tale Review* (2006): 136.
19 *Ibid.*, 139.
20 Cristina Bacchilega, *Postmodern Fairy Tales: Gender and Narrative Strategies* (Philadelphia: University of Pennsylvania Press, 1997): 50.
21 Cathy Lynn Preston, "Disrupting the Boundaries of Genre and Gender: Postmodernism and the Fairy Tale," *Fairy Tales and Feminism: New Approaches*, ed. Donald Haase (Detroit: Wayne State University Press, 2004), 211–212.
22 Moi, "Appropriating Bourdieu," 1022.

7 Storytelling as Spectacle in the Globalized World

1 Carl Ewald, "The Story of the Fairy Tale," trans. Alexander Teixeira de Mattos, in *Spells of Enchantment: The Wondrous Fairy Tales of Western Culture*, ed. Jack Zipes (New York: Viking, 1991): 564–565. I have adapted the translation of Ewald's text. Here is the original translation:

Once upon a time, ever so many years ago, Truth suddenly vanished from out of the world.

When people perceived this, they were greatly alarmed and at once sent five wise men in search of Truth. They set out, one in this direction and one in that, all plentifully equipped with traveling expenses and good intentions. They sought for ten long years. Then they returned, each separately. While still at a distance, they waved their hats and shouted that they had found Truth.

The first stepped forward and declared that Truth was Science. He was not able to finish his report, however; for before he had done, another thrust him aside and shouted that that was a lie, that Truth was Theology and that he had found it. Now while these two were at loggerheads—for the Science man replied to the attack vigorously—there came a third and said, in beautiful words, that Love was Truth, without a doubt. Then came the fourth and stated, quite curtly, that he had Truth in his pocket, that it was Gold, that all the rest was childish nonsense. At last came the fifth. He could not stand on his legs, gave a gurgling laugh, and said that Truth was Wine. He had found Truth in Wine, after looking everywhere.

Then the five wise men began to fight, and they pummeled one another so lustily that it was horrible to see. Science had its head broken, and Love was so greatly ill-treated that it had to change its clothes before it could show itself in respectable society. Gold was so thoroughly stripped of every covering that people felt awkward about knowing it; and when the bottle broke, Wine flowed away into the mud. But Theology came off worst of all: everybody had a blow at it and it received such a basting that it became the laughingstock of all beholders.

And people took sides, some with this one and some with that, and they shouted so loud that they could neither see nor hear for the din. But far away, at the extreme end of the earth, sat a few and mourned because they thought that Truth had gone to pieces and would never be made whole again.

Now as they sat there, a little girl came running up and said that she had found Truth. If they would just come with her—it was not very far—Truth was sitting in the midst of the world, in a green meadow.

Then there came a pause in the fighting, for the little girl looked so very sweet. First one went with her; then another; and ever more. . . . At last, they were all in the meadow and there discovered a figure the like of which they had never seen before. There was no distinguishing whether it was a man or a woman, an adult or a child. Its forehead was pure as that of one who knows no sin; its eyes deep and serious as those of one who has read into the heart of the whole world. Its mouth opened with the brightest smile and then quivered with a sadness greater than any could describe. Its hand was soft as a mother's and strong as the hand of a king; its foot trod the earth firmly, yet crushed not a flower. And then the figure had large, soft wings, like the birds that fly at night.

Now as they stood there and stared, the figure drew itself erect and cried, in a voice that sounded like bells ringing:

"I am Truth!"

"It's a Fairy Tale!" said Science.

"It's a Fairy Tale!" cried Theology and Love and Gold and Wine.

Then the five wise men and their followers went away, and they continued to fight until the world was shaken to its center. But a few old and weary men and a few young men with ardent and eager souls and many women and thousands of children with great wide eyes: these remained in the meadow where the Fairy Tale was.

2 Zygmunt Bauman, *Globalization: The Human Consequences* (New York: Columbia University Press, 1998): 18.

3 Zygmunt Bauman, *Community: Seeking Safety in an Insecure World* (Cambridge: Polity Press, 2001):98–99.

4 *Ibid.*, 131.

5 *Ibid.*, 150.

6 Patrick Ryan, "The Storyteller in Context: Identity and Storytelling Experience," *Storytelling, Self, Society* 4.2 (May–August 2008): 74–75.

7 Jo A. Tyler, "Storytelling and Organizations: Introduction to the Special Issue," *Storytelling, Self, Society* 2.2 (Spring 2006): 2.

8 Neil Lanham, "Orality & Metaphor," *Storylines* (Winter 2006): 8.

Bibliography

Critical Studies, Monographs, and Reference Works

Aarne, Antti. *The Types of the Folktales. A Classification and Bibliography*. Rev. and enlarged by Stith Thompson. 2nd rev. ed. FF Communications Nr. 3. Helsinki: Suomalainen Tiedeakatemia, 1961.

Adorno, Theodor. *Aesthetic Theory*. Trans. Robert Hullot-Kentor. Minneapolis, MN: University of Minnesota, 1997.

Agamben, Giorgio. *Il Regno e la Gloria: Per una genealogia teologica dell'economia e del governo*. Venice: Nero Pozza, 2007.

Alterman, Eric. "Out of Print: The Death and Life of the American Newspaper." *The New Yorker* (March 31, 2008): 48–59.

Altwerger, Bess, ed. *Reading for Profit: How the Bottom Line Leaves Kids Behind*. Portsmouth, NH: Heinemann, 2005.

Alverman, Donna, ed. *Adolescents and Literacies in a Digital World*. New York: Peter Lang, 2002.

Anderson, Graham. *Fairytale in the Ancient World*. London: Routledge, 2000.

——. *Greek and Roman Folklore: A Handbook*. Westport, CT: Greenwood Press, 2006.

Anderson, Marilyn. *Never Kiss a Frog: A Girl's Guide to Creatures from the Dating Swamp*. New York: Red Rock Press, 2003.

Argilli, Marcello. *Gianni Rodari: Una biografia*. Turin: Einaudi, 1990.

Armitt, Lucy. *Theorising the Fantastic*. London: Arnold, 1996.

Ashliman, D. L. "Symbolic Sex-Role Reversals in Grimms' Fairy Tales." In *Forms of the Fantastic: Selected Essays from the Third International Conference on the Fantastic in Literature and Film*. Eds. Jan Hokenson and Howard Pearce. New York: Greenwood Press, 1986, 193–198.

Aunger, Robert. *The Electric Meme: A New Theory of How We Think*. New York: Free Press, 2002.

Bacchilega, Cristina. *Postmodern Fairy Tales: Gender and Narrative Strategies*. Philadelphia, PA: University of Pennsylvania Press, 1997.

——. "Reflections on Recent English-Language Fairy-Tale Fiction by Women. Extrapolating from Nalo Hopkinson's 'SkinFolk.'" *Fabula* 47.3/4 (2006): 201–210.

Bakow, J., Leda Cosmides, and John Tooby, eds. *The Adapted Mind: Evolutionary Psychology and the Generation of Culture*. New York: Oxford University Press, 1992.

Bandler, Richard and John Grinder. *Frogs into Princes: Neuro Linguistic Programming*. Ed. John O. Stevens. Moab, UH: Real People Press, 1979.

Bauman, Zygmunt. *Globalization: The Human Consequences*. New York: Columbia University Press, 1998.

——. *Community: Seeking Safety in an Insecure World*. London: Polity Press, 2001.

——. *Liquid Life*. London: Polity Press, 2005.

——. *Consuming Life*. London: Polity Press, 2007.

——. *Does Ethics Have a Chance in a World of Consumers?* Cambridge, MA: Harvard University Press, 2008.

Bearne, Eve and Victor Watson, eds. *Where Texts and Children Meet*. London: Routledge, 2000.

Beitter, Ursula. "Identity Crisis in Fairy-Tale Land: The Grimm Fairy Tales and Their Uses by Modern-Day Imitators." In *Imagination, Emblems and Expressions: Essays on Latin American, Caribbean and Continental Culture and Identity*. Ed. Helen Ryan-Ransom. Bowling Green, OH: Bowling Green State University Popular Press, 1993, 274–282.

Bernheimer, Kate, ed. *Mirror, Mirror on the Wall: Women Writers Explore their Favorite Fairy Tales*. New York: Anchor, 1998; exp. 2nd ed. 2002.

Bettelheim. Bruno. *The Uses of Enchantment: The Meaning and Importance of Fairy Tales*. New York: Knopf, 1976.

Birkerts, Sven. *The Gutenberg Elegies: The Fate of Reading in an Electronic Age*. New York: Fawcett Columbine, 1994.

——. "The Fate of the Book." In *Tolstoy's Dictaphone: Technology and the Muse*. St. Paul, MN: Gray Wolf Press, 1996, 189–199.

Blackmore, Susan. *The Meme Machine*. Oxford: Oxford University Press, 1999.

Blair, Walter. "The Funny Fondled Fairytale Frog." *Studies in American Humor*. 1 (1982): 17–23.

Bloch, Ernst. *Heritage of Our Times*. Trans. Neville and Stephen Plaice. Berkeley, CA: University of California Press, 1991.

Boero, Pino and Carmine De Luca. *La letteratura per l'infanzia*. Rome-Bari: Laterza, 1995.

Bottomore, Tom, ed. *A Dictionary of Marxist Thought*. Cambridge, MA: Harvard University Press, 1983.

Bourdieu, Pierre. *The Field of Cultural Production: Essays on Art and Literature*. Trans. Randal Johnson. New York: Columbia University Press, 1993.

Boyd, Robert and Peter Richerson. *Culture and the Evolutionary Process*. Chicago, IL: University of Chicago Press, 1985.

Bradshaw, Tom and Bonnie Nichols. *Reading at Risk: A Survey of Literary Reading in America*. Washington, DC: National Endowment for the Arts, 2004.

Brewer, Derek. *Symbolic Stories: Traditional Narratives of Family Drama in English Literature*. Cambridge: D. S. Brewer, 1980.

Brooks, Karen. *Consuming Innocence: Popular Culture and Our Children*. Queensland, Australia: University of Queensland Press, 2008.

Bruner, Jerome. *Actual Minds, Possible Worlds*. Cambridge, MA: Harvard University Press, 1986.

Bruner, Jerome and Helen Haste, eds. *Making Sense: The Child's Construction of the World*. London: Routledge, 1987.

Buss, David M. *The Evolution of Desire: Strategies of Human Mating*. Rev. and exp. ed. New York: Basic Books, 2003.

Caniglia, Julia. "The All-Seeing Eye: Questions for Steven Heller—Writer, Teacher, Art Director." *The Rake* 6.69 (November, 2007): 20–21.

Carroll, Joseph. *Evolution and Literary Criticism*. Columbia, MO: University of Missouri Press, 1995.

——, ed. *Literary Darwinism: Evolution, Human Nature, and Literature*. New York: Routledge, 2004.

Cashdan, Elizabeth. "Women's Mating Strategies." *Evolutionary Anthropology* 5 (1996): 134–143.

Castells, Manuel. *The Rise of the Network Society*. Malden, MA: Blackwell, 1996.

Cavalli Sforza, Luigi Luca. *L'evoluzione della cultura*. Turin: Codice, 2004.

Cavalli Sforza, Luigi Luca and Marcus Feldman. *Cultural Transmission and Evolution: A Quantitative Approach*. Princeton, NJ: Princeton University Press, 1981.

Cladière, Nicolas and Dan Sperber. "The Role of Attraction in Cultural Revolution (Reply to J. Henrich and R. Boyd, 'On Modeling Cognition and Culture,' *Journal of Cognition and Culture*, 2 (2), 2002)." To appear in *Biology and Philosophy* (forthcoming). See: http://dan.sperber.com/on%20Richerson%20&%20Boyd.htm.

Clark, Beverly Lyon and Margaret R. Higonnet, eds. *Girls, Boys, Books, Toys: Gender in Children's Literature and Culture*. Baltimore: Johns Hopkins University Press, 1999.

Clark, William and Michael Grunstein. *Are We Hardwired? The Role of Genes in Human Behavior*. New York: Oxford University Press, 2000.

Clouston, W. A. "The Story of 'The Frog Prince': Breton Variant, and Some Analogues." *Folk-Lore Quarterly Review* 3 (September 1890): 493–506.

Cook, Daniel Thomas, ed. *Symbolic Childhood*. New York: Peter Lang, 2002.

——. *The Commodification of Childhood: The Children's Clothing Industry and the Rise of the Child Consumer*. Durham, NC: Duke University Press, 2004.

——. "Beyond Either/or." *Journal of Consumer Culture* 4.2 (2004): 147–153.

Cook, Daniel Thomas and Kaiser, Susan. "Betwixt and Be Tween: Age Ambiguity and the Sexualization of the Female Consuming Subject." *Journal of Consumer Culture* 4.2 (2004): 203–227.

Cooper, J. C. *Fairy Tales: Allegories of the Inner Life*. Wellingborough, UK: Aquarian Press, 1983.

Coyne, Jerry A. "His Tale Is True." *Times Literary Supplement* (June 16, 2006): 7–9.

Cox, Trudy Liebke. *The Fairy Tale as the Tree of Knowledge: Freudian, Jungian, and Feminist Approaches to "The Frog Prince."* Charlotte, NC: MA Thesis, University of North Carolina at Charlotte, 1984.

Crain, Caleb. "Twilight of the Books. What will life be like if people stop reading?" *The New Yorker* (December 24 & 31, 2007): 134–139.

Critser, Greg. "Let Them Eat Fat: The Heavy Truths About American Obesity." *Harper's* 300 (March 2000): 41–47.

Cross, Gary. *Kids' Stuff: Toys and the Changing World of American Childhood*. Cambridge, MA: Harvard University Press, 1997.

——. "Wondrous Innocence: Print Advertising and the Origins of Permissive Child Rearing in the US." *Journal of Consumer Consumption* 4.2 (2004): 183–201.

——. *The Cute and the Cool: Wondrous Innocence and Modern American Children's Culture*. New York: Oxford University Press, 2004.

Dawkins, Richard. *The Selfish Gene*. Oxford: Oxford University Press, 1976. Rev. ed. 1989. Thirtieth anniversary edition 2006.

——. *The God Delusion*. Boston, MA: Houghton Mifflin, 2006.

Debord, Guy. *The Society of the Spectacle*, Trans. Donald Nicholson-Smith. New York: Zone Books, 1995.

Dench, Geoff. *The Frog, the Prince and the Problem of Men*. London: Neanderthal Books, 1994.

Dennett, Daniel. *Darwin's Dangerous Idea*. New York: Simon & Schuster, 1995.

——. "The Evolution of Culture." *Monist* 84.3 (2001): 305–324.

——. "The New Replicators." In Mark Pagel, ed., *Encyclopedia of Evolution*. Vol. 1. Oxford: Oxford University Press, 2001. E83–92.

——. *Freedom Evolves.* New York: Viking Penguin, 2003.

——. "From Typo to Thinko: When Evolution Graduated to Semantic Norms." In *Culture and Evolution*. Eds. S. Levinson and P. Jaisson. Cambridge, MA: MIT Press, 2005.

——. *Breaking the Spell: Religion as a Natural Phenomenon*. New York: Viking, 2006.

Derungs, Kurt, ed. *Die ursprünglichen Märchen der Brüder Grimm*. Bern: Amalia, 1999.

Dresang, Eliza. *Radical Change: Books for Youth in a Digital Age*. New York: H. H. Wilson, 1999.

Drewermann, Eugen. *Der Froschkönig: Grimms Märchen tiefenpsychologisch gedeutet*. Zurich: Walter Verlag, 2003.

Dyson, Anne Haas. *Writing Superheroes: Contemporary Childhood, Popular Culture, and Classroom Literacy*. New York: Teachers College Press, 1997.

Elias, Norbert. *The Civilizing Process: The History of Manners*. Trans. Edmund Jephcott. New York: Urizen, 1978.

Ewers, Hans-Heino. *Literatur für Kinder und Jugendliche: Eine Einführung*. Munich: Fink, 2000.

Fass, Paula. *Children of a New World: Society, Culture, and Globalization*. New York: New York University Press, 2007.

Finders, Margaret and Alfred Tatum. "Hybridization of Literacy Practices: A Review of What They Don't Learn in School: Literacy in the Lives of Urban Youth." *Reading Research Quarterly* 40.3 (2005): 388–397.

Fischer, Steven Roger. *A History of Reading*. London: Reaktion Books, 2003.

Fisher, Helen. *Anatomy of Love: A Natural History of Mating, Marriage, and Why We Stray*. New York: Ballantine, 1994.

Freire, Paulo. *Pedagogy of Hope: Reliving Pedagogy of the Oppressed*. Trans. Robert R. Barr. New York: Continuum, 1997.

Freud, Sigmund. *The 'Uncanny'*. Trans. James Strachey. London: Penguin, 1985.

Gannon, Susan R. "Children's Literature Studies in a New Century." *Signal* 91 (January 2000): 25–40.

George, Nelson. *Hip Hop America*. New York: Viking Penguin, 1998.

Gilligan, Carol. *In a Different Voice: Psychological Theory and Women's Development*. Cambridge, MA: Harvard University Press, 1982.

Gottschall, Jonathan. "Quantitative Literary Study: A Modest Manifesto and Testing the Hypotheses of Feminist Fairy Tale Studies." In *The Literary Animal: Evolution and the Nature of Narrative*. Eds. Jonathan Gottschall and David Sloan Wilson. Evanston, IL: Northwestern University Press, 2005, 199–224.

Gottschall, Jonathan and David Sloan Wilson, eds. *The Literary Animal: Evolution and the Nature of Narrative*. Evanston, IL: Northwestern University Press, 2005.

Gould, Joan. *Spinning Straw into Gold: What Fairy Tales Reveal about the Transformations in a Woman's Life*. New York: Random House, 2005.

Gowaty, Patricia Adair. "Evolutionary Biology and Feminism." *Nature* 3.3 (1992): 217–249.

Grafen, Alan and Mark Ridley, eds. *Richard Dawkins: How a Scientist Changed the Way We Think*. Oxford: Oxford University, 2006.

Graff, Harvey J. *The Legacies of Literacy: Continuities and Contradictions in Western Culture and Society*. Bloomington, IN: Indiana University Press, 1987.

——. *The Labyrinths of Literacy: Reflections on Literacy Past and Present*. Rev. ed. Pittsburgh, PA: University of Pittsburgh Press, 1995.

——. *The Literacy Myth: Cultural Integration and Social Structure in the Nineteenth Century*. New Brunswick, NJ: Transaction, 1991.

Haas, Christina. *Writing Technology: Studies on the Materiality of Literacy*. Mahwah, NJ: Lawrence Erlbaum, 1996.

Haase, Donald, ed. *Fairy Tales and Feminism: New Approaches*. Detroit, MI: Wayne State University Press, 2004.

Haddad, Wadi. "What Next for World Literacy: An Afterword." In *The Future of Literacy in a Changing World*. Ed. Daniel A. Wagner, rev. ed. Cresskill, NJ: Hampton Press, 1999, 397–398.

Haig, David. "The Gene Meme." In *Richard Dawkins: How a Scientist Changed the Way We Think*. Eds. Alan Grafen and Mark Ridley, Oxford: Oxford University Press, 2006, 50–65.

Hallford, Deborah and Edgardo Zaghini, eds. *Outside In: Children's Books in Translation*. Chicago, IL: Milet, 2005.

Hardaway, Kathleen. *I Kissed a Lot of Frogs: But the Prince Hasn't Come*. Chicago, IL: Moody Press, 2002.

Hawisher, Gail E. and Cynthia L. Selfe. *Global Literacies and the World-Wide Web*. New York: Routledge, 2000.

Heller, Steven and Véronique Vienne, eds. *Citizen Designer: Perspectives on Design Responsibility*. New York: Allworth Press, 2003.

Henrich, Joseph and Robert Boyd. "On Modeling Cognition and Culture: Why Replicators Are Not Necessary for Cultural Evolution." *Culture and Cognition* 2.67 (2002): 87–112.

Higonnet, Anne. *Pictures of Innocence: The History and Crisis of Ideal Childhood*. London: Thames & Hudson, 1998.

Hilton, Mary, Morag Styles, and Victor Watson, eds. *Opening the Nursery Door: Reading, Writing and Childhood 1600–1900*. London: Routledge, 1997.

Hintz, Carrie and Elaine Ostry, eds. *Utopian and Dystopian Writing for Children and Young Adults*. New York: Routledge, 2003.

Houston, R. A. *Literacy in Early Modern Europe: Culture and Education 1500–1800*. 2nd ed. London: Longman, 2002.

Hume, Kathryn. *Fantasy and Mimesis: Responses to Reality in Western Literature*. New York: Methuen, 1984.

Hunt, Peter, ed. *International Companion Encyclopedia of Children's Literature*. London: Routledge, 1996.

Hymowitz, Kay S. *Liberation's Children: Parents and Kids in a Postmodern Age*. Chicago, IL: Ivan R. Dee, 2003.

Irwin, W. R. *The Game of the Impossible: A Rhetoric of Fantasy*. Urbana, IL: University of Illinois Press, 1976.

Iyengar, Sunil, ed. *To Read or Not to Read: A Question of National Consequence*. Washington, DC: National Endowment for the Arts, 2007.

Jackson, Rosemary. *Fantasy: The Literature of Subversion*. London: Methuen, 1981.

Jacobs, Joseph. *English Fairy Tales and More English Fairy Tales*. Ed. Donald Haase. Santa Barbara, CA: ABC-CLIO, 2002.

Jenkins, Henry, ed. *The Children's Culture Reader*. New York: New York University Press, 1999.

Kapur, Jyotsna. *Coining for Capital: Movies, Marketing, and the Transformation of Childhood*. New Brunswick, NJ: Rutgers University Press, 2005.

Kasson, John. *Amusing the Million: Coney Island at the Turn of the Century*. New York: Hill & Wang, 1978.

Kellner, Douglas. "New Life Conditions, Subjectivities and Literacies; Some Comments on the Lukes' Reconstructive Project." *Journal of Early Childhood Literacy* 2.1 (2002): 105–112.

Kinder, Marsha, ed. *Kids' Media Culture*. Durham, NC: Duke University Press, 1999.

Kline, Stephen. *Out of the Garden: Toys and Children's Culture in the Age of TV Marketing*. London: Verso, 1993.

Kline, Stephen, Dyer-Witheford, Nick, and de Peuter, Greig. *Digital Play: The Interaction of Technology, Culture, and Marketing*. Montreal: McGill-Queen's University Press, 2003.

Klugman, Karen. "A Bad Hair Day for G.I. Joe." In *Girls, Boys, Books, Toys: Gender in Children's Literature and Culture*. Eds. Beverley Lyon Clark and Margaret R. Higonnet. Baltimore, MD: Johns Hopkins University Press, 1999, 169–182.

Kress, Gunther. *Literacy in the New Media Age*. London: Routledge, 2003.

Lambert, Lydia. *Kissing Frogs: The Path to a Prince*. New York: iUniverse, 2005.

Langer, Beryl. "The Business of Branded Enchantment: Ambivalence and Disjuncture in the Global Children's Culture Industry." *Journal of Consumer Culture* 4.2 (2004): 251–277.

Lanham, Neil. "Orality & Metaphor." *Storylines* (Winter 2006): 8.

Lankshear, Colin with James Paul Gee, Michele Knobel, and Chris Searle. *Changing Literacies*. Buckingham, UK: Open University Press, 2002.

Lapham, Lewis. "Mudville." *Harper's Magazine* (March 2008): 11–14.

Lathey, Gillian, ed. *The Translation of Children's Literature: A Reader*. Toronto: Multilingual Matters, Ltd., 2006.

Le Guin, Ursula K. "Staying Awake: Notes on the Alleged Decline of Reading." *Harper's Magazine* 316.1893 (February 2008): 33–38.

Lentricchia, Frank and Thomas McLaughlin, eds. *Critical Terms for Literary Study*. 2nd ed. Chicago, IL: University of Chicago Press, 1995.

Levine, Gail Carson. *The Fairy Dust and the Quest for the Egg*. Illustr. David Christiana. New York: Disney Press, 2006.

Lewis, Cynthia and Bettina Fabos. "Instant Messaging, Literacies, and Social Identities." *Reading Research Quarterly* 40.4 (2005): 470–501.

Linn, Susan. *Consuming Kids: Protecting Our Children from the Onslaught of Marketing and Advertising*. New York: Anchor, 2004.

Lipman, Doug. "Three Waves of Storytelling Awareness." *Storytelling, Self, Society* 2.2 (Spring 2006): 121–126.

Lipson, Greta, Eric Lipson, and Susan Kropa. *The Scoop on Frogs and Princes: Newspaper Commentaries on Classics Retold*. Carthage, IL: Good Apple, 1993.

Little, William, H. W. Fowler, and J. Couldson, eds. *The Oxford Universal Dictionary*. 3rd ed. Oxford: Clarendon Press, 1955.

Lombreglia, Ralph. "Humanity's Humanity in the Digital Twenty-First." In *Tolstoy's Dictaphone: Technology and the Muse*. Ed. Sven Birkerts. St. Paul, MN: Graywolf Press, 1996, 231–246.

Luke, Allan and Carmen Luke. "Adolescence Lost/Childhood Regained: On Early Intervention and the Emergence of the Techno-Subject." *Journal of Early Childhood Literacy* 1.1 (2001): 91–120.

Luke, Allan and Peter Freebody. "A Map of Possible Practices: Further Notes on the Four Resources Model." *Practically Primary* 4 (1999): 5–8.

Luke, Allan and Susan Grieshaber. "New Adventures in the Politics of Literacy." *Journal of Early Childhood Literacy* 4.1 (2004): 5–9.

Mackey, "Little Women Go to Market: Shifting Texts and Changing Readers." Children's Literature in Education 29 (September 1998): 153–173.

Mahiri, Jabari, ed. *What They Don't Learn in School: Literacy in the Lives of Urban Youth.* New York: Peter Lang, 2004.

Marin, Louis. *Utopics: Spatial Play.* Trans. Robert A. Vollrath. Atlantic Highlands, NJ: Humanities Press, 1984.

Martens, Lydia, Dale Southerton, and Sue Scott. "Bringing Children (and Parents) into the Sociology of Consumption." *Journal of Consumer Culture* 4.2 (2004): 155–182.

Mattenklott, Gundel. *Zauberkreide: Kinderliteratur seit 1945.* Frankfurt am Main: Fischer, 1994.

McChesney, Robert W. *Rich Media, Poor Democracy: Communication Politics in Dubious Times.* Urbana, IL: University of Illinois Press, 1999.

McEneaney, John. "Agent-Based Literacy Theory." *Reading Research Quarterly* 41 (2006): 352–371.

McGahey, Michael. *Why Kiss a Frog? Your Prince Is Out There! Every Woman's Complete Self-Help Guide to Friends, Lovers, and the Search for her Perfect Partner!* Miami, FL: Broken Bottle Entertainment, 2002.

McNaughton, Stuart. "On Making Early Interventions Problematic: A Comment on Luke and Luke (2001)." *Journal of Early Childhood Literacy* 2.1 (2002): 97–103.

Mieder, Wolfgang, ed. *Grimms Märchen—modern: Prosa, Gedichte, Karikaturen.* Stuttgart: Reclam, 1979.

——. "Modern Anglo-American Variants of the Frog Prince (AaTh 440)." *New York Folklore* 6 (1980): 111–135.

Miller, Geoffrey. *The Mating Mind.* New York: Doubleday, 2000.

Miller, G. Wayne. *Toy Wars: The Epic Struggle Between G. I. Joe, Barbie, and the Companies that Make Them.* Holbrook, MA: Adams Media Corporation, 1998.

Miller, Laura, *Reluctant Capitalists: Bookselling and the Culture of Consumption.* Chicago, IL: University of Chicago Press, 2007.

Moi, Toril. "Appropriating Bourdieu: Feminist Theory and Pierre Bourdieu's Sociology of Culture." *New Literary History* 22 (1991): 1017–1049.

Morpurgo, Michael. "On Teaching Children to Read." *The Royal Society of Literature Review* (2008): 3–4.

Murray, Gail. *American Children's Literature and the Construction of Childhood.* New York: Twayne, 1998.

Nikolajeva, Maria. *Beyond Babar: The European Tradition in Children's Literature.* Lanham, MD: Scarecrow Press, 2006.

Nikolajeva, Maria and Carole Scott. *How Picturebooks Work.* New York: Routledge, 2001.

Onishi, Normimitsui. "Thumbs Race as Japan's Best Sellers Go Cellular." *The New York Times* (January 20, 2008), http//www.nytimes.com/2008/01/20/world/asia/20japan.html.

O'Sullivan, Emer. *Comparative Children's Literature.* London: Routledge, 2005.

Outhwaite, William. "Culture." In *A Dictionary of Marxist Thought.* Ed. Tom Bottomore. Cambridge, MA: Harvard University Press, 1983, 109–112.

Paul, Lissa. *Reading Other Ways.* Woodchester, Stroud: Thimble Press, 1998.

Perrot, Jean. *Jeux et enjeux du livre d'enfance et de jeunesse.* Paris: Éditions du Cercle de la Librairie, 1999.

Phillips, Adam. *Equals.* London: Faber & Faber, 2002.

Phillips, Ashley. "Will Cell Phone Novels Come Stateside?" *ABC News* (January 23, 2008) http// abcnews.go.com/Technology/GadgetGuide/story?id=417182.

Pigliucci, Massimo and Jonathan Kaplan. *Making Sense of Evolution: The Conceptual Foundations of Evolutionary Biology.* Chicago, IL: University of Chicago Press, 2006.

Pléh, Csaba. "Thoughts on the Distribution of Thoughts: Memes or Eipidemies." *Journal of Cultural and Evolutionary Psychology* 1 (2003): 21–51.

Preston, Cathy Lynn. "Disrupting the Boundaries of Genre and Gender: Postmodernism and the Fairy Tale." In *Fairy Tales and Feminism: New Approaches.* Ed. Donald Haase. Detroit, MI: Wayne State University Press, 2004, 197–212.

Pullman, Philip. "Introduction." In *Outside In: Children's Books in Translation.* Eds. Deborah Hallford and Edgardo Zaghini. Chicago, IL: Milet, 2005, 6–9.

Renonciat, Annie, ed. *The Changing Face of Children's Literature in France/Livres d'enfance, livres de France.* Paris: Hachette, 1998.

Richerson, Peter J. and Robert Boyd. *Not by Genes Alone: How Culture Transformed Human Evolution.* Chicago, IL: University of Chicago Press, 2005.

Ritzer, George. *Enchanting a Disenchanted World: Revolutionizing the Means of Consumption.* Thousand Oaks, CA: Pine Forge Press, 1999.

Rizzini, Irene and Bush, Malcolm. "Globalization and Children." *Childhood* 9.4 (2002): 371–374.

Rodari, Gianni. *Grammatica della fantasia: Introduzione all'arte di inventare storie.* Turin: Einaudi, 1973.

——. *The Grammar of Fantasy.* Trans. Jack Zipes. New York: Teachers and Writers Collaborative, 1996.

Röhrich, Lutz. *Wage es, den Frosch zu küssen! Das Grimmsche Märchen Nummer Eins in seinen Wandlungen.* Cologne: Diederichs, 1987.

——. "Froschkönig (AaTh 440)." *Enzyklopädie des Märchens.* Vol. 5. Ed. Rolf Wilhelm Brednich. Berlin: de Gruyter, 1999, 410–422.

Rosen, Judith. "Where the Sales Are: The Changing Landscape of Children's Book Outlets." *Publishers Weekly* 247 (February 14, 2000): 95–97.

Rosenblatt, Stephen. "Culture." In *Critical Terms for Literary Study.* Eds. Frank Lentricchia and Thomas McLaughlin. 2nd ed. Chicago, IL: University of Chicago Press, 1995, 225–32.

Ruddell, Robert and Norman Unrau, eds. *Theoretical Models and Processes of Reading.* 5th ed. Newark, DE: International Reading Association, 2004.

Ryan, Patrick. "The Storyteller in Context: Identity and Storytelling Experience." *Storytelling, Self, Society* 4.2 (May–August, 2008): 64–87.

Schor, Juliet. *Born to Buy.* New York: Scribner, 2004.

Seiter, Ellen. *Sold Separately: Parents & Children in Consumer Culture.* New Brunswick, NJ: Rutgers University Press, 1995.

——. *Television and New Media Audiences.* Oxford: Oxford University Press, 1999.

——. *The Internet Playground: Children's Access, Entertainment, and Mis-Education.* New York: Peter Lang, 2005.

Shami, Nailah. *Do Not Talk To, Touch, Marry or Otherwise Fiddle with Frogs: How to Find Prince Charming by Finding Yourself.* New York: Plume Books, 2001.

Shannon, Patrick. *Reading Poverty.* Portsmouth, NH: Heinemann, 1998.

——. *Reading Against Democracy: The Broken Promises of Reading Instruction.* Portsmouth, NH: Heinemann, 2007.

Shoemaker, Joel. "Hungry . . . for M. T. Anderson: An Interview with M. T. Anderson." VOYA 27.2 (June 2004): 98–102.

Skidelsky, Robert. "Gloomy about Globalization." *The New York Review of Books* 45.6 (April 17, 2008): 60–64.

Small, Meredith. "The Evolution of Female Sexuality and Mate Selection in Humans." *Nature* 3.2 (1992): 133–156.

——. *Female Choices: Sexual Behavior of Female Primates*. Ithaca, NY: Cornell University Press, 1993.

——. *What's Love Got to Do with It? The Evolution of Human Mating*. New York: Doubleday, 1995.

Smith, Janet Adam. *Children's Illustrated Books*. London: Collins, 1948.

Smuts, Barbara. "Male Aggression against Women: An Evolutionary Perspective." *Nature* 3.1 (1992): 1–44.

Sperber, Dan. *Explaining Culture: A Naturalistic Approach*. London: Blackwell, 1996.

Sperber, Dan and Nicolas Cladière. "Defining and Explaining Culture (Comments on Richerson and Boyd, *Not by Genes Alone*) to appear in *Biology and Culture* (forthcoming). See http://.dan.sperber.com/on%20Richerson%%%20Boyd.htm.

Sperber, Dan and Deirdre Wilson. *Relevance: Communication and Cognition*. 2nd ed. London: Blackwell, 1995.

Spitz, Ellen Handler. *The Brightening Glance: Imagination and Childhood*. New York: Pantheon, 2006.

Steinberg, Shirley R. and Joe L. Kincheloe, eds. *Kinderculture: The Corporate Construction of Childhood*. Boulder, CO: Westview, 1997.

Stiglitz, Joseph. *Globalization and Its Discontents*. New York: Norton, 2002.

——. *The Roaring Nineties*. New York: Norton, 2003.

——. *Making Globalization Work*. New York: Norton, 2008.

Sutton, Martin. "A Prince Transformed: The Grimms 'Froschkönig' in English." *Seminar* 24.2 (1990): 119–137.

Swinfen, Ann. *In Defense of Fantasy: A Study of the Genre in English and American Literature since 1945*. London: Routledge & Kegan Paul, 1984.

Talairach-Vielmas, Laurence. *Moulding the Female Body in Victorian Fairy Tales and Sensation Novels*. Aldershot, UK: Ashgate, 2007.

Todorov, Tzvetan. *The Fantastic: A Structural Approach to a Literary Genre*. Trans. Richard Howard. Ithaca, NY: Cornell University Press, 1975.

Tomlinson, Carl, ed. *Children's Books from Other Countries*. Lanham, MD: Scarecrow Press, 1998.

Tyler, Jo A. "Storytelling and Organizations: Introduction to the Special Issue." *Storytelling, Self, Society* 2.2 (Spring 2006): 1–4.

Uther, Hans-Jörg. *The Types of International Folktales: A Classification and Bibliography*. 3 vols. Ff Communications No. 284. Helsinki: Suomalainen Tiedeakatemia, 2004.

——. *Handbuch zu den "Kinder-und Hausmärchen" der Brüder Grimm*. Berlin: De Gruyter, 2008.

Van Coillie, Jan and Walter Verschueren, eds. *Children's Literature in Translation: Challenges and Strategies*. Manchester: St. Jerome Publishing, 2006.

Vickers, Joanne and Barbara Thomas. *No More Frogs, No More Princes: Women Making Creative Choices at Midlife*. Freedom, CA: Crossing Press, 1993.

Volkmann, Helga and Ulrich Freund, eds. *Der Froschkönig . . . und andere Erlösungsbedürftige*. Hohengehren: Schneider Verlag, 2000.

Vos, Gail de and Anna E. Altmann. *New Tales for Old: Folktales as Literary Fictions for Young Adults*. Englewood, CO: Libraries Unlimited, 1999.

Wedderburn, Robert. *The Complaynt of Scotland (c. 1550)*. Edinburgh: The Scottish Text Society, 1979.

Wilson, Edward. *Sociobiology: The New Synthesis*. Cambridge, MA: Harvard University Press, 1975.

——. *Consilience: The Unity of Knowledge*. New York: Knopf, 1998.

Wilson, Michael. *Storytelling and Theatre*. Basingstoke, UK: Palgrave, 2005.

Wolf, Maryanne. *Proust and the Squid: The Story and Science of the Reading Brain*. New York: HarperCollins, 2007.

Wolf, Naomi. "Young Adult Fiction: Wild Things," *The New York Times* (March 12, 2006), http://www.nytimes.com/200603/12/books/review/12wolf.html.

Wolf, Shelby Anne and Shirley Brice Heath. *The Braid of Literature: Children's Worlds of Reading*. Cambridge, MA: Harvard University Press, 1992.

Yashinsky, Dan. *Suddenly They Heard Footsteps: Storytelling for the Twenty-First Century*. Toronto: Vintage, 2004.

Zelizer, Viviana. "Kids and Commerce." *Childhood* 9.4 (2002): 375–396.

Zipes, Jack. *Creative Storytelling: Building Community/Changing Lives*. New York: Routledge, 1995.

——. *Happily Ever After: Fairy Tales, Children, and the Culture Industry*. New York: Routledge, 1997.

——. *When Dreams Came True: Classical Fairy Tales and Their Tradition*. New York: Routledge, 1999.

——. *Sticks and Stones: The Troublesome Success of Children's Literature from Slovenly Peter to Harry Potter*. New York: Routledge, 2000.

——. *Speaking Out: Storytelling and Creative Drama for Children*. New York: Routledge, 2004.

——. *Why Fairy Tales Stick: The Evolution and Relevance of a Genre*. New York: Routledge, 2006.

Selected Fiction and Poetry

Adler, C. S. *Willie, The Frog Prince*. New York: Clairon, 1994.

Almond, David. *The Savage*. Illustr. Dave McKean. London: Walker Books, 2008.

Anderson, Marilyn. *Never Kiss a Frog*. New York: Red Rock Press, 2003.

Anderson, M. T. *Feed*. New York: Miramax Books. 2002.

Anno, Mitsumasa. *All in a Day*. Illustrs. Mitsumasa Anno, Raymond Briggs, Ron Brooks, Gian Calvi, Eric Carle, Zhu Chenglian, Leo and Diane Dillon, Akiko Hayashi, and Nicolai Ye. Popov. London: Hamish Hamilton, 1986.

Atwood, Margaret. *Good Bones and Simple Murders*. New York: Doubleday, 1994.

——. *Princess Prunella and the Purple Peanut*. Illustr. Maryann Kovalsiki. Toronto: Key Porter Books, 1995.

Bail, Murray. *Eucalyptus*. London: Harvill, 1998.

Baker, E. D. *The Frog Princess*. New York: Bloomsbury, 2002.

Beaumont, Jeanne Marie and Claudia Carlson, eds. *The Poets' Grimm: 20th Century Poems from Grimm Fairy Tales*. Ashland, OR: Story Line Press, 2003.

Beckett, M. E. "Near Beauty." In *Black Thorn, White Rose*. Eds. Ellen Datlow and Terry Windling. New York: Avon, 1993.

Bender, Aimee. *The Girl in the Flammable Skirt*. New York: Doubleday, 1998.

——. *Willful Creatures*. New York: Doubleday, 2005.

Berenzy, Alix. *A Frog Prince*. New York: Henry Holt, 1989.

Bernheimer, Kate. *The Complete Tales of Ketzia Gold*. Tallahassee, FL: Florida State University Press, 2001.

——. *The Complete Tales of Merry Gold*. Tuscaloosa, AL: University of Alabama Press, 2006.

Black, Fiona. *The Frog Prince*. Kansas City, MO: Andrews and McNeel, 1991.

Block, Francesca Lia. *Dangerous Angels: The Weetzie Bat Books.* New York: HarperCollins, 1998.

——. *I Was a Teenage Fairy.* New York: HarperCollins, 1998.

——. *The Rose and the Beast: Fairy Tales Retold.* New York: HarperCollins, 2000.

Blundell, Tony. *Beware of Boys.* London: Viking Children's Books, 1991.

Boie, Kristen, *Erwachsene reden. Marco hat was getan.* Hamburg: Friedrich Oetinger, 1994.

——. *Abschiedskuss für Saurus.* Hamburg: Oetinger, 1994.

Brooke, William J. "A Prince in the Throat." *Untold Tales.* New York: HarperCollins, 1992.

Bucak, Ayse Papaatya. "Once There Was, Once There Wasn't." *Fairy Tale Review* (2006): 53–54.

Campbell, J. F. *Popular Tales of the West Highlands.* London: Alexander Gardner, 1890.

Canfield, Jane White. *The Frog Prince: A True Story.* New York: Harper & Row, 1970.

Carryl, Guy Wetmore. *Grimm Tales Made Gay.* Boston, MA: Houghton, Mifflin & Co., 1902.

Carter, Angela. *The Bloody Chamber and Other Stories.* London: Penguin, 1979.

Carter, Angela, ed. *The Virago Book of Fairy Tales.* Illustr. Corinna Sargood. London: Virago, 1990. Reprinted as *The Old Wives Fairy Tale Book.* New York: Pantheon, 1990.

Clark, Simon. "Now Fetch Me an Axe." In *Once Upon a Crime.* Eds. Ed Gorman and Martin H. Greenberg. New York: Berkeley, 1998.

Conford, Ellen. *The Frog Princess of Pelham.* New York: Litle Brown and Company, 1997.

Coover, Robert. *Briar Rose.* New York: Grove Press, 1996.

Coville, Bruce. *The World's Worst Fairy Godmother.* New York: Pocket Books, 1996.

Crane, Walker. *The Story Book I.* London: Routledge, 1874–1876.

Datlow, Ellen and Terri Windling, eds. *Black Thorn, White Rose.* New York: Avon, 1993.

——. *Snow White, Blood Red.* New York: Avon, 1994.

——. *Ruby Slippers, Golden Tears.* New York: Avon, 1995.

——. *Silver Birch, Blood Moon.* New York: Avon, 1999.

——. *Black Heart, Ivory Bones.* New York: Avon, 2000.

——. *A Wolf at the Door and Other Retold Fairy Tales.* New York: Simon & Schuster, 2000.

Davies, Adam. *The Frog King.* New York: Riverhead Books, 2002.

Dick, Philip. *Time Out of Joint.* Philadelphia, PA: Lipincott, 1959.

Donoghue, Emma. *Kissing the Witch: Old Tales in New Skins.* New York: HarperCollins, 1997.

Easton, Patricia Harrison. *Davey's Blue-Eyed Frog.* New York: Clarion, 2003.

Eisner, Will. *The Princess and the Frog.* New York: Nantier, Bell, Minoustchine, 1999.

Ewald, Carl. "The Story of the Fairy Tale." In: *Spells of Enchantment: The Wonder Tales of Western Culture.* New York: Viking, 1991, 564–565.

Farmer, Nancy. *The House of the Scorpion.* New York: Atheneum, 2002.

Fisher, David. "Frog Prince v. Wicked Witch." *Legally Correct Fairy Tales.* New York: Warner, 1996.

Fleischman, Paul. *Glass Slipper, Gold Sandal: A Worldwide Cinderella.* Illustr. Julie Paschkis. New York: Henry Holt, 2007.

Fühmann, Franz. "Die Prinzessin und der Frosch." *Die Richtung der Märchen.* Berlin: Aufbau Verlag, 1962, 146–147.

Gag, Wanda. *Tales from Grimm.* New York: Coward-McCann, 1936.

Gaiman, Neil. *The Wolves in the Walls.* Illustr. Dave McKean. New York: HarperCollins, 2003.

Galdone, Paul. *The Frog Prince.* New York: McGraw-Hill, 1974.

Garner, James Finn. "The Frog Prince." *Politically Correct Bedtime Stories for Our Life and Times.* Hungry Minds, 1994.

Greenberg, Martin H. and John Helfers, eds. *Little Red Riding Hood in the Big Bad City*. New York: DAW, 2004.

Greenberg, Martin H. and Kerrie Hughes, eds. *Crone*. New York: DAW, 2005.

Greenberg, Martin H. and Russell Davis, eds. *Faerie Tales*. New York: DAW, 2004.

Gripari, Pierre. *La Sorcière de la rue Mouffetard et autre contes de la rue Broca*. Illustr. Fernando Puig Rosado. Paris: Gallimard, 1967.

———. *Contes de la rue Broca*. Paris: La Table Ronde, 1967. Translated by Emily Arnold McCully as *Tales of the Rue Broca*. Indianapolis, IN: Bobbs-Merrill, 1969.

———. *Contes de la rue Folie-Mércourt*. Illustr. Claude Lapointe. Paris: Grasset et Fasquelle, 1983.

———. *Patrouille du conte*. Illustr. Marcel Laverdet. Lausanne: L'Age d'homme, 1983.

Halliwell, James Orchard. *Popular Rhymes and Nursery Tales*. London: John Russell Smith, 1849.

Hay, Sara Henderson. "The Marriage." *Story Hour*. Fayetteville, AS: University of Arkansas Press, 1998.

Hoffman, Nina Kirki. "Mallificent." In *Little Red Riding Hood in the Big Bad City*. Eds. Martin H. Greenberg and John Helfers, New York: DAW, 2004, 4–30.

———. "Switched." In *Rotten Relations*. Ed. Denise Little. New York: DAW, 2004.

Hohler, Franz. *Der Riese und die Erbeerkonfitüre und andere Geschichten*. Illustr. Nikolaus Heidelbach. Ravensburg: Otto Maier, 1993.

Hopkins, Jackie Mims. *The Horned Toad Prince*. Atlanta: Peachtree, 2000.

Horowitz, Elinor Lander. *The Strange Story of the Frog Who Became a Prince*. Illustr. John Heinly. New York: Delacorte Press, 1971.

Husain, Shahrukh. *Women Who Wear Breeches: Delicious and Dangerous Tales*. London: Virago, 1995.

———. *Temptresses: The Virago Book of Evil Women*. London: Virago, 1998.

Isaacs, Bernard, trans. *The Frog Princess*. Moscow: Goznak Central Board, Ministry of Finance of the USSR, 1974.

Jacobs, A. J. "The Frog Prince." *Fractured Fairy Tales*. New York: Bantam, 1997.

Janosch. *Janosch erzählt Grimm's Märchen* [1972]. Revised ed. Weinheim: Beltz & Gelberg, 1991.

———. *Not Quite as Grimm*. Trans. Patricia Crampton. London: Abelard-Schuhman, 1974.

Kaschnitz, Marie Luise. "Bräutigam Froschkönig." *Überallnie. Ausgewählte Gedichte 1928–1965*. Munich: Deutscher Taschenbuch Verlag, 1969, 150.

Kickiss, Rebecca. *Never After*. New York: Ace, 2002.

Kilworth, Garry. "The Frog Chauffeur." In *Silver Birch, Blood Moon*. Eds. Ellen Datlow and Terri Windling. New York: Avon, 1999.

Langley, Jonathan. *The Princess and the Frog*. London: HarperCollins, 1993.

Lee, Tanith. "The Princess and Her Future." *Red as Blood, Or Tales from the Sisters Grimmer*. New York: DAW, 1983.

———. "Kiss Kiss." In *Silver Birch, Blood Moon*. Eds. Ellen Datlow and Terri Windling. New York: Avon, 1999.

———. *White as Snow*. New York: TOR, 2000.

Le Fanu, Brinsley. *The Frog Prince and Other Stories from Grimm's Fairy Tales*. London: Review of Reviews Office, 1897.

Levine, Gail Carson. *Ella Enchanted*. New York: HarperCollins, 1997.

———. *The Fairy's Test*. Illustr. Mark Elliott. New York: HarperCollins, 1999.

———. *The Princess Test*. Illustr. Mark Elliott. New York: HarperCollins, 1999.

———. *Princess Sonora and the Long Sleep*. Illustr. Mark Elliott. New York: HarperCollins, 1999.

———. *Cinderellis and the Glass Hill*. Illustr. Mark Elliott. New York: HarperCollins, 2000.

——. *For Biddle's Sake*. New York: HarperCollins, 2002.

Link, Kelly. *Stranger Things Happen*. Brooklyn, NY: Small Beer Press, 2001.

——. *Magic for Beginners*. New York: Harcourt, 2005.

Little, Denise, ed. *The Sorcerer's Academy*. New York: DAW, 2003.

——, ed. *Rotten Relations*. New York: DAW, 2004.

——, ed. *Hags, Sirens, and Other Bad Girls of Fantasy*. New York: DAW, 2006.

Maas, Selve. *The Moon Painters, and other Estonian Folk Tales*. New York: Viking, 1971.

MacLachlan, Patricia. *Moon, Stars, Frogs and Friends*. New York: Pantheon, 1980.

Märchen der Brüder Grimm. Illustr. Nikolaus Heidelbach. Weinheim: Beltz & Gelberg, 1995.

Maguire, Gregory. *Confessions of an Ugly Stepsister*. Illustr. Bill Sanderson. New York: Regan Books, 1999.

Malamud, Bernard. *God's Grace*. New York: Farrar, Straus and Giroux, 1982.

Mamet, David. *The Frog Prince*. 1986.

Mann, Pamela. *The Frog Princess?* Milwaukee, WI: Gareth Stevens, 1995.

McKillip, Patricia. "Toad." In *Silver Birch, Blood Moon*. Eds. Ellen Datlow and Terri Windling. New York: Avon, 1999.

McKinley, Robin. "The Princess and the Frog." *The Door in the Hedge*. New York: Greenwillow Books, 1981.

——. *Spindle's End*. New York: G. P. Putnam's Sons, 2000.

Medley, Linda. *Castle Waiting* [1996]. Seattle, WA: Fantagraphics, 2006.

Mieder, Wolfgang, ed. *Disenchantments: An Anthology of Modern Fairy Tale Poetry*. Hanover, NH: University Press of New England, 1985.

Mitchell, Stephen. *The Frog Prince: A Fairy Tale for Consenting Adults*. New York: Harmony Books, 1999.

Moore, John. *The Unhandsome Prince*. New York: Ace, 2005.

Mourlevant, Jean-Claude. *L'enfant Océan*. Paris: Pocket, 1999.

Napoli, Donna Jo. *The Prince of the Pond: Otherwise Known as De Fawg Pin*. New York: Dutton, 1992.

——. *The Magic Circle*. New York: Dutton, 1993.

——. *Jimmy, the Pickpocket of the Palace*. New York: Dutton, 1995.

——. *Sirena*. New York: Scholastic, 1998.

——. *Zel*. New York: Dutton, 1998.

——. *Crazy Jack*. New York: Delacorte, 1999.

——. *Beast*. New York: Atheneum, 2000.

——. *Gracie, the Pixie of the Puddle*. New York: Dutton, 2004.

Napoli, Donna Jo and Richard Tchen. *Spinners*. New York: Dutton, 1999.

Oertel, Liya Lev. "The Fairy Godfather." In *Newfangled Fairy Tales: Book #2*. Ed. Bruce Lansky. New York: Meadowbrook Press, 1998.

Oster, Christian. *La grève des fées*. Paris: L'école ds loisirs, 2001.

Panzer, Friedrich, ed. *Kinder- und Hausmärchen der Brüder Grimm: Vollständige Ausgabe in der Urfassung*. Wiesbaden: Emil Vollmer Verlag, n.d.

Paterson, Katherine. *The Wide-Awake Princess*. Illustr. Vladimir Vagin. New York: Clarion, 2000.

Piumini, Roberto. *The Store*. Illustr. Tiziana Zanetti. Honesdale, PA: Boyds Mills Press, 1988.

——. *The Saint and the Circus*. Illustr. Barry Root. New York: Tambourine Books, 1991.

——. *Lo Stralisco*. Trieste: Einaudi Ragazzi, 1993.

——. *Mattie and Grandpa*. London: Puffin, 1993.

——. *The Knot in the Tracks*. Illustr. Mikhail Fedorov. New York: Tambourine Books, 1993.

——. *Doctor Me Di Cin*. Illustr. Piet Grobler. Ashville, NC: Front Street, 2001.

Porter, Jane. *The Frog Prince*. New York: Warner Books, 2005.

Quinn, Daniel. "The Frog King, or Iron Henry." In *Black Thorn, White Rose*. Eds Ellen Datlow and Terri Windling. New York: Avon, 1993.

Radunsky, Vladimir. *Manneken Pis: A Simple Story of a Boy Who Peed on a War*. New York: Atheneum, 2002.

——. *Le grand bazar*. Paris: Éditions du Panama, 2006.

Ragan, Kathleen, ed. *Fearless Girls, Wise Women and Beloved Sisters: Heroines in Folktales from Around the World*. New York: Norton, 1998.

Rodari, Gianni. *Telephone Tales*. Trans. Patrick Creagh. London: Harrap, 1965.

——. *The Befana's Toy Shop: A Twelfth Night Tale*. Trans. Patrick Creagh. London: Dent, 1970.

——. *Tante storie per giocare*. Rome: Riuniti, 1971.

——. *A Pie in the Sky*. London: Dent, 1971.

——. *Tales Told by a Machine*. London: Abelard and Shulman, 1976.

Rölleke, Hans, ed. *Die älteste Märchensammlung der Brüder Grimm*. Cologny-Genève: Fondation Martin Bodmer, 1975.

Rosen, Michael, ed. *The Oxfam Book of Children's Stories: South and North, East and West*. Cambridge, MA: Candlewick, 1994.

Roth, Mary Jane. *His Majesty, the Frog*. New York: Morrow, 1971.

Sargent, Pamela, ed. *Conqueror Fantastic*. New York: DAW, 2004.

Schami, Rafik. *Das Schaf im Wolfspelz: Märchen und Fabeln*. Kiel: Neuer Malik Verlag, 1986.

——. *Der Schnabelsteher*. Zurich: Nord-Süd, 1995. Translated by Anthea Bell as *The Crow Who Stood on his Beak*. Illustr. Els Coob. New York: North-South Books, 1996.

Schlachter, Rita. "The Frog Princess." In *Newfanlged Fairy Tales: Book #1*. Ed. Bruce Lansky. New York: Meadowbrook Press, 1997.

Schroeder, B. *The Frog Prince*. New York: North-South Books, 1998.

Schumacher, Clair. *Brave Lily*. New York: Morrow, 1985.

Schwedhelm, Joachim. "Mini-Märchen." *Die Zeit* 37 (September 13, 1974): 23.

Scieszka, Jon. *The Frog Prince Continued*. Illustr. Steve Johnson. New York: Viking, 1991.

Sexton, Anne. *Transformations*. Boston, MA: Houghton, Mifflin Co., 1979.

Sherman, Josepha. "Feeding Frenzy or The Further Adventures of the Frog Prince." In *Twice Upon a Time*. Ed. Denise Little. New York: DAW, 1999.

Sherwood, Frances. *Everything You've Heard Is True*. Baltimore, MD: Johns Hopkins University Press, 1989.

Sís, Peter. *Madlenka*. New York: Farrar, Straus and Giroux, 2000.

——. *The Wall: Growing Up Behind the Iron Curtain*. New York: Farrar, Straus and Giroux, 2007.

Slater, Lauren. *Blue Beyond Blue: Extraordinary Tales for Ordinary Dilemmas*. Illustr. Stephanie Knowles. New York: W. W. Norton, 2005.

Smith, Carmen Giminez. "Finding the Lark." *Fairy Tale Review* (2006): 136–139.

Solotareff, Grégoire. *The Ogre and the Frog King*. New York: Greenwillow Books, 1988.

Springer, Nancy. *Fair Peril*. New York: Avon, 1996.

Stanley, Diane. *Rumpelstiltskin's Daughter*. New York: William Morrow, 1997.

Starkey, Mike. *Frogs and Princes: Poems*. London: MARC Europe, 1987.

Steig, William. *Shrek!* New York: Farrar, Straus and Giroux, 1990.

Storr, Catherine. *It Shouldn't Happen to a Frog and Other Stories*. Illustr. Priscilla Lamont. London: Piccolo Books, 1987.

Straus, Gwen. *Trail of Stones*. New York: Knopf, 1990.

Tan, Shaun. *The Lost Thing*. Sydney: Lothian Books, 2000.

——. *The Arrival*. Sydney: Lothian Books, 2006.

Tarcov, Edith H. *The Frog Prince*. Illustr. James Marshall. New York: Scholastic Book Services, 1974.

Tchana, Katrin. *The Serpent Slayer and Other Stories of Strong Women*. Illustr. Trina Schart Hyman. Boston, MA: Little Brown, 2000.

Thomas, Jean. *Devil's Ditties: Being Stories of the Kentucky Mountain People*. Chicago, IL: Hatfield, 1931.

Vande Velde, Vivian. "Frog." *Tales from the Brothers Grimm and the Sisters Weird*. San Diego, CA: Harcourt Brace, 1995.

——. *The Rumpelstiltskin Problem*. Boston, MA: Houghton Mifflin, 2000.

Vesy, A. *The Princess and the Frog*. New York: Atlantic Monthly Press, 1985.

Wedge, Chris. *Out of Picture: Art from the Outside Looking In*. New York: Villard, 2007.

Walker, Barbara. "The Frog Princess." *Feminist Fairy Tales*. San Francisco, CA: Harper, 1996.

Weyn, Suzanne. *Water Song*. New York: Simon Pulse, 2006.

Wilson, Gahan. "The Frog Prince." In *Snow White, Blood Red*. Eds. Ellen Datlow and Terri Windling. New York: Avon, 1994.

Windling, Terri, ed. *The Armless Maiden and Other Tales for Childhood's Survivors*. New York: Tor, 1995.

Yolen, Jane. *Briar Rose*. New York: TOR, 1992.

——. *Not One Damsel in Distress: World Folktales for Strong Girls*. Illustr. Susan Guevara. San Diego, CA: Silver Whistle/Harcourt, 2000.

Yolen, Jane and Heidi Stemple. *Mirror, Mirror: Forty Folktales for Mothers and Daughters to Share*. New York: Viking, 2000.

Ziegesgar, Cecily von. *It Had to Be You*. New York: Poppy Publishing/Hachette, 2007.

Zipes, Jack. *Don't Bet on the Prince. Contemporary Feminist Fairy Tales in North America and England*, New York: Methuen, and London: Gower, 1986.

——, ed. and trans. *The Complete Fairy Tales of the Brothers Grimm*. 3rd ed. New York: Bantam, 2003.

Filmography

Black XXX-mas (2000)
Director: Peter Van Hees
In: *Best of AtomFilms 2000: Cinema with an Edge* (AtomFilms).

The Truman Show (1998)
Director: Peter Weir

The following films are "Frog Prince" versions.

Frog Prince (1954)
Director: Lotte Reiniger

Tales from Muppetland: The Frog Prince (1972)
Director: Jim Henson

The Frog King (1981)
Director: Tom Davenport

The Tale of the Frog Prince (1982)
Director: Eric Idle

The Frog Prince (1987)
Director: Jackson Hunsicker

Froschkönig (1987)
East Germany, color
Director: Walter Beck.

The Frog King (1994)
Director: David Kaplan

Prince Charming (2001)
Director: Allan Arkush

Index